A Compendium And Concordance Of The Complete Works Of Shakespeare: Also, An Index Of Every Character In The Dramas And Where They Appear

George A. Smith

WILLIAM SHAKESPEARE.

(Chandos Portrait)

A COMPENDIUM AND CONCORDANCE

OF

THE COMPLETE WORKS

OF

SHAKESPEARE

ALSO, AN INDEX OF EVERY CHARACTER IN THE DRAMAS AND WHERE THEY APPEAR

COMPILED BY GEO. A. SMITH, B. A.

(EDITOR OF THE NEW BURLESQUE HOMER, THE ILLUSTRATED HISTORY OF ROME, ETC.)

ILLUSTRATED BY 37 OUTLINE DRAWINGS (ONE TO EACH PLAY)
BY FRANK HOWARD

PHILADELPHIA
GEBBIE & CO.
1889

PREFACE.

IT is the intention of the publishers to make this COMPENDIUM such a perfect summary of Shakespeare's Dramas as will enable the student to comprehend the whole plot of each play at a glance. This will be found a great advantage to the general reader, and will prove a still greater boon to the theatre-goer who may be about to witness on the stage one of Shakespeare's plays which he may not have read, or read so long ago as to need refreshing his memory thereon. Each drama will be treated separately in the rotation in which they appear in the *Dr. Johnson edition of Shakespeare's Works* published by Gebbie & Co., but it will serve equally well for any other edition. The following will be the method of treatment of each drama:

1st. A historical notice of when the play was written, or first appeared in print, or was first acted, and the sources from whence Shakespeare most probably drew his work.

2d. The plot of the play summarized and the *dramatis personæ* in this connection repeated in detail.

3d. A few brief notes on the most prominent characters in each drama, to enable the reader more readily to measure and estimate the relative importance and position of the chief actors engaged.

This arrangement for busy men and women will possess at least the recommendation of novelty, and we think will be found generally useful, when any play of Shakespeare is spoken of, to be able at a few minutes' notice to compass an understanding of all the chief characters and the plot of the drama.

The CONCORDANCE embodies all the familiar phrases most currently quoted—treated by *catchwords*, leading to the quotations, alphabetically arranged; and these quotations are furthermore elaborately indexed, so that if any important word of any popular quotation be remembered, the searcher is likely to find it in this CONCORDANCE.

A separate CONCORDANCE OR INDEX OF CHARACTERS will be found following the general Concordance of Familiar Quotations. This, we believe, is the first time that all the characters in Shakespeare's works have been brought together and registered each in the proper place.

GEBBIE & CO.

Philadelphia, July 6, 1889.

CONTENTS.

LIST OF ILLUSTRATIONS.

THE TEMPEST. ACT III. SCENE I.

HISTORICAL SUMMARY OF THE TEMPEST.

No one has hitherto been fortunate enough to discover the romance, on which Shakespeare founded this play. Mr. Collins, the poet, issaid indeed to have informed Mr. T. Warton, that it was founded on an old romance called 'Aurelio and Isabella,' printed in Italian, Spanish, French and English in 1588; but as no such work could be discovered by the acute and learned writer to whom this information was communicated, it was reasonably inferred by him, that Collins, in consequence of the failure of memory during his last illness, had substituted the name of one novel for another.

It seems probable, that the event, which immediately gave rise to the composition of this drama, was the voyage of Sir George Somers, who was shipwrecked on the Bermudas in 1609, and whose adventures were given to the public by Silvester Jourdan, one of his crew, with the following title: 'A Discovery of the Bermudas, otherwise called the Isle of Divels: by Sir Thomas Gates, Sir George Somers, and Captayne Newport, and divers others.' In this publication Jourdan informs us, that 'the islands of the Bermudas, as every man knoweth, that hath heard or read of them, were never inhabited by any Christian or heathen people; but ever esteemed and reputed a most prodigious and enchanted place, affording nothing but gusts, stormes and foul weather; which made every navigator and mariner to avoid them as Scylla and Charybdis, or as they would shun the devil himselfe.' It has hence been concluded that this play was written towards the close of 1611, and that it was brought on the stage early in the succeeding year.

Mr. Hunter says, there is an island in the Mediterranean named Lampedosa, which is near to the coast of Tunis, and from its description in Dapper, was the probable track of the King of Naples' voyage in Shakespeare's 'Tempest.' This island is known to sailors as the enchanted island, and if the Italian novel or its translations should ever be discovered, it will be found that this surmise is correct.

It is remarked by Dr. Drake, that 'the 'Tempest' is, next to Macbeth, the noblest product of our author's genius. Never were the wild and the wonderful, the pathetic and the sublime, more artfully and gracefully combined with the sportive sallies of a playful imagination, than in this enchantingly attractive drama. Nor is it less remarkable, that all these excellences of the highest order are connected with a plot, which, in its mechanism, and in the preservation of the unities, is perfectly classical and correct.'

PERSONS REPRESENTED.

ALONSO, king of Naples.
SEBASTIAN, his brother.
PROSPERO, the rightful duke of Milan.
ANTONIO, his brother, the usurping duke of Milan.
FERDINAND, son to the king of Naples.

GONZALO, an honest old counsellor of Naples.

ADRIAN, } lords.
FRANCISCO, }

CALIBAN, a savage and deformed slave, found by Prospero on the desert island.

TRINCULO, a jester.

STEPHANO, a drunken butler.

MASTER of a ship, BOATSWAIN, and MARINERS.

MIRANDA, daughter to Prospero.

ARIEL, an airy spirit.

IRIS,
CERES,
JUNO, } spirits.
NYMPHS,
REAPERS,

Other spirits attending on Prospero.

SCENE, the sea, with a ship; afterwards an uninhabited island.

COMPENDIUM OF THE PLAY.

PROSPERO, duke of Milan, being fond of study and retirement, intrusts the public business of the state to his younger brother Antonio, who secretly engages with Alonso, king of Naples, to hold Milan as a fief of the Neapolitan crown, in consideration of his assistance in dethroning his unsuspecting brother. Not daring publicly to deprive Prospero of life, on account of his great popularity, the conspirators force him and his daughter Miranda, an infant three years old, into a crazy boat; and with a small supply of provisions abandon them to the fury of the elements. Being cast on a desert island, where no human creature is found but a savage named Caliban, Prospero puts into practice the necromantic art, with which he had formerly experimented, with great success, and employed his leisure hours with the education of Miranda. About twelve years after these transactions, Alonso, having agreed to marry his daughter to the king of Tunis, conducts her to that country, accompanied by the usurping duke of Milan, and a numerous train. Having left the lady with her husband at Tunis, they embark on their return to Naples; and the drama commences with a great tempest raised by Prospero, who, by the agency of a spirit named Ariel, wrecks the king's ship in such a manner, that none of the passengers are lost, and they are all landed on Prospero's island. Ferdinand, the king's son, is separated from his father, who supposes him drowned; while Prospero, discovering him after the shipwreck, conducts him to his cell, where he and Miranda become mutually enamored. In the mean time, Alonso, Antonio and their immediate followers, terrified by spectral illusions raised by the injured duke, run distracted, till at length, Prospero, satisfied with making them sensible of their former guilt, and with the resumption of his dignity, generously remits further punishment; extends his mercy to Caliban and his drunken companions, who had conspired to murder him; and, having restored Ferdinand to his disconsolate parent, abjures forever the magic art, and proceeds to Naples to solemnize the nuptials of the youthful pair. Like the 'Midsummer Night's

Dream,' with which it has been classed, the 'Tempest' is one of those romantic dramas, which defy analytical criticism, and would lose in effect by being subjected to a rigid examination of realities. Although the unities are preserved, perhaps more by accident than design, no play owes less allegiance to the exact sciences; and the interest is not weakened by trivial incongruities in the author's conduct of time and space. A hag-born monster, a young lady educated by a magician prince in a desolate island, and an attendant spirit, capable of the assumption of any form, who not only treads the oose of the salt deep, runs on the sharp wind of the north, works in the frosted earth, and rides on the curled clouds, but in his lighter moods, rides on the bat's back, or reposes in a cowslip's bell, are singular materials for a drama, the simplicity of whose construction exhibits in strong outline the boundless skill by which it is made so irresistibly attractive. It required the genius of Shakespeare to reconcile these apparently discordant elements, and construct out of them an harmonious structure. If, however, the reader imagines a defect exists, and agreeing with some critics in the opinion that Ariel was not an 'ethereal featureless angel,' observes an inconsistency in the development of his character, let us entreat him to merge it into the romantic conduct of the plot, and regard the whole drama as a purely imaginative construction formed on the idea of retributive justice, to which no one but Shakespeare has made necromancy subservient, without in some degree injuring the cause of virtue.

HISTORICAL SUMMARY OF THE TWO GENTLEMEN OF VERONA.

Mr. Steevens conjectures that some of the incidents of this play were taken by Shakespeare from the 'Arcadia,' book i. chap. 6, where Pyrocles consents to head the Helots; to which tale the adventures of Valentine with the outlaws, in this drama, bear a striking resemblance. But however this question may be disposed of, there can be little doubt that the episode of Felismena, in the Diana of George of Montemayor, a romance translated from the Spanish, and published in the year 1598, was the source whence the principal part of the plot of the 'Two Gentlemen of Verona' has been derived. The story of Proteus and Julia, in this play, closely corresponds with its prototype; and in several passages the dramatist has copied the very language of the pastoral.

The authenticity of this drama has been disputed by Hanmer, Theobald, and Upton, who condemn it as a very inferior production: but Dr. Johnson, in ascribing it to the pen of Shakespeare, asks, 'if it be taken from him, to whom shall it be given?' justly remarking, that 'it will be found more creditable that Shakespeare might sometimes sink below his highest flights, than that any other should rise up to his lowest.' 'It is observable,' says Pope, 'that the style of this comedy is less figurative, and more natural and unaffected, than the greater part of this author's, though supposed to be one of the first he wrote.'

TWO GENTLEMEN OF VERONA. ACT III. SCENE I.

Valentine detected by the Duke on the treacherous information of Proteus.

The 'Two Gentlemen of Verona' was not printed until it appeared in the folio of 1623, but is mentioned in Meres' 'Wits' Treasury,' printed in 1598.

PERSONS REPRESENTED.

DUKE of Milan, father to Silvia.
VALENTINE, PROTEUS, } gentlemen of Verona.
ANTONIO, father to Proteus.
THURIO, a foolish rival to Valentine.
EGLAMOUR, agent for Silvia in her escape.
SPEED, a clownish servant to Valentine.
LAUNCE, servant to Proteus.
PANTHINO, servant to Antonio.
HOST, where Julia lodges in Milan.
OUTLAWS.

JULIA, a lady of Verona, beloved by Proteus.
SILVIA, the duke's daughter, beloved by Valentine.
LUCETTA, waiting-woman to Julia.

Servants, Musicians.

SCENE, sometimes in Verona; sometimes in Milan; and on the frontiers of Mantua.

COMPENDIUM OF THE PLAY.

A young gentleman of Verona, named Valentine, after taking leave of his friend Proteus, visits the court of Milan, where he becomes captivated by the charms of Silvia, the duke's daughter, who secretly favors his addresses, in preference to those of a rich suitor provided by her father. In the mean time, Proteus, who had become enamored of Julia, a Veronese lady, successfully prosecutes his suit, and obtains from his mistress assurances of mutual regard. The satisfaction of these lovers is soon interrupted by the young gentleman's father, who, ignorant of his son's attachment, is anxious to send him to Milan, where Valentine still resides. After quitting Julia with professions of unalterable constancy, Proteus joins his friend, who receives him with the utmost tenderness; confides to him the secret of his love; and, having introduced him into the presence of Silvia, informs him of his intended elopement with her: but he has soon reason to repent his misplaced confidence; for Proteus, a very inferior character, who by this time had forgotten his vows to Julia, and was resolved to supplant Valentine, treacherously informs the duke of his daughter's proposed flight, which procures the banishment of Valentine and the imprisonment of Silvia. During this period, Julia, unable to endure the absence of her lover, travels to Milan in the disguise of a youth, and contrives to hire herself as a page to Proteus, whose perfidy she soon discovers. Silvia soon after effects her escape from confinement, but is overtaken in a forest by Proteus, who endeavors to obtain her consent by threats of violence, when she is unexpectedly rescued by Valentine, whose life had recently been spared by a band of outlaws settled here, on condition of becoming their leader. The remonstrances of Valentine awaken the remorse of Proteus: he entreats forgiveness, which is readily granted him; and Julia, having discovered herself, is united to her lover; while the duke, after pardoning the outlaws and recalling them from exile, willingly consents to the nuptials of his daughter with Valentine. Speed and Launce, servants respectively to Valentine and Proteus, are droll fellows—Launce with his dog in the fourth act is a masterpiece of wit and funny invention. Mr. Halliwell says, "Although probably not quite the 'first heir' of Shakespeare's dramatic invention, the 'Two Gentlemen of Verona' exhibits a deficiency of effective situation, and to some extent a crudity of construction, which would most likely have been avoided by a practised writer for the stage. But these defects are unnoticed by the reader in the richness of its poetical beauties and overflowing humor; its romance and pathos. The tale is based on love and friendship. Valentine is the ideal personification of both, of pure love to Silvia, and romantic attachment to the friend of his youth. Proteus, on the contrary, selfish and sensual, suffers himself to be guided by his passions, and concludes his inconstancy to his love with perfidious treachery to his friend. Valentine, noble and brave, but timid before the mistress of his affections, adoring Silvia's glove, and too diffident even to interpret her stratagem of the letter: Proteus, daring all, and losing his integrity, in the excess of a tumultuous passion. If Shakespeare has painted these elements in an outline something too bold for the extreme refinement of the present day, the error must be ascribed to his era, not to himself; and if it be also objected to in this play, that the female characters are germs only of more powerful creations in 'Twelfth Night' or 'Cymbeline,' the reader must bear in mind they are perhaps more suitable to the extreme simplicity of the story, that the chief object of the dramatist is directed to the development of the characters of Valentine and Proteus, and, above all, that the play should be judged by itself. There are few, indeed, who would be willing to miss the 'Two Gentlemen of Verona,' for it is, nevertheless, a gem, though it may not shine quite as brilliantly as some others in the Shakesperian cabinet."

MERRY WIVES OF WINDSOR. ACT V. SCENE V.

Falstaff, disguised as Herne the Hunter, meets the Merry Wives in the forest

HISTORICAL SUMMARY OF THE MERRY WIVES OF WINDSOR.

An old translation of 'Il Pecorone,' by Giovanni Florentino, is supposed to have furnished Shakespeare with some of the incidents of this comedy.

Mr. Rowe informs us that Queen Elizabeth was so well pleased with the admirable character of Falstaff in the two parts of Henry IV. that she commanded our author to continue it for one play more, and to show him in love; a task which he is said to have completed in a fortnight, to the admiration of his royal patroness, who was afterwards very well pleased at the representation. This information, it is probable, came originally from Dryden, who, from his intimacy with Sir William Davenant, had an opportunity of learning many particulars concerning Shakespeare. Mr. Chalmers has endeavored to set aside the general tradition relative to this comedy, but does not appear to have succeeded.

Speaking of this play, Dr. Johnson remarks that 'no task is harder than that of writing to the ideas of another. Shakespeare knew what the queen, if the story be true, seems not to have known;—that by any real passion of tenderness, the selfish craft, the careless jollity, and the lazy luxury of Falstaff must have suffered so much abatement that little of his former cast would have remained. Falstaff could not love but by ceasing to be Falstaff. He could only counterfeit love; and his professions could be prompted, not by the love of pleasure, but of money. Thus the poet approached as near as he could to the work enjoined him: yet having, perhaps, in his former plays completed his own idea, seems not to have been able to give Falstaff all his former power of entertainment.

This comedy was not printed in its present form till 1623, when it was published with the rest of Shakespeare's plays in the folio edition. An imperfect copy had been printed in 1602.

PERSONS REPRESENTED.

Sir JOHN FALSTAFF.
FENTON, a young gentleman in love with Anne Page.
SHALLOW, a country justice.
SLENDER, cousin to Shallow.
Mr. FORD, } two gentlemen dwelling at Windsor.
Mr. PAGE, }
WILLIAM PAGE, a boy, son to Mr. Page.
Sir HUGH EVANS, a Welsh parson.
Dr. CAIUS, a French physician.
HOST of the Garter Inn.
BARDOLPH, }
PISTOL, } followers of Falstaff.
NYM, }
ROBIN, page to Falstaff.
SIMPLE, servant to Slender.
RUGBY, servant to Dr. Caius.

Mrs. FORD, } the merry wives.
Mrs. PAGE, }

Mrs. ANNE PAGE, her daughter, in love with Fenton.
Mrs. QUICKLY, servant to Dr. Caius.

Servants to Page, Ford, etc.

SCENE, Windsor, and the parts adjacent.

COMPENDIUM OF THE PLAY.

THE vanity of Sir John Falstaff having misinterpreted the hospitable attentions of two ladies (The Merry Wives) at Windsor into an admiration for his person, he resolves to profit by his good fortune, but is betrayed by some discarded domestics (Pistol and Bardolph) who revenge their dismissal by revealing their master's designs to the husbands of his mistresses. Page disregards the information altogether; while Ford, who had, for some time past, entertained unfounded suspicions of his wife's honor, resolves to ascertain the truth of the information. For this purpose, under the assumed name of Brook, he causes himself to be introduced to Falstaff, whom he artfully draws into the confession of an assignation which he had just before made with mistress Ford, who in the meantime had conspired with her friend to punish the knight for his infamous proposals. Ford, supposing that he has sufficiently detected the infidelity of his wife, assembles his neighbors, in order to surprise Falstaff at the appointed interview: he is, however, conveyed away, by the contrivance of the two wives, in a basket with foul linen, and thrown into the Thames, where he narrowly escapes drowning. The suspicions of Ford are now somewhat abated; but when he again repairs to Falstaff as Brook, and learns the deception that has been practised on him, and the arrangements which have been made by his wife for a second visit from her admirer, his fury rekindles; he again solicits his friends to accompany him home, whence Falstaff again escapes in the disguise of an old witch, though not without suffering a severe cudgelling at the hands of the enraged Ford as a fortune-teller. A third assignation is now made with him in Windsor forest at midnight, where Falstaff, representing the spirit of Herne the huntsman, with horns on his head, having agreed to assume this disguise for a meeting with Mrs. Ford and Mrs. Page, is severely pinched by the accomplices of the plot, in the garb of fairies and hobgoblins; when the husbands, who are now made acquainted with the intention of their wives, rush from the place of their concealment; and, having sufficiently exposed and derided him, forgive him. The remainder of this comedy is occupied by the rivalry of Slender and Caius, for the hand of Page's daughter Anne, who prefers a young gentleman named Fenton, whom she marries. Mr. Singer says, "the bustle and variety of the incidents, the rich assemblage of characters, and the skilful conduct of the plot of this delightful comedy, are unrivalled in any drama, ancient or modern. Falstaff, the inimitable Falstaff, here 'lards the lean earth,' a butt and a wit, a humorist, and a man of humor, a touchstone and a laughing-stock, a jester and a jest—the most perfect comic character that ever was exhibited.' The jealous Ford, the uxorious Page, and their two merry wives are admirably drawn; Sir Hugh Evans and Dr. Caius no less so, and the duel scene between them irresistibly comic. The swaggering jolly Boniface, mine host of the Garter; and last, though not least, Master Slender and his cousin Shallow, are such a group as were never yet equalled by the pen or pencil of genius."

HISTORICAL SUMMARY OF 'TWELFTH NIGHT.'

THE comic scenes of this play appear to have been entirely the production of our author; while the serious part is founded on a story in the fourth volume of 'Belleforest's Histoires Tragiques,' which he took from Bandello. Malone, however, is of opinion that the plot of this comedy was rather derived from the 'Historie of Apolonius and Silla;' which tale is to be found in a collection, by Barnaby Rich, which first appeared in the year 1583. But little doubt can remain of the identity of the story of Bandello with the incidents of 'Twelfth Night,' after a perusal of the comparison of both compositions from the pen of Mrs. Lennox:—

'Sebastian and Viola, in the play, are the same with Paolo and Nicuola in the novel: both are twins, and both remarkably like each other. Viola is parted from her brother by a shipwreck, and supposes him to be drowned; Nicuola loses her brother at the sacking of Rome, and for a long time is ignorant whether he is alive or dead. Viola serves the duke, with whom she is in love, in the habit of a page; Nicuola, in the same disguise, attends Lattantio, who had forsaken her for Catella. The duke sends Viola to solicit his mistress in his favor; Lattantio commissions Nicuola to plead for him with Catella. The duke's mistress falls in

TWELFTH NIGHT. ACT III. SCENE IV.

Malvolio before Olivia in the cross-gartered yellow stockings.

love with Viola, supposing her to be a man; and Catella, by the like mistake, is enamored of Nicuola: and, lastly, the two ladies in the play, as well as in the novel, marry their lovers whom they had waited on in disguise, and their brothers wed the ladies who had been enamored of them.'

Mr. Collier and Mr, Hunter almost simultaneously discovered, in a manuscript diary of a student of the Middle Temple, among the Harleian Manuscripts, dating from 1601 to 1603, the following passage, which shows that all previous speculations, with regard to the date of the composition of this play, had assigned it to too late a period:—

"Feb. 2, 1601 [2.]

"At our feast, wee had a play called Twelve Night, or What You Will. Much like the Comedy of Errors, or Menechuri in Plautus; but most like and neere to that in Italian called Ingauni. A good practice in it to make the steward believe his lady widowe was in love with him, by counterfayting a letter as from his lady in general terms, telling him what she liked best in him, and prescribing his gesture in smiling, his apparraile, etc., and then when he came to practice making him believe they took him to be mad," etc.

Mr. Hunter by unwearied investigation, and an ingenious inductive process, ascertained that the writing of the diary was that of John Manningham, who was entered of the Middle Temple in 1597.

The play had most probably been publicly acted before this private performance, at the Candlemas feast of the Middle Temple in 1601-2; and from the absence of it in the list of Shakespeare's plays enumerated by Meres in 1598, the inference is that it was composed in 1599 or 1600.

PERSONS REPRESENTED.

ORSINO, duke of Illyria, in love with Olivia.
SEBASTIAN, a young gentleman, brother to Viola.
ANTONIO, a sea captain, friend to Sebastian.
A SEA CAPTAIN, friend to Viola.
VALENTINE, CURIO, } gentlemen attending on the duke.
SIR TOBY BELCH, uncle of Olivia.
SIR ANDREW AGUE-CHEEK, boon companion of Sir Toby.
MALVOLIO, steward to Olivia.
FABIAN, CLOWN, } servants to Olivia.

OLIVIA, a rich countess.
VIOLA, in love with the duke.
MARIA, Olivia's woman.

Lords, Priests, Sailors, Officers, Musicians, and other Attendants.

SCENE, a city in Illyria, and the sea-coast near it.

COMPENDIUM OF THE PLAY.

SEBASTIAN and Viola, twin children of a gentleman

of Messaline, and remarkable for an exact resemblance of features, being deprived of both their parents, quit their native country: they are encountered at sea by a violent tempest, which destroys the vessel and most of the crew, while Viola, the captain, and a few passengers betake themselves to the boat, which conveys them in safety to the sea-coast of Illyria. The lady, thus deprived of her brother, clothes herself in male attire, and enters into the service of Prince Orsino, who is at this time engaged in the unsuccessful pursuit of a neighboring lady, named Olivia. The talents of the disguised page soon render her so great a favorite of her master, that she is selected to intercede with the obdurate Olivia; who, though deaf to the solicitations of the prince, is seized with a sudden passion for the messenger, which meets with a repulse. Viola, on her return home, is waylaid by Sir Andrew Ague-cheek, a foolish suitor of Olivia, favored by her uncle, Sir Toby Belch, who persuades him to challenge the youth, in order to beget in his mistress a favorable opinion of his courage. Viola, as may well be supposed, is averse to a rencontre of this description; when she is rescued from her embarrassment by the arrival of a sea captain, who, having saved her brother Sebastian from the wreck, had since supplied him with considerable sums of money for his exigencies; but, in consequence of an unexpected arrest, is compelled to solicit a moiety of the loan: he accordingly applies to Viola, believing that he is addressing his friend Sebastian; and, when she denies all knowledge of his person, reproaches her with her ingratitude. In the meantime, Sebastian arrives; and the foolish knight, with his confederate, supposing him to be the page of Orsino, who had before declined the combat, assault him; but their violence is repaid with interest, and the combatants are parted by Olivia, whose advances to the supposed page are now received with mutual affection, and they are married without delay. Viola, arriving soon after with her master at the house of Olivia, is mistaken by the lady for her husband, by whose appearance the mystery is at length cleared up, and Viola is united to the prince. The bye-play of the pranks of Maria, the waiting-maid of Viola, and Sir Toby Belch with Malvolio, the major-domo of Viola's household, is one of the brightest bits of fun in Shakespeare's works. In the character of Malvolio some of the best Shakespearian actors have appeared, among others Charles Barron and Henry Irving. What is the subject of the comedy? Love: the Duke's love for Olivia—the love of Viola for the Duke—the new-born love of Olivia for the disguised Viola; and there is a sly penchant growing between Sir Toby and Maria—they are assimilated together by their love of fun; and Malvolio's ridiculous love for his mistress Olivia. The artist is not seen endeavoring to force a catastrophe: the characters fall into their places with a natural ease and grace, as if they were our veritable neighbors, and we already knew all about them. A noble-natured lady, mourning for her brother's death, will not for grief listen to the manly and ardent wooing of the Duke, and Viola, 'beautiful exceedingly,' whose heart has become a shrine, where in turn love for the Duke burns with a calm, undecaying constancy, yet having little or no hope of return, so that when we hear her urging Orsino's suit into Olivia's unwilling ears, we sympathize the more strongly with her, knowing that all this time runs a trembling through her voice, which speaks more of suffering than could many complaining words. There is a magic in it, too, for all that; and even the cold Olivia feels it as the tones fall around her heart, and she, that could not, or would not love, for very excess of grief, now loves in despite of it, as 'twere against her will; and we see that she had not forgotten her woman's wit and tact, when she sends Malvolio after the 'peevish messenger' with her ring. Illyria is a warm and sunny clime, peculiarly so at the bright 'season of the year,' when love most rejoices, and smiles in the bright and beauteous face of nature with a serener joy. The comedy is rich, hearty, rollicking, abandoned; actually glorious in its wild, mad revelry.

HISTORICAL SUMMARY OF 'MEASURE FOR MEASURE.'

THE primary source of the fable of this play is to be traced to a story in the Ecatommithi of Giraldi Cinthio, which was repeated in the tragic histories of Belleforest; but Shakespeare's immediate original was the play of 'Promos and Cassandra' of George Whetstone, published in 1578. 'This story,' says Mr. Steevens, 'which, in the hands of Whetstone, produced little more than barren insipidity, under the culture of Shakespeare, became fertile of entertainment. The old play of 'Promos and Cassandra' exhibits an almost complete embryo of 'Measure for Measure;' yet the hints on which it is formed are so slight, that it is nearly as impossible to detect them as it is to point out in the acorn the future ramifications of the oak.'

Dr. Johnson, speaking of this play, says, 'I cannot but suspect that some other had new-modelled the novel of Cinthio, or written a story, which in some particulars resembled it, and that Cinthio was not the author whom Shakespeare immediately followed. The emperor in Cinthio is named Maximine: the duke, in Shakespeare's enumeration of the persons of the drama, is called Vincentio. This appears a very slight remark; but since the duke has no name in the play, nor is ever mentioned but by his title, why should he be called Vincentio among the persons but because the

MEASURE FOR MEASURE. ACT III. SCENE II.

The Duke's return and punishment of Angelo, etc.

name was copied from the story, and placed superfluously at the head of the list by the mere habit of transcription? It is therefore likely that there was then a story of Vincentio, duke of Vienna, different from that of Maximine, emperor of the Romans.

'Of this play, the light or comic part is very natural and pleasing; but the grave scenes, if a few passages be excepted, have more labor than elegance. The plot is rather intricate than artful.'

Malone concludes that 'Measure for Measure' was written in 1603–1604. In the latter year it was first performed by 'His Majesty's Players' at Whitehall. It was first printed in the folio edition of 1623.

PERSONS REPRESENTED.

VINCENTIO, duke of Vienna.
ANGELO, lord deputy in the duke's absence.
ESCALUS, an ancient lord, joined with Angelo in the deputation.
CLAUDIO, a young gentleman.
LUCIO, a fantastic.
Two other like GENTLEMEN.
VARRIUS,* a gentleman, servant to the duke.
PROVOST.
THOMAS, } two friars.
PETER, }
A JUSTICE.

* Varrius might be omitted, for he is only once spoken to, and says nothing in reply.

ELBOW, a simple constable.
FROTH, a foolish gentleman.
CLOWN, servant to Mrs. Over-done.
ABHORSON, an executioner.
BARNARDINE, a dissolute prisoner

ISABELLA, sister to Claudio.
MARIANA, betrothed to Angelo.
JULIET, beloved by Claudio.
FRANCISCA, a nun, with whom Isabella is as a novitiate.
Mrs. OVER-DONE, a bawd.

Lords, Gentlemen, Guards, Officers, and other Attendants.

SCENE, Vienna.

COMPENDIUM OF THE PLAY.

VINCENTIO, duke of Vienna, anxious to reform the laxity of public morals, which too great remissness on the part of his government had introduced, invests Angelo, an officer renowned for rigid justice, with unlimited authority during his pretended absence; and, having assumed the habit of a friar, is enabled in this disguise to view attentively the proceedings of his deputy. A young lady of the city, named Juliet, proves pregnant by her betrothed lover, Claudio, who, according to an old penal enactment, is sentenced by the severe governor to lose his head. Isabella, the sister of the culprit, intercedes for the life of her brother with Angelo, who becomes deeply enamored with her, and proposes her dishonor as the price of his compliance with her petition. The virtuous maiden spurns the proffered terms, and flies to Claudio, to whom she relates the perfidy of the governor, exhorting him to submit to his fate with fortitude; but the fear of death overpowers his resolution, and he implores his sister to yield to the solicitations of the deputy, which request she rejects with abhorrence. In the meantime the disguised duke has become acquainted with Mariana, a lady formerly affianced to Angelo, who is persuaded to keep a private assignation with her husband (Angelo), which Isabella has feigned to make in her own name, to secure the safety of her brother. The inhuman tyrant, supposing that he has now achieved his object, and dreading the vengeance of the injured Claudio, determines to disregard his promise of mercy, and sends orders to the prison for his immediate execution. The duke now pretends to return from his travels, and Angelo is publicly convicted of murder and seduction both by Isabella and his master; and is about to suffer the punishment of his crimes, when the entreaties of his deserted wife, and the unexpected appearance of Claudio, who had been rescued from death by the interposition of the disguised duke, preserves him from the fate which he has so justly merited. As a relief to the more serious business of the play there are amusing scenes in which Froth, Elbow, a clown, and others perform delightful low comedy. Mr. Halliwell says: 'I think it will be found a serious error has been committed by nearly all who have treated on the play, in estimating the extent of the crime for which Claudio was condemned. Ulrici says he had 'seduced his mistress before marriage.' This is, however, erroneous. In Shakespeare's time the ceremony of betrothment was usually supposed to confer the power of matrimonial union. Claudio obtained possession of Julietta on 'a true contract;' and provided marriage was celebrated within a reasonable time afterwards, no criminality could be alleged after the contract had been formally made. So, likewise, the duke tells Mariana it was no sin to meet Angelo, for he was her 'husband on a pre-contract.' The story would be more properly analyzed by representing Claudio's error as venial and Angelo's strictness so much the more severe, thus involving a greater antithesis in his fall. The only painful scene in the play is the subject of the argument between Angelo and Isabella; but Shakespeare is not to be blamed for the direction it takes. On the contrary, he has infinitely purified a barbarous tale which the taste of the age authorized as a subject of dramatic representation. The scenes between the lower characters would have been readily tolerated by a female audience in the time of the first James, and although they must now be passed over, we can hardly censure the poet for not foreseeing the extreme delicacy of a later age. The offences chiefly consist of a few gross words, which no one but literary antiquarians will comprehend, and are purposely left without explanation. Bearing in mind that the improprieties of language above alluded to are faults of the age, not of the poet's judgment, and that a similar apology may be advanced for the choice of subject, the moral conveyed by 'Measure for Measure' is of a deeply religious character. It exhibits in an outline of wonderful power how ineffective are the strongest resolutions against the insidious temptation of beauty, when they are not firmly strengthened and guarded by religion. The prayers of Angelo came from his lips, not from his heart, and he fell. Isabella, on the contrary, is preserved by virtue grounded on religious faith. Her character is presented as nearly approaching perfection as is consistent with possible reality; and we rejoice that such a being should be snatched from the gloomy cloister to exercise her mild influence in a more useful station. The minor characters complete the picture of one of the chief phases of human life, the conflict of incontinence and chastity.'

HISTORICAL SUMMARY OF 'MUCH ADO ABOUT NOTHING.'

A STORY in some respects similar to this drama may be found in the fifth book of 'Orlando Furioso,' and likewise in the second book of 'Spenser's Fairy Queen;' but it is most probable that Shakespeare derived the principal incident of this comedy from a version of Belleforest, who copied the Italian novelist Bandello. In the 22d tale of the first part of Bandello, and the 18th history of the third volume of Belleforest, a story is related, the events of which nearly resemble those attendant on the marriage of Claudio and Hero.

As this play was printed in quarto in 1600, and is not mentioned by Meres in his list of Shakespeare's works published about the end of 1598, Mr. Malone conjectures that the year 1600 may be accurately assigned as the time of its production. It is reported to have been formerly known under the name of 'Benedick and Beatrice.'

'This play,' says Steevens, 'may be justly said to contain two of the most sprightly characters that Shakespeare ever drew. The wit, the humorist, the gentleman, and the soldier are combined in Benedick. It is to be lamented, indeed, that the first and most splendid of these distinctions is disgraced by unnecessary profaneness; for the goodness of his heart is hardly sufficient to atone for the license of his tongue. The too sarcastic levity which flashes out in the conversation of Beatrice may be excused on account of the

MUCH ADO ABOUT NOTHING. ACT V. SCENE IV.

Claudio about to be married to a supposed niece of Leonato in reparation for his calumny on Hero.

steadiness and friendship to her cousin, so apparent in her behavior, when she urges her lover to risk his life by a challenge to Claudio.' Heminge, the player, received on the 20th of May, 1613, the sum of £40 and £20 more as his Majesty's gratuity for exhibiting six plays at Hampton Court, among which was this comedy.

PERSONS REPRESENTED.

DON PEDRO, prince of Arragon.
DON JOHN, his bastard brother.
CLAUDIO, a young lord of Florence, favorite to Don Pedro.
BENEDICK, a young lord of Padua, favorite likewise of Don Pedro.
LEONATO, governor of Messina.
ANTONIO, his brother.
BALTHAZAR, servant to Don Pedro.
BORACHIO, CONRADE, } followers of Don John.
DOGBERRY, VERGES, } two foolish officers.
A SEXTON.
A FRIAR.
A BOY.

HERO, daughter to Leonato.
BEATRICE, niece to Leonato.
MARGARET, URSULA, } gentlewomen attendir

Messengers, Watch, and A

SCENE, Messin

COMPENDIUM OF THE PLAY.

LEONATO, a gentleman of Messina, has an only daughter named Hero, whose beauty and accomplishments captivate the affections of count Claudio, a favorite of the prince then on a visit to her father, who willingly gives his consent to a union so promising. In the meantime, Don John, a natural brother of the prince, who has long viewed the elevation of Claudio with a eye of jealousy, accuses the lady of inconstancy; and, in confirmation of his assertion, introduces his brother and his friend to her chamber window at midnight: the artifice of an attendant of Don John, named Borachio, who contrives to address the waiting-maid stationed at the window by the name of Hero, appears to leave no room for doubt, and the enraged lover repudiates his affianced
'le at the very moment of the nuptials: Hero
; and, by the advice of the friar, a false report
death is circulated. During the progress of
nts Borachio reveals the success of his
s to a fellow-servant whom he meets in
nd their conversation is overheard by
who convey the culprits to Leonato's
a full confession is made by the re-
chio. Claudio now entreats forgive-
insulted father, which is granted on
of his union with a cousin of his
s, whose face he is not permitted to
ompletion of the marriage ceremony,
ess is made perfect by finding him-
l of the innocent Hero. A very
f this play is occupied with the

deception which is practised to betray Benedick and Beatrice, two rival wits and professed marriage-haters, into a mutual passion for each other, which is at length accomplished, and they are both content to renounce their prejudices against marriage. Dogberry and Verges vary the notes of comedy by inimitable folly and pretension.

It is not unworthy of remark, that Shakespeare's muse appears to be more inventive in comedy than in tragedy. In the latter, he has usually seized upon some well-known story for his plot; but his comedies often are traceable to no source whatever, other than his own wonderful genius, which seems to enjoy and revel in wild rollicking fun and mad-cap diversion. In 'Much Ado About Nothing' he descends to broad farce with our learned friend Dogberry, who assures us that he is 'a wise fellow; and, which is more, an officer; and, which is more, an householder; and, which is more, as pretty a piece of flesh as any is in Messina; and one that knows the law-go to; and a rich fellow enough-go to; and a fellow that hath had losses; and one that hath two gowns, and everything handsome about him.' And his fellow-officer, the feeble old Verges, who is, indeed, verging upon the edge of the grave, but yet still clings to his parochial dignity and gives his concurrence to the wise conclusions of his friend Dogberry, and thanks God that he is 'as honest as any man living, that is an old man, and no honester than he.' Then from this merriment we are transported, without effort, to the interior of the church, with its solemn sepulchral statuary, its heraldic emblazonment, and its funereal-looking banners; where stands the monument which is supposed to cover the corpse of Hero. Here, at midnight, enters the repentant Claudio, preceded by attendants with dim-burning tapers, and sad music, to—

'Hang her an epitaph upon her tomb,
And sing it to her bones.'

Indeed the serious portion of this play is exquisitely conceived, the disgrace of the gentle Hero by her lover's casting her off, and branding her with infamy, even within the holy precincts of the church, where he should have taken her to his heart; the astonishment of the guests, and that of Benedick, who exclaims:—

'This looks not like a nuptial;'

and the hysterical answer of the terror-stricken girl: 'True, O God!' would be altogether too tragic for introduction into a comedy, but that the spectator knows that the discovery of her innocence is already made, although not yet revealed to her lover and her friends. The agony and shame of her aged father are painted in a manner worthy of our poet.

The discovery of the villany of Don John, who has caused all the sorrow, is remarkable; Shakespeare never omits an opportunity of illustrating his favorite doctrine of the omnipresence of a jealous Providence, which works through common means and unsuspected channels, and returns to all men good for good, evil for evil. It is most true

'Our indiscretion sometimes serves us well
When our deep plots do pall; and that should teach us,
There's a divinity that shapes our ends
Rough-hew them how we will.'

For what the wisdom of Leonato, Claudio, and the

rest could not discover, was dragged from pitchy darkness, and revealed in the full blaze of day by the foolish and imbecile constables of the watch, Dogberry and his ancient friend Verges. But the chief interest of the play circles round Benedick and Beatrice; it originally bore their names instead of 'Much Ado,' etc.; they have won for it its great popularity; they love each other from the first, but they do not know it; each of them has forsworn love because they conceive it to be a cause of melancholy; the lady says she would 'rather hear a dog bark at a cow than a man swear he loves her,' while Benedick tells us: 'I will not be sworn but love may transform me to an oyster; but I'll take my oath on it, till he have made an oyster of me, he shall never make me such a fool.' It was a wild jest, and worthy of the brain of Shakespeare, to bring two such avowed infidels to love together, and entangle them in the rose-linked meshes of Hymen; but this is effected by the merry stratagem of making both believe that each is the object of the concealed passion of the other. So that after Benedick has declared of his cousin that:—'She speaks poniards, and every word stabs: if her breath were as terrible as her terminations, there were no living near her, she would infect to the north star; I would not marry her though she were endowed with all that Adam had left him before he transgressed;' he offers her his hand and heart, and loves her with as much warmth and sincerity, though certainly not with so much youthful heart and passion, as the young ill-starred Romeo did his mistress, Juliet. Their mutual declaration of affection is exquisite and in admirable keeping:—

Benedick—I protest I love thee.
Beatrice—Why, then, God forgive me!
Benedick—What offence, sweet Beatrice?
Beatrice—You have staid me in a happy hour;
I was about to protest I loved you.

Many a lady might learn a winning lesson from this delightful frankness.

MIDSUMMER-NIGHT'S DREAM. ACT III. SCENE I.

The "Translation" of Bottom.

HISTORICAL SUMMARY OF 'A MIDSUMMER-NIGHT'S DREAM.'

THE Knight's Tale, in Chaucer, is supposed by Steevens to have been the prototype whence Shakespeare derived the leading features of this play: the same writer conjectures that the doggerel verses of Bottom and his associates are nothing more than an extract from 'the boke of Perymus and Thesbye,' printed in 1562; while Mr. Capell thinks our author indebted to a fantastical poem of Drayton, called Nymphidia, or the Court of Fairy, for his notions of those aërial beings.

The title of this drama was probably suggested (like 'Twelfth Night' and 'The Winter's Tale') by the season of the year at which it was first represented: no other ground, indeed, can be assigned for the name which it has received, since the action is distinctly pointed out as occurring on the night preceding May-day.

Of the 'Midsummer Night's-Dream' there are two editions in quarto; one printed for Thomas Fisher, the other for James Roberts, both in 1600. Neither of these editions deserves much praise for correctness. Fisher is sometimes preferable; but Roberts was followed, though not without some variations, by Hemings and Condell, and they by all the folios that succeeded them.

'Wild and fanciful as this play is,' says Dr. Johnson, 'all the parts in their various modes are well written, and give the kind of pleasure which the author designed. Fairies in his time were much in fashion: common tradition had made them familiar, and Spenser's poem had made them great.'

PERSONS REPRESENTED.

THESEUS, duke of Athens.
EGEUS, father to Hermia.
LYSANDER, } in love with Hermia.
DEMETRIUS, }
PHILOSTRATE, master of the revels to Theseus.
QUINCE, the carpenter.
SNUG, the joiner.
BOTTOM, the weaver.
FLUTE, the bellows-mender.
SNOUT, the tinker.
STARVELING, the tailor.

HIPPOLYTA, queen of the Amazons, betrothed to Theseus.
HERMIA, daughter to Egeus, in love with Lysander.
HELENA, in love with Demetrius.
OBERON, king of the fairies.
TITANIA, queen of the fairies.
PUCK, or ROBIN-GOODFELLOW, a fairy.
PEAS-BLOSSOM, }
COBWEB, } fairies.
MOTH, }
MUSTARD-SEED, }
PYRAMUS, }
THISBE, }
WALL, } characters in the interlude performed by the clowns.
MOONSHINE, }
LION, }

Other fairies attending their king and queen.
Attendants on Theseus and Hippolyta.

SCENE, Athens, and a wood not far from it.

COMPENDIUM OF THE PLAY.

Oberon, king of the fairies, requests his queen Titania to bestow on him a favorite page to execute the office of train-bearer; which she refusing, he, in revenge, moistens her eyes during sleep with a liquor, which possesses the singular property of enamoring her of the first person she sees: the object which her eyes first encounter is an ignorant Athenian weaver, named Bottom, who, together with his associates, are preparing to represent a play at the approaching nuptials of Theseus and Hippolyta; when a waggish spirit of Oberon, named Puck, covers Bottom with the head of an ass;—a transformation which terrifies the rustic swains, and fulfils the intention of his master, in the dotage of his queen. During this period, a young couple, Lysander and Hermia, flying from a cruel father, and the rigor of the Athenian laws, which forbid their union, enter the enchanted wood, whither they are pursued by Demetrius, whose suit is favored by the father of the fugitive damsel, and who is himself beloved by another lady following him, named Helena, whom he treats with disdain. Oberon, in pity to Helena, commands Puck to anoint the eyes of the churlish Demetrius with the charmed liquor during sleep; but he by mistake enchants Lysander. Demetrius soon after becomes the subject of the same operation, while Helena is presented to each of the awakened lovers: the object of their affections becomes now instantly changed, and the hitherto favored Hermia is rejected by both; till Oberon at length disenchants Lysander, restores the weaver to his pristine form, and becomes reconciled to his queen. The play concludes with the union of Hippolyta to Theseus, by whose mediation the father of Hermia consents to his daughter's marriage with Lysander, while Demetrius becomes the husband of Helena. Schlegel says: 'The different parts of the plot; the wedding of Theseus, the disagreement of Oberon and Titania, the flight of the two pair of lovers, and the theatrical operations of the mechanics, are so lightly and happily interwoven, that they seem necessary to each other for the formation of a whole. Oberon is desirous of relieving the lovers from their perplexities, and greatly adds to them through the misapprehension of his servant, till he at last comes to the aid of their fruitless amorous pain, their inconstancy and jealousy, and restores fidelity to its old rights. The extremes of fanciful and vulgar are united when the enchanted Titania awakes and falls in love with a coarse mechanic with an ass's head, who represents or rather disfigures the part of a tragical lover. The droll wonder of the transmutation of Bottom is merely the translation of a metaphor in its literal sense; but, in his behavior during the tender homage of the Fairy Queen, we have a most amusing proof how much the consciousness of such a head-dress heightens the effect of his usual folly. Theseus and Hippolyta are, as it were, a splendid frame for the picture; they take no part in the action, but appear with stately pomp. The discourse of the hero and his Amazon, as they course through the forest with their noisy hunting train, works upon the imagination like the fresh breath of morning, before which the shapes of night disappear.'

LOVE'S LABOR'S LOST. ACT IV. SCENE III.

HISTORICAL SUMMARY OF 'LOVE'S LABOR'S LOST.'

No traces have yet been discovered of any novel or tale from which the incidents of this comedy have been borrowed. The fable, however, does not appear to be a work of pure invention, and most probably is indebted for its origin to some romance, now no longer in existence. The character of Holofernes is supposed to be the portrait of an individual; and some of his quotations have induced commentators to infer that John Florio, a pedantic teacher of Italian, was the object of the poet's satire.

Malone conjectures that 'Love's Labor's Lost' was first written in 1594, of which no exact transcript is preserved; for in the earliest edition which has hitherto been found of this play, namely that of 1598, it is said in the title page to be 'newly corrected and augmented,' with the farther information, that it had been 'presented before her highness the last Christmas;' facts, which show, that we are in possession, not of the first draught or edition of this comedy, but only of that copy which represents it as it was revived and improved for the entertainment of Queen Elizabeth in 1597. That this was one of Shakespeare's earliest essays in dramatic writing is clearly proved by the frequent rhymes, the imperfect versification, and the irregularity of the composition.

'It must be confessed,' says Dr. Johnson, 'that

there are many passages in this play, mean, childish, and vulgar; and some which ought not to have been exhibited, as we are told they were, to a maiden queen. But there are scattered through the whole many sparks of genius; nor is there any play that has more evident marks of the hand of Shakespeare.'

PERSONS REPRESENTED.

FERDINAND, king of Navarre.
BIRON, LONGAVILLE, DUMAIN, } lords attending on the king.
BOYET, MERCADE, } lords attending on the princess of France.
DON ADRIANO DE ARMADO, a fantastical Spaniard.
SIR NATHANIEL, a curate.
HOLOFERNES, a schoolmaster.
DULL, a constable.
COSTARD, a clown.
MOTH, page to Armado.
A FORESTER.

PRINCESS OF FRANCE.
ROSALINE, MARIA, KATHARINE, } ladies attending on the princess.
JAQUENETTA, a country wench.

Officers and others, attendants on the king and princess.

SCENE, Navarre.

COMPENDIUM OF THE PLAY.

FERDINAND, king of Navarre, having devoted himself to the study of philosophy, prevails on three of his courtiers, Biron, Longaville, and Dumain, to renounce with him the pleasures of society; exacting an oath from each, that for the space of three years they would sedulously attend to the culture of their minds, separate themselves entirely from the company of females, and practise the utmost simplicity in their apparel and diet. At this critical juncture the princess of France arrives at the palace of Navarre on an embassy from the king, her father, attended by three ladies in her train: her personal charms and mental endowments soon make a powerful impression on the heart of the secluded monarch; and he has the satisfaction of perceiving that his fellow-students are not insensible to the attractions of the ladies of the French court; but are equally anxious with himself to obtain a dispensation of their rash vow. An immediate prosecution of their suit is now resolved on, which exposes them to the raillery of their mistresses, who, after reproaching the repentant devotees with their perjury, insist on subjecting the permanence of their attachments to the trial of a whole year; at the expiration of which period they consent to become their wives. Costard, a clown, and Moth, the page of Armado, are the broad humorists of the play, assisted therein by Jaquenetta, a country wench.

Singer says, 'the scene in which the king and his companions detect each other's breach of their mutual vow is capitally contrived. The discovery of

Biron's love-letter while rallying his friends, and the manner in which he extricates himself, by ridiculing the folly of the vow, are admirable.'

The grotesque characters, Don Adriano de Armado, a braggadochio, such as we find frequently in Italian comedies, Nathaniel the curate, and Holofernes, that prince of pedants (whom Warburton thought was intended as a ridicule of the resolute John Florio), with the humors of Costard the clown, are well contrasted with the sprightly wit of the principal characters in the play. It has been observed that 'Biron and Rosaline suffer much in comparison with Benedick and Beatrice,' and it must be confessed that there is some justice in the observation. Yet Biron, 'that merry mad-cap lord,' is not overrated in Rosaline's admirable character of him—

'A merrier man,
Within the limit of becoming mirth,
I never spent an hour's talk withal;
His eye begets occasion for his wit;
For every object that the one doth catch
The other turns to a mirth-moving jest;—
So sweet and voluble is his discourse.'

There are other immortal characters in the play—Dull, the obtuse constable, on whom Shakespeare improved in Dogberry, and Moth, the page, that 'most acute juvenal,' are, both, original creations and thoroughly Shakespearian.

MERCHANT OF VENICE. ACT II. SCENE V.

HISTORICAL SUMMARY OF THE 'MERCHANT OF VENICE.'

It is generally believed that Shakespeare was indebted to several sources for the materials of this admirable play. The story of the bond is taken from a tale in the Pecorone of Sir Giovanni, a Florentine novelist, who wrote in 1378, three years after the death of Boccace. This book was probably known to our author through the medium of some translation no longer extant. The coincidences between these productions are too striking to be overlooked. Thus, the scene being laid at Venice; the residence of the lady at Belmont; the introduction of a person bound for the principal; the taking more or less than a pound of flesh, and the shedding of blood; together with the incident of the ring, are common to the novel and the play.

The choice of the caskets, in this comedy, is borrowed from chapter 49 of the English *Gesta Romanorum*, where three vessels are placed before the daughter of the king of Apulia for her choice, to prove whether she is worthy to receive the hand of the son of Anselmus, emperor of Rome. The princess, after praying to God for assistance, rejects the gold and silver caskets, and chooses the leaden, which being opened, and found to be full of gold and precious stones, the emperor informs her that she has chosen as he wished, and immediately unites her to his son.

The love and elopement of Jessica and Lorenzo have been noticed by Mr. Dunlop as bearing a similitude to the fourteenth tale of Massuccio di Salerno, who flourished about 1470. In that tale we meet with an avaricious father, a daughter carefully shut up, her elopement with her lover by the intervention of a servant, her robbing her father of his money, together with his grief on the discovery;—a grief, divided equally between the loss of his daughter and the loss of his ducats.

Malone places the date of the composition of this play in 1598. It is mentioned by Meres in his list published in 1598 to be printed by James Roberts, if license were first had from the Lord Chamberlain. It was not printed by Roberts until 1600.

PERSONS REPRESENTED.

DUKE OF VENICE.
PRINCE OF MOROCCO, PRINCE OF ARRAGON, } suitors to Portia.
ANTONIO, the merchant of Venice.
BASSANIO, his friend.
SALANIO, SALARINO, GRATIANO, } friends to Antonio and Bassanio.
LORENZO, in love with Jessica.
SHYLOCK, a Jew.
TUBAL, a Jew, his friend.
LAUNCELOT GOBBO, a clown, servant to Shylock.
OLD GOBBO, father to Launcelot.

Salerio, a messenger from Venice.
Leonardo, servant to Bassanio.
Balthazar, } servants to Portia.
Stephano, }

Portia, a rich heiress.
Nerissa, her waiting-maid.
Jessica, daughter to Shylock.

Magnificoes of Venice, Officers of the court of justice, Jailer, Servants, and other Attendants.

Scene, partly at Venice, and partly at Belmont, the country-seat of Portia.

COMPENDIUM OF THE PLAY.

A rich and beautiful heiress residing at Belmont, named Portia, is compelled by the will of her deceased father to subject every suitor to the choice, by random guess, of a golden, silver, or leaden casket: in the latter is enclosed a portrait of the lady, who is to become the wife of its fortunate selector. Bassanio, a young Venetian gentleman, at length obtains the prize, and is scarcely united to his bride, when he receives intelligence from Venice that his dear friend Antonio, from whose liberality he has procured the means of prosecuting his suit, is completely ruined; and that a bond, which he has executed with a Jew for the payment of a sum of money within a certain period, on forfeiture of a pound of flesh nearest his heart, is now demanded by his inexorable creditor. After receiving a ring from his bride with professions of constancy, Bassanio flies to the relief of his patron: the lady, in the meantime, procures letters of recommendation from an eminent jurist, and, in the disguise of a doctor of laws, is introduced to the duke, as a person well qualified to decide the cause pending between the merchant and the Jew; and at length, by her ingenuity, the unfortunate debtor is delivered from his savage persecutor. The disguised lawyer persists in refusing all pecuniary recompense, but entreats from Bassanio the ring which she had presented to him at his departure, which he reluctantly yields: the same expedient is successfully tried by the waiting-maid, who is the wife of Gratiano, disguised as a lawyer's clerk. The lady and her attendant now hasten home; and, on the arrival of their husbands, amuse themselves with witnessing their confusion at the loss of their love tokens, till the stratagem is at length fully explained. The remainder of this play is occupied with the elopement of Jessica, the daughter of the Jew, with a young man named Lorenzo, who procures from his father-in-law the reversion of his whole property. Gratiano is the bright, light-hearted friend of Antonio and Bassanio, who weds Nerissa. Shylock is not more cruel than his age; for Antonio, honest merchant as he is, would have converted the Jews to Christianity by means of the inquisition; and when Shylock is every way defeated and humbled, insists on his apostatizing from his religious faith, or he will take from him the remaining moiety of his wealth. We do not participate largely in the general sympathy for Antonio; he is full of the prejudices of conventionality, rather dogmatic, melancholy without a cause, and of an unsocial nature. The rattling Gratiano gives him wholesome advice, and although Antonio pretends to despise it, the lively jester is the wiser of the two. Antonio is a bad political economist; he lends money without interest, because he does not understand its value as a commodity in merchandise, as well as its use as a medium of exchange; but he has no right to rail on Shylock, because he declines to follow a profitless and erroneous example. He had gratified his hate to the Jew by many mean and insolent provocations, altogether unworthy of the conduct of a Venetian gentleman; and the act of spitting upon the bread of the Israelite was little short of absolute ruffianism. Still the amiable Antonio justifies this conduct, and says he is likely to repeat it. 'After this,' as Mr. Hazlitt well remarks, 'the appeal to the Jew's mercy, as if there were any common principle of right and wrong between them, is the rankest hypocrisy, or the blindest prejudice.' Mrs. Jamieson (a delightful and very acute writer) is angry with Hazlitt because he thinks Portia a clever woman, and because he says she has a degree of affectation about her which is not usual in Shakespeare's representation of women. She exclaims—'Portia clever! why the word clever implies something common-place, inasmuch as it speaks the presence of the active and perceptive, with a deficiency of the feeling and reflective powers.' 'Portia,' she eloquently continues, 'hangs beside the terrible inexorable Jew, the brilliant lights of her character set off by the shadowy power of his, like a magnificent beauty-breathing Titian by the side of a gorgeous Rembrandt.' Notwithstanding Mrs. Jamieson's appeal in behalf of Portia, we are somewhat inclined to side with Hazlitt in his estimate of the character; she is too quick and sarcastic, and a little too forward. Many of her speeches are very beautiful, and all of them are evidence that she is a woman of great intellect. Nerissa is a pert imitator of her mistress—a copy in water-colors of a fine oil painting. Jessica is not an amiable creation; she runs away from her father to marry one of a race he detests; this is an offence, but still, under the peculiar circumstances, not an unforgivable one: but she robs her father, and wantonly wastes the proceeds of her dishonesty. She has no compunction in leaving her home thus stealthily; on the contrary, her last thought before quitting it is, that she has not helped herself sufficiently to her father's stores. There is a selfishness about this that is disgusting, but the usurer's love of money descended to his offspring, and that which is greedily accumulated by the father is idly dissipated by the daughter. The trial scene is a masterpiece of dramatic construction, a play in itself; with every character perfectly developed. Shylock defends his own cause, and urges his claim with consummate skill; he stands like a rock, unshaken by the waves of argument which repeatedly dash against him. His answers are admirable; elated by a feeling of assured success—triumphing in the anticipated death of his enemy whom he contemplates offering as a sacrifice to the insulted genius of his people, he at first replies in a bantering vein—he'll not answer—it is his humor: but when the duke appeals to his religious feelings, he enters freely into argument—denies that he falls within the censure of the sacred law—he has as much right to a pound of the body of Antonio, which is his by purchase, as they have to the bodies of their domestic slaves. Shylock has the best of the argument; and he feels that he has. The duke cannot answer him, but talks about dismissing the court; when Portia opportunely arrives. At her appearance—taking her for a youth, and, therefore, an inexperienced lawyer—he regards her with a smile of triumph—he is the more certain of his revenge. Already, in imagination, does he see the once haughty, scoffing merchant quivering and fainting beneath his weapon. Gratiano utters a violent invective against him: he answers, with derisive scorn and a bitter wit—

> 'Till thou can'st rail the seal from off my bond,
> Thou but offend'st thy lungs to speak so loud.'

Portia then appeals to his sense of humanity, but his heart is closed; he is offered thrice his money, but avarice is overpowered and swallowed up by a gigantic desire of revenge. Portia makes one final attempt to arouse his feelings;—he will at least have at hand a surgeon, lest Antonio should bleed to death; but he cannot find it so nominated in the bond, and he adheres to the strict letter of the law. It is now that our feelings turn against the Jew; a revenge so implacable seems fiendish, we forget his wrongs, and our sympathy is lost to him. He demands judgment, and flourishing his knife, exclaims to his intended victim, in a voice of vindictive malice, 'Come, prepare.' The scale is now turned; he is told to cut off the pound of flesh, but, adds Portia—

> 'This bond doth give thee here no jot of blood,' etc.

Shylock at once perceives himself defeated, ruined, and triumphed over; his wealth is confiscated and his life is ostentatiously pardoned, but on such conditions, that in the agony of his soul, he solicits them to take that too; and finally, with a bitter, heart-broken sigh, he totters from the court, to hide his sorrow in his lonely and deserted house, a childless, ruined man. We hear no more of Shylock, but the interest is well sustained during the remaining act, and as poetry, it is perhaps superior to the rest of the play; it is like a strain of exquisite melody to soothe the ruffled spirit of the spectator after the excitement of the trial. The light buffoon of the play is Launcelot Gobbo. It is as impossible for Shakespeare to get along without a clown, as for a circus of the present day to omit that amusing feature of the performance.

AS YOU LIKE IT. ACT I. SCENE II.

HISTORICAL SUMMARY OF 'AS YOU LIKE IT.'

The plot of this beautiful and romantic comedy has been attributed by Dr. Grey and Mr. Upton to the Coke's Tale of Gamelyn, erroneously called Chaucer's; but no printed edition of that work made its appearance till near a century after the death of our author, who contented himself with borrowing his story from a novel, or rather pastoral romance, entitled 'Euphues' Golden Legacy,' written in a very fantastical style by Dr. Thomas Lodge, and by him first published in 1590. In addition to the fable, which is pretty exactly followed, the outlines of the principal characters may be traced in the novel, with the exception of Jaques, Touchstone, and Audrey, who are generally admitted to be the creation of the poet.

The first publication of 'As You Like It' appears to have been the folio of 1623. It is supposed by Malone to have been written after 1596, and before 1600. We learn by tradition that Shakespeare himself performed the part of Adam.

'Of this play,' writes Dr. Johnson, 'the fable is wild and pleasing. I know not how the ladies will approve the facility with which both Rosalind and Celia give away their hearts. To Celia much may be forgiven for the heroism of her friendship. The character of Jaques is one of force and originality. The comic dialogue is very sprightly, with less mixture of low buffoonery than in some other plays; and the graver part is elegant and harmonious. By hastening to the end of his work, Shakespeare suppressed the dialogue between the usurper and the hermit, and lost an opportunity of exhibiting a moral lesson, in which he might have found matter worthy of his highest powers.'

PERSONS REPRESENTED.

DUKE, living in exile.
FREDERICK, brother to the Duke, and usurper of his dominions.
AMIENS, JAQUES, } lords attending upon the Duke in his banishment.
LE BEAU, a courtier attending upon Frederick.
CHARLES, his wrestler.
OLIVER, ORLANDO, } sons of Sir Rowland de Bois.
ADAM, DENNIS, } servants to Oliver.
TOUCHSTONE, a clown.
SIR OLIVER MAR-TEXT, a vicar.
CORIN, SYLVIUS, } shepherds.
WILLIAM, a country fellow, in love with Audrey.
A person representing HYMEN.

ROSALIND, daughter to the banished Duke.
CELIA, daughter to Frederick.

PHEBE, a shepherdess.
AUDREY, a country wench.

Lords belonging to the two Dukes; Pages, Foresters, and other Attendants.

The SCENE lies, first, near Oliver's house; afterwards, partly in the usurper's court, and partly in the forest of Arden.

COMPENDIUM OF THE PLAY.

A DUKE of France, being dispossessed of his dominions by Frederick, his younger brother, retires to the forest of Arden with a few faithful adherents, leaving behind him his daughter Rosalind, who is detained at the court of the usurper to be a companion to her cousin Celia. While here, Rosalind becomes enamored of young Orlando, son of Sir Roland de Bois, the old duke's friend, who signalizes himself in wrestling before the court. The accomplishments and popularity of Rosalind soon, however, excite the apprehensions of her uncle, who banishes her from his territories: the affection of Celia prompts her to accompany her kinswoman, and she makes her escape in the disguise of a shepherdess, while Rosalind assumes the habit of a man. Arrived at the forest of Arden, the two friends purchase a house and grounds, where they reside for some time as brother and sister: here they are agreeably surprised at the presence of Orlando, who, in order to guard his life from the machinations of Oliver, his elder brother, is compelled to join the company of the banished Duke. Rosalind, after, by delightful strategy, satisfying herself of the attachment of her lover, and the willingness of her father to consent to their union, resumes her female apparel, and bestows her hand on Orlando, while Celia becomes the wife of the repentant Oliver, whose life is preserved from the fury of a lion by the bravery of his injured brother. In the meantime Duke Frederick, jealous of the increasing number of his opponents, arrives with a large army for the purpose of exterminating them: on the skirts of the forest he is encountered by an old hermit, who dissuades him from the prosecution of his cruel enterprise. Struck with remorse, he voluntarily resigns his dukedom, and retires from the world, while the exiles are reinstated in their former dignities. The character of Jaques is natural and well preserved—one of the most pleasant philosophers the world has ever seen. Touchstone is the most intellectual of the fools of Shakespeare; he is a great lover of argument; there is no broad farcical fun about him, but a grave humor which is admirable. He is a moral teacher, too, in his way, and regrets 'that fools may not speak wisely what wise men do foolishly.' Some of his sayings are aphorisms of considerable wisdom, as, 'Rich honesty dwells like a miser, sir, in a poor house; as your pearl in your foul oyster;' and 'Your *If* is your only peacemaker; much virtue in an *If*.' In the introduction of Sir Oliver Mar-text (a character seldom played), our poet indulges in a sly hit against the Puritan and itinerant ministers, whom he appears to have regarded with aversion. The concluding observation of the curate stamps him as a man not properly qualified for the clerical profession. Audrey is a country lass, as ignorant as might be supposed from a life of so isolated a nature, but there is something really winning in the poor girl's natural simplicity. Touchstone, regretting her want of an appreciative understanding of his humorous sallies, wishes that the gods had made her poetical, to which she replies: 'I do not know what poetical is; is it honest in deed and word? Is it a true thing?' This character is often misunderstood upon the stage, being represented as a coarse country gawky; a little consideration of the poet will show that she is an artless, comely peasant-girl, ignorant enough, but attractive from her fresh rural simplicity and unreserved sincerity.

HISTORICAL SUMMARY OF 'ALL'S WELL THAT ENDS WELL.'

The fable of this comedy is taken from a novel, of which Boccace is the original author; but which was immediately derived by Shakespeare from the tale of Giletta of Narbonne, in the first volume of William Painter's 'Palace of Pleasure,' printed at London in 1566. To this novel, however, the poet was only indebted for the leading features of the more serious parts of his drama: the comic characters, and especially that of Parolles, appear to be entirely of his own formation.

A supposed allusion to the fanaticism of the Puritans induced Malone to assign the date of 1606 to the composition of this play; but the many passages of rhyme scattered throughout seem to mark it as an earlier production. In 1598 Meres refers to a play of Shakespeare, called 'Love's Labor Wonne,' which very accurately applies to this, but to no other of our author's productions: we have reason therefore to conclude that it was intended as a counter-title to 'Love's Labor's Lost;' and that the present proverbial appellation was suggested in consequence of the adage itself being found in the body of the play.

'This play,' says Dr. Johnson, 'has many delightful and some happy characters, though not new, nor produced by any deep knowledge of human nature. Parolles is a boaster and a coward, such as has always

ALL'S WELL THAT ENDS WELL. ACT III. SCENE II.

Bertram repudiating Helena after his marriage to her.

been the sport of the stage; but perhaps never raised more laughter or contempt than in the hands of Shakespeare. I cannot reconcile my heart to Bertram; a man noble without generosity, and young without truth: who marries Helena as a coward, and leaves her as a profligate: when she is dead by his unkindness, sneaks home to a second marriage; is accused by a woman whom he has wronged; defends himself by falsehood; and is dismissed to happiness.'

PERSONS REPRESENTED.

KING OF FRANCE.
DUKE OF FLORENCE.
BERTRAM, count of Rousillon.
LAFEU, an old lord.
PAROLLES, a follower of Bertram.
Several young French Lords, that serve with Bertram in the Florentine war.
STEWARD, CLOWN, A PAGE, } servants to the countess of Rousillon.

COUNTESS OF ROUSILLON, mother to Bertram.
HELENA, a gentlewoman protected by the countess.
An old WIDOW of Florence.
DIANA, daughter to the widow.
VIOLENTA, MARIANA, } neighbors and friends to the widow.

Lords attending on the king; Officers, Soldiers, etc., French and Florentine.

SCENE, partly in France and partly in Tuscany.

COMPENDIUM OF THE PLAY.

HELENA, the daughter of a celebrated physician, conceives a violent attachment to Bertram, count of Rousillon, who on the death of his father repairs to Paris, as a ward of the king of France, at this time languishing under the influence of a distemper which has been pronounced incurable. Directed by the medical knowledge she has received from her father, Helena procures an audience of the monarch, and undertakes to effect his cure, on condition of choosing for herself a husband, with reservation only of the royal family. The king is restored to health, and the lady fixes her choice on Bertram. Unable to resist, the young count reluctantly consents to the nuptials, which are no sooner performed, than he dismisses his bride to her home, and sets out for Florence, whence he sends her a letter intimating his determination of never cohabiting with her till (what he considers to be an impossibility) she obtains a ring which he wears on his finger, and is pregnant by him. The receipt of this epistle induces Helena to quit the castle of Rousillon, and proceed to Italy, where she hears of her husband's unsuccessful attempts on the chastity of a widow's daughter, on whom she prevails to pretend to accede to his solicitations, and Helena is afterwards introduced in her stead to the bed of Bertram, and there contrives to exchange rings with him. Soon after Bertram, having received intelligence of the death of Helena, returns to France, and is reconciled to the king, who is about to consent to his union with the daughter of a favorite courtier, when he detects a ring in his possession, which he had formerly presented to Helena, who had contrived to place it on her husband's finger during his supposed assignation with his Italian mistress. Failing to give any satisfactory account of the means by which he obtained it, he is suspected of having murdered his wife, when Helena appears, satisfies her husband of the fulfilment of his requisitions, and is publicly acknowledged by the repentant Bertram. We could have wished that the long discussion between Parolles and Helena in the first act had been given to some other character; it profanes the otherwise delicate modesty of her nature, which is on no other occasion overstepped or laid aside; even in her strange plan to obtain the affections of her husband. This coarse dialogue, witty and ingenious as it is, would have been better omitted; it was one of Shakespeare's numerous concessions to the sensuality of his audiences. The Countess, mother of Bertram, is a highly interesting character; Shakespeare invests all his matrons with dignity; he is no ungallant poet who represents the young only as attractive. The amiability and wisdom of the Countess win our admiration, and her directions to her son on his leaving her for the court, though brief, may be justly placed in comparison with Polonius's sage and excellent advice to Laertes on a similar occasion. The king is a philosophical invalid, who utters many valuable moral truths; his expostulation with Bertram on his pride of birth is a piece of powerful reasoning. It is equally true as strange that, despite our lofty pretensions and cherished ancestral dignities, our blood poured altogether 'would quite confound distinction.' Parolles is the great comic creation of the piece, a fop, a fool, a liar, a braggart, and every way a knave; and yet, with all these vices, amusing enough. He is too contemptible for anger; we almost pity him when he is discovered and disgraced, and even when he is exposed to the unmerciful raillery of the jovial old Lord Lafeu, who says 'there can be no kernel in this light nut; the soul of this man is his clothes.' His adventure in search of the lost drum, which he swears he will recover or perish in attempting to do so, and then goes out for a walk at night to devise some account of his expedition, is a piece of admirable comedy. But his being taken prisoner by his own companions (who suspect his cowardice), blindfolded, and made to confess to them the secrets of their own camp, is irresistibly amusing; equal in broad fun to Falstaff's midnight adventure at Gadshill. But Parolles cannot extricate himself from a difficulty with the same dexterity that is evinced by the jovial fat knight; once discovered he is disgraced forever, and he resolves to give up military pretensions and live 'safest in shame.' He turns parasite and gets his bread by flattery. In this new capacity he shows great dexterity, and when he enters in soiled and ragged attire, he propitiates the old Lord Lafeu in his favor by a delicate compliment, 'O my good Lord, you were the first that found me;' that is, your strong sense and discernment first discovered me to be a braggart and no soldier. The shrewd old noble is flattered into compassion, and exclaims: 'Though you are a fool and a knave, you shall eat: go to, follow.'

Monsieur Lavatch, the clown, with his answer that suits all questions, adds to the comic interest of the play, and may fairly take rank with Touchstone and Feste for humor and equivocating wit.

In noticing the beauties of this comedy, the scene where the young Count Bertram woos Diana to yield to his impetuous and unlawful love should not be forgotten; a finer lesson on maiden purity was never preached; a holier caution to young and susceptible beauty never fell from the lips of moralist or sage.

HISTORICAL SUMMARY OF THE 'TAMING OF THE SHREW.'

NOTHING appears to invalidate the conclusion of Malone that this was one of Shakespeare's earlier plays, although Warburton and Farmer have disputed its authenticity. It abounds with the doggerel measure and tedious play on words, so observable in 'The Comedy of Errors,' and 'Love's Labor's Lost,' which Shakespeare took occasion to condemn in one of his subsequent comedies. The year 1596 is the probable date of its production, since in 1594, an old play, on which the present drama is supposed to be founded, was entered at Stationers' Hall, entitled 'Taming of a Shrew,' which is attributed to the pen of George Peele or Robert Greene. The plots of these two pieces are found to be essentially the same.

The story of Lucentio, and his artifice to obtain the hand of Bianca, is formed on a comedy of George Gascoigne, from the Italian of Ariosto, called 'Supposes,' which was performed by the gentlemen of Gray's Inn in 1566; and the Induction is borrowed from Goulart's *Histoires Admirables de nôtre Temps*, translated from the Latin of Heuterus, who relates a similar delusion, which was practised on the credulity of a poor artisan at Brussels by Philip the Good, duke of Burgundy.

TAMING OF THE SHREW. INDUCTION, SCENE II.

Christopher Sly seated to witness the Play.

PERSONS REPRESENTED.

A LORD.

CHRISTOPHER SLY, a drunken tinker. Hostess, Page, Players, Huntsmen, and other servants attending on the lord.	Persons in the Induction.

BAPTISTA, a rich gentleman of Padua.
VINCENTIO, an old gentleman of Pisa.
LUCENTIO, son to Vincentio, in love with Bianca.
PETRUCHIO, a gentleman of Verona, a suitor to Katharina.

GREMIO, HORTENSIO,	suitors to Bianca.
TRANIO, BIONDELLO,	servants to Lucentio.
GRUMIO, CURTIS,	servants to Petruchio.

PEDANT, an old fellow set up to personate Vincentio.

KATHARINA, the shrew, BIANCA, her sister,	daughters to Baptista.

WIDOW.

Tailor, Haberdasher, and Servants attending on Baptista and Petruchio.

SCENE, sometimes in Padua; and sometimes in Petruchio's house in the country.

COMPENDIUM OF THE PLAY.

A NOBLEMAN, returning from the chase, finds an ignorant tinker, named Sly, lying on the bench of an alehouse, dead-drunk, and causes him to be conveyed home, laid on one of his richest beds, and arrayed in the most costly apparel. When the drunkard awakes, he is surrounded by attendants, who succeed in persuading him that he is a nobleman, who for many years has been laboring under mental delusion. The conviction of Sly that he is 'a lord indeed' is succeeded by the introduction of a company of players, who entertain him with the representation of a comedy, of which the following is a brief outline: A citizen of Padua, named Baptista, the father of Katharina and Bianca, refuses to listen to the numerous admirers of the latter till after the marriage of her elder sister, whose violence of temper effectually deters all suitors; and the lovers of Bianca are compelled to resort to the expedient of procuring a husband for Katharina, which they accomplish, in the person of Petruchio. By a rough and singular method of courtship the shrew is won, and at length tamed by a perseverance in the same course of treatment. In the meantime, Lucentio, a young gentleman of Pisa, introduces himself to Bianca in the disguise of a classical tutor, and succeeds in obtaining her hand by the intervention of his servant Tranio, who assumes the name and apparel of his master in order to forward his designs. The presence of Lucentio's father becomes necessary, and Tranio devises the scheme of engaging a schoolmaster to represent him. At this critical juncture the real father unexpectedly arrives, and encounters his son's servant in his master's clothes. Tranio impudently disclaims all knowledge of his master's father, who is about to be committed to jail as an impostor, when his son enters with his bride, and a reconciliation is speedily effected. Schlegel thinks that the latter part of Shakespeare's play of 'Taming of a Shrew' has been lost, or that the remarks of the tinker during the progress of the play were left to the judgment of the actor, though he also admits that it is unlikely that the poet should have left to chance the conclusion of that which he had so carefully commenced. The character of Sly in the introduction is drawn with a broad pencil, and in a style of the richest humor; he is very sceptical of the truth and reality of his newly acquired rank, and asks incredulously—'am I not Christopher Sly, old Sly's son of Burton-heath; by birth, a pedlar; by education, a card-maker; by transmutation, a bear-herd; and now, by present profession, a tinker!' To dissipate his doubts, his deceivers call in the aid of music, and description in language exquisitely glowing, of the pleasures which await him. They describe his horses, hawks, and hounds, his pictures:

'Adonis, painted by a running brook;
And Cytherea all in sedges hid;
Which seem to move and wanton with her breath,
Even as the waving sedges play with wind.'

And lastly his wife, whom they describe as—

'A lady far more beautiful
Than any woman in this waning age.'

The poor tinker is bewildered and convinced, and determines to celebrate, what he supposes to be his return to reason, with 'a pot o' the smallest ale.' In the play itself, Petruchio and Katharina are eminently Shakespearian creations. Petruchio, Benedick, and Mercutio, etc., are a class of characters peculiar to our poet, and which could only have been written by a man with a natural cheerfulness and love of humanity. In drawing the character of Katharina, Shakespeare has pictured a woman naturally of a kind though irritable disposition, made a complete scold by early indulgence and a bad education. Petruchio undertakes to re-educate her, and he does so with a happy effect: the virago becomes a gentle and obedient wife. Her lecture, after she has been tamed, in the banquet scene, to her sister and the widow, on the duty which a woman owes her husband, is a fine moral sermon, dressed in language of the loftiest poetry. Beaumont and Fletcher's comedy of 'The Woman's Prize; or, the Tamer Tam'd,' is a continuation of the 'Taming of the Shrew,' and in it Petruchio is in his turn subdued by a second wife.

WINTER'S TALE. ACT III. SCENE II.

The Trial of Hermione. The oracle of Apollo having been consulted, the answer is read in court.

HISTORICAL SUMMARY OF 'THE WINTER'S TALE.'

The story of this play is taken from Robert Greene's 'Pleasant History of Dorastus and Fawnia,' which was published in 1588. Shakespeare has, however, changed the names of the characters, and added the parts of Antigonus, Paulina, and Autolycus from his own invention.

'The Winter's Tale' was not entered on the Stationers' books, or printed till 1623, while we learn from Vertue's manuscripts that it was acted at court in 1613. Malone attributes the composition to the year 1611; but Lord Orford assigns to it a much earlier date, and conjectures that it was written during the lifetime of Elizabeth, and that it was intended as an indirect apology for Anne Boleyn; in which light it might be considered as a sequel to 'King Henry VIII.'

Much censure has been cast on our author by Dryden and Pope for his disregard of the classical unities, which are nowhere so daringly violated as in this production, where we meet with a young woman becoming a bride, who, but a few minutes before, had been deposited on the sea-shore, a new-born infant.

Schlegel has observed of this drama that its title is happily adapted to its subject, being 'one of those tales which are peculiarly calculated to beguile the dreary leisure of a long winter evening, which is even attractive and intelligible to childhood, and which, animated by fervent truth in the delineation of character and passion, invested with the decoration of a poetry lowering itself, as it were, to the simplicity of the subject, transport even manhood back to the golden age of imagination.'

PERSONS REPRESENTED.

LEONTES, king of Sicilia.
MAMILLIUS, his son.
CAMILLO, ANTIGONUS, CLEOMENES, DION, } Sicilian lords.
Another Sicilian Lord.
ROGERO, a Sicilian gentleman.
An Attendant on the young prince Mamillius.
Officers of a court of judicature.
POLIXENES, king of Bohemia.
FLORIZEL, his son.
ARCHIDAMUS, a Bohemian lord.
A MARINER.
JAILER.
An old SHEPHERD, reputed father of Perdita.
CLOWN, his son.
Servant to the old Shepherd.
AUTOLYCUS, a rogue.
TIME, as chorus.

HERMIONE, queen to Leontes.
PERDITA, daughter to Leontes and Hermione.
PAULINA, wife to Antigonus.
EMILIA, a lady, Two other Ladies, } attending the queen.

MOPSA, DORCAS, } shepherdesses.

Lords, Ladies and Attendants; Satyrs for a dance; Shepherds, Shepherdesses, Guards, etc.

SCENE, sometimes in Sicilia; sometimes in Bohemia.

COMPENDIUM OF THE PLAY.

POLIXENES, king of Bohemia, during a visit to his friend Leontes, king of Sicily, awakens the jealousy of his host, who unjustly suspects him of an intrigue with his wife Hermione, and endeavors to prevail on a courtier, named Camillo, to poison his guest: instead, however, of complying with his request, Camillo informs the unsuspecting monarch of his danger, and accompanies him in his flight to Bohemia. Leontes now vents his rage on the innocent Hermione, who is debarred from the society of her son, and confined in prison, where she is delivered of a daughter named Perdita, who is considered by Leontes as spurious, and ordered to be exposed for death. Antigonus, to whose custody the infant is committed, reaches the Bohemian territories, and during his progress is strangled by a bear, while the child is found by a poor shepherd, who rears it as his own. In the meantime, the character of Hermione is completely vindicated by the answer of the oracle of Delphi, which informs Leontes that he shall want an heir to his kingdom till the lost infant is found; and in confirmation of its truth, his son suddenly expires immediately after the arrival of the commissioners. The spirits of the queen are unable to sustain this last shock; she nearly dies, and the intelligence of her death is soon after conveyed to her repentant husband. At the age of sixteen, Perdita captivates the affections of Florizel, the son of Polixenes, who contrives to escape from Bohemia with his affianced bride, and reaches the coast of Sicily, whither he is pursued by his enraged father: the apparel and jewels, which were found with the infant at the time of its exposure, are now produced by the shepherd, and Perdita is recognized as the daughter of Leontes, and bestowed in marriage on her lover. Paulina, the widow of Antigonus, invites her master and his guests to inspect a statue of Hermione, which excites unbounded admiration as a triumph of art, when the supposed marble becomes animated, and Leontes recovers his amiable wife, who had in retirement awaited the fulfilment of the oracle. Antolycus, the rogue, and the young shepherd and his two sweethearts, Mopsa and Dorcas, are a source of pleasant relief and merriment.

Henry Tyrrell says: Shakespeare has been much censured on account of his utter disregard of the unities of time and place in this play, and for his anachronisms and geographical errors. Sixteen years elapse between the third and fourth acts; which circumstance so shocked Dryden that, speaking of this and some other productions of Shakespeare, he said they 'were either grounded on impossibilities, or so meanly written, that the comedy neither caused your mirth nor the serious part your concernment.'

The master-spirit of the drama is not to be measured with a foot-rule and bound down by frigid regulations, which every powerful imagination makes use of only so far as they are consistent with and favorable to his own design. Mr. Steevens has justly remarked that Shakespeare 'was not ignorant of these rules, but disregarded them.'

With respect to the geographical error of making Bohemia a sea-bounded country, and opening a water communication between it and Sicilia, the poet doubtless erred from ignorance. Greene, from whose story of 'Pandosta' he had borrowed the subject, had previously fallen into the same error, and Shakespeare has copied it without examination. We are willing to grant this freely, but it takes nothing from the exquisite beauty of the play; it is none the less one of the finest comedies in existence although it contains a geographical error. It is the critic's duty to point out such literal imperfections, that they might not mislead the uninformed; but it betrays a pert and hasty judgment, when, presuming on the existence of such errors, he proceeds to condemn the work. It is as if a man finding among many precious pearls a few worthless pebbles should condemn them all as valueless.

Leontes is justly punished for his suspicion; his infant and dearly loved son pines and dies in consequence of his mother's disgrace; his daughter is bred up by rude shepherds at a distance from her stricken father, and his queen lost to him for a period of sixteen years, during which he bitterly reproaches himself as the cause of her supposed death. His remorse is not diminished by time; when the long separation is about to cease, and Paulina reminds him of the perfections of the woman he had killed, he answers mournfully:

> 'She I kill'd? I did so; but thou strik'st me
> Sorely, to say I did.'

Shakespeare had the materials of a tragedy in his hand, had he been so disposed to treat the subject, but he chose to make it, like life, a mingled yarn of good and evil, smiles and tears; and the sense of gloom produced by the sad effects of Leontes' jealousy is dissipated by the charm of rustic, yet still majestic, beauty, which surrounds Perdita, as the queen of the rural feast, distributing flowers and discoursing sweetly on their names and nature; by the quaint humor of the rogue, Autolycus, who, like his namesake, the son of Mercury, is 'a snapper up of unconsidered trifles;' and by the hearty merriment of the young shepherd and his two sweethearts, Mopsa and Dorcas. The court and the cottage are brought closely together, and while suspicion and remorse abide with princes, cheerfulness and mirth dwell with peasants.

All throughout this play the language is in the poet's most mature and perfect style; it is profuse in beauty, wanton and luxuriant in exquisite imaginations and aphorisms of deep wisdom. How admirable is Paulina's taunt to the passionate monarch, when he threatens to condemn her to the stake:

> 'I care not;
> It is an heretic that makes the fire,
> Not she which burns in it.'

And for beauty, the whole of the third scene of the fourth act may be quoted as being almost without a parallel. The concluding scene also, where the supposed statue of Hermione is exhibited, and where, at the word of Paulina, it assumes animation, and the still living queen is restored to the embraces of her repentant husband, and her daughter, who had been estranged from her from the first hour of her birth, is an admirable and touching invention of Shakespeare's own inspiration.

COMEDY OF ERRORS. ACT V. SCENE I.

The Abbess brings on Antipholus and Dromio of Syracuse.

HISTORICAL SUMMARY OF THE 'COMEDY OF ERRORS.'

SHAKESPEARE appears to have taken the general plan of this comedy from a translation of the 'Menæchmi of Plautus,' by W. W., i. e. (according to Wood), William Warner, in 1595, whose version of the argument is as follows:—

'Two twinne-borne sons a Sicill marchant had,
  Menechmus one, and Sosicles the other:
The first his father lost, a little lad;
  The grandsire namde the latter like his brother.
This, growne a man, long travell tooke to seeke
  His brother, and to Epidamnum came,
Where th' other dwelt inricht, and him so like,
  That citizens there take him for the same;
Father, wife, neighbours, each mistaking either,
  Much pleasant error, ere they meete togither.'

Perhaps the last of these lines suggested to Shakespeare the title for his piece.

'In this play,' says Mr. Steevens, 'we find more intricacy of plot than distinction of character; and our attention is less forcibly engaged, because we can guess, in great measure, how the *dénouement* will be brought about. Yet the subject appears to have been reluctantly dismissed, even in the last and unnecessary scene, where the same mistakes are continued, till they have lost the power of affording any entertainment at all.'

Dr. Drake, in defending our author from the indiscriminate censure of Steevens, observes, that 'if we consider the construction of the fable, the narrowness of its basis, and that its powers of entertainment are almost exclusively confined to a continued deception of the external senses, we must confess that Shakespeare has not only improved on the Plautian model, but, making allowance for a somewhat too coarse vein of humor, has given to his production all the interest and variety that the nature and the limits of his subject would permit.'

PERSONS REPRESENTED.

SOLINUS, duke of Ephesus.
ÆGEON, a merchant of Syracuse.
ANTIPHOLUS of Ephesus, } Twin brothers, and sons to Ægeon and Æmilia, but unknown to each other.
ANTIPHOLUS of Syracuse, }
DROMIO of Ephesus, } Twin brothers, and attendants on the two Antipholuses.
DROMIO of Syracuse, }
BALTHAZAR, a merchant.
ANGELO, a goldsmith.
A MERCHANT, creditor to Angelo.
PINCH, a schoolmaster and conjurer.

ÆMILIA, wife to Ægeon, an abbess at Ephesus.
ADRIANA, wife to Antipholus of Ephesus.
LUCIANA, her sister.

LUCE, her servant.
A COURTEZAN.

Jailer, Officers, and other Attendants.

SCENE, Ephesus.

COMPENDIUM OF THE PLAY.

A RICH merchant of Syracuse, named Ægeon, and a poor man of the same city, became the fathers of twin sons, each pair exactly resembling each other in feature: the children of the latter are purchased by the citizen, who bestows them on his sons as attendants. Ægeon, with his wife and family, shortly after visits Epidamnum; and on their return, the ship in which they sail is split asunder by a violent storm, which separates the husband from the wife, and each of the twin brothers from their respective counterparts. Ægeon, with his younger son and attendant, is rescued from his perilous condition, and conveyed to Syracuse. Arrived at years of maturity, the young man is anxious to procure some intelligence of his mother and brother, and, with the consent of his father, quits his home, and at length, in company with his servant, arrives at Ephesus, where the elder Antipholus, who separated from his mother, has long resided, in high favor with the duke, at whose desire he has united himself to a lady of fortune, who now mistakes the stranger for her husband, insisting that he shall accompany her home to dinner: the real husband arrives during the repast, and finds his own doors barred against his entrance. The perplexities, arising from the confusion of the masters and their servants, induce the Syracusan youth to suppose himself under the influence of witchcraft, and he takes refuge in a religious house, whither his mother had retired, and had long presided as abbess. The Ephesian dame, supposing the refugee to be her husband, complains to the duke of the conduct of the abbess, who refuses to deliver him up to the custody of his wife. The simultaneous appearance of the young men and their servants now unravels the mystery. In the mean time, Ægeon lands at Ephesus, and is about to lose his head for a violation of the law in entering a hostile city, when he is ransomed by his son, from whom he had parted at Syracuse; and recognizes, in the person of the abbess, his long-lost wife, Æmilia.

J. O. Halliwell says: The materials of which the 'Comedy of Errors' is constructed chiefly belong to the cycle of farce, but they have been worked into a comedy by a wonderful effort of dramatic power; the lighter character, however, remaining prominent in particular scenes. Comedy would allow the two Antipholuses with a license similar to that which sanctions the resemblance between Sebastian and Viola in 'Twelfth Night;' but the two Dromios, in conjunction with the former, certainly belong to farce. The admirable manner in which the mistakes arising from these identities are conducted, and the dignity given to the whole by the introduction of fine poetry most artistically interwoven, are indicative of that high dramatic genius which belongs almost exclusively to Shakespeare. The poetical conversation between Luciana and Antipholus of Syracuse reminds us forcibly of the 'Sonnets,' and the similar ideas in the former are strengthened in power by being associated with a dramatic narrative; for had Shakespeare not been a dramatist, he would scarcely have ranked as so great a poet. No play of Shakespeare's, whether either effectively read or acted, affords as many subjects for broad merriment as this.

HISTORICAL SUMMARY OF 'MACBETH.'

MALONE has assigned to the year 1606 the composition of this great effort of our author's genius, which has been regarded as the medium of dexterous and graceful flattery to James I., a lineal descendant of Banquo, who is charged by the old historians with a participation in the murder of Duncan, although for very obvious reasons Shakespeare has here represented him as innocent of that cruel deed.

The original narrative of these events is contained in the *Scotorum Historiæ* of Hector Boethius, whence it was translated into the Scottish dialect by John Bellenden, and afterwards into English by Holinshed, from whose Chronicles Shakespeare closely followed it. The awful incantations and mysterious agency of the witches in this tragedy could not fail to be highly gratifying to the pedantic vanity of a monarch, whose prejudices in favor of the reality of witchcraft or enchantment are well known.

'This play,' says Dr. Johnson, 'is deservedly celebrated for the propriety of its fictions, and solemnity, grandeur, and variety of its action ; but it has no nice discriminations of character : the events are too great to admit the influence of particular dispositions ; and the course of the action necessarily determines the conduct of the agents. The danger of ambition is well described ; and I know not whether it may not be said, in defence of some parts which now seem improbable,

MACBETH. ACT III. SCENE IV.

Macbeth at the banquet sees a ghost.

that in Shakespeare's time it was necessary to warn credulity against vain and illusive predictions. The passions are directed to their true end. Lady Macbeth is merely detested; and though the courage of Macbeth preserves some esteem, yet every reader rejoices at his fall.'

PERSONS REPRESENTED.

DUNCAN, king of Scotland.
MALCOLM, DONALBAIN, } his sons.
MACBETH, BANQUO, } generals of the king's army.
MACDUFF, LENOX, ROSSE, MENTETH, ANGUS, CATHNESS, } noblemen of Scotland.
FLEANCE, son to Banquo.
SIWARD, earl of Northumberland, general of the English forces.
YOUNG SIWARD, his son.
SEYTON, an officer attending on Macbeth.
SON TO MACDUFF.
AN ENGLISH DOCTOR. A SCOTCH DOCTOR.
A SOLDIER. A PORTER. AN OLD MAN.

LADY MACBETH.
LADY MACDUFF.

GENTLEWOMAN attending on Lady Macbeth.
HECATE, and THREE WITCHES.

Lords, Gentlemen, Officers, Soldiers, Murderers, Attendants, and Messengers.

The Ghost of Banquo, and several other Apparitions.

SCENE, in the end of the fourth act, lies in England; through the rest of the play, in Scotland; and, chiefly, at Macbeth's castle.

COMPENDIUM OF THE PLAY.

DUNCAN, king of Scotland, is rescued from the calamities of foreign invasion and domestic treason by the valor of his generals Macbeth and Banquo, who, after the defeat of the enemy, are returning in triumph, when they are arrested in their progress by three witches, who salute Macbeth by the titles of Cawdor and king; at the same time foretelling that Banquo shall be the father of a race of kings, although he shall never be in possession of the crown. After the announcement of these prophecies, the witches vanish, and messengers arrive from Duncan with the intelligence that the rebellious thane of Cawdor is condemned to death, and that his title is conferred on Macbeth, whose ambition is now panting for the fulfilment of the remainder of the prediction: overcome by the suggestions of his wife, he murders his sovereign in his sleep, during a visit with which he honors him. By the artful contrivances of the guilty pair, the king's two sons, Malcolm and Donalbain, are suspected of parricide, and compelled to purchase their safety by flight. The sovereignty now devolves on Macbeth, who, fearful of the prophecy which assigns the crown to the posterity of Banquo, resolves to free himself of his apprehensions by the assassination both of him and his only son: the father is slain, but his son Fleance escapes under favor of the night. In the meantime, Malcolm, the eldest son of Duncan, resides in the English court, under the protection of Edward the Confessor, who raises a large army in his behalf, under command of Siward, Earl of Northumberland, which is strengthened by the arrival of Macduff, the thane of Fife, who, in consequence of Macbeth's jealousy, is compelled to quit his country: after his departure, the inhuman tyrant wreaks his vengeance on that nobleman's wife and children, all of whom he causes to be murdered. The two friends, with their English auxiliaries, now proceed towards Scotland, where they are joined by a number of discontented nobles. Macbeth is defeated and slain; his wretched wife, tormented with remorse, puts a period to her existence; and Malcolm is restored to the throne of his ancestors.

Let us give a brief analysis of its principal characters; it may be called a sublime homily on the weakness of human nature—a startling warning, spoken as it were, in words of thunder, and written in characters of blood, against dallying with temptation. Macbeth is gradually led to do that which he persuades himself he cannot avoid—he consents to become a murderer, because he believes that fate has willed it so; he is not the first or the last great criminal who has cast his sins upon a supposed fatal and indisputable ordinance, and who believes, or professes to believe, that he was predestined to evil. He is brave and just before he is tempted, but when tempted strongly, he yields, and falls from the warrior to the tyrant—timorous, cunning and blood-thirsty. When he slays the unoffending Duncan he first reasons strongly against the act, tries to escape from its commission—his conscience wrestles with him, and represents the virtues of the meek king pleading like angels 'against the deep damnation' of the deed; and when the act is done, it is instantly repented, and the murderer stands aghast at his soul-destroying work. The poet has here presented us with an awful picture of the terrors of conscience—the shuddering murderer trembling at every sound, and peopling the air with avenging voices uttering strange and fearful threatenings; but after Macbeth becomes deeply steeped in blood and familiar with crime, we may observe the savage premeditation of his murders. When giving directions for the death of Banquo, he addresses the assassins thus: 'Was it not yesterday we spoke together?' evincing a perfect indifference to the intended destruction of his old associate and fellow-soldier; he has altogether got rid of the 'compunctious visitings' which shook him when engaged in the murder of Duncan. It has been said that a man who commits one murder, and escapes detection or punishment, seldom remains single in his crime—he is hounded on by his impetuous and savage desires again to imbrue his hands in blood; thus is it with Macbeth: he feels that for him there is no retreat, and he adds crime to crime, until he becomes a mere vulgar tyrant, surrounding his nobility with spies, and, in his fear, devoting to death even the innocent, whom he merely suspected to be dangerous.

Lady Macbeth is such a character as Shakespeare alone, of all dramatists, could have painted—terrible even to sublimity in her determinate wickedness—fiend-like in the savage obduracy of her nature; the bitter scoffer of the irresolute pleadings of departing virtue, and the expiring throes of conscience in her guilty partner; still she is never utterly beyond our sympathy. She urges her husband to the murder of Duncan, but she bears no hatred to the mild old king: he is an obstacle in her path to greatness, and must be removed. When bending over his couch, on the fearful night of his murder, when, amidst the howlings of the storm and the rack of the elements, there were

'Lamentings heard i' the air; strange screams of death
And prophesying, with accents terrible'—

even then, unmoved by all these horrors, she contemplates his destruction by her own hand; but the resemblance between him and her aged father shoots athwart her mind, and she experiences a momentary tenderness for the unsuspecting and defenceless monarch. She is a woman still. But this softening of her stern nature is but transient; it does not last long enough to interfere with her dread resolve; she feels, but smothers human sympathies, and brings them into bondage to her adamantine will. This fearful woman is a faithful and affectionate wife: we view her with none of the abhorrence which is excited in us towards Regan and Goneril, the cruel and unnatural daughters of the aged Lear, whom, with an exquisite probability, Shakespeare also makes unchaste and treacherous wives. When, at the banquet, Macbeth raves about the ghost of Banquo, who glares horribly upon him and points to the

'Twenty trenched gashes on his head,'

she dismisses the guests in confusion; but when they are gone, she utters not one word of reproach, but gently tells him that he lacks rest.

She has shown no sign of repentance—spoken no word of compunction; yet we see her punishment is begun; the torture of the mind tells on the fevered frame; the seed which she had sown in blood, though it had grown to be a vigorous plant, had borne no fruit; and when she next comes upon the scene, it is when brokenhearted and dying she utters in her sleep those fearful thoughts which, in her watchful moments, she had kept closed up in her own sad, yet hardened heart.

After Macbeth and his ambitious wife, there are few strongly marked characters in the play, except Macduff, thane of Fife, who had fled with Malcolm and Donalbain, and on whom Macbeth wreaks vengeance by destroying his wife and children. Macduff gladly joins Malcolm in his vengeance on Macbeth, and at one point of the play Macduff, in the hands of a good actor, overshadows Macbeth in the grandeur of his declamation for revenge. Duncan is a mild and virtuous sovereign; but he calls for little further comment: the softness of his nature is traceable in the timid characters of his two sons, who, by their disgraceful flight, at first incur the suspicion of being his murderers. Banquo is the opposite of Macbeth, being both a brave and virtuous general. The witches solicit him also during sleep to some horrible act, but he prays against a repetition of the temptation, while Macbeth is on the watch for opportunity.

This great tragedy conveys a grand moral precept: poetical justice is dealt out rigidly to its chief actors.

Lady Macbeth, as the greatest criminal, is the greatest sufferer: madness, and a supposed suicide, close her career of guilt and gloom; and her husband meets his death by the same violent means as those by which he had attained his regal but wretched eminence, while the punishment of both is brought about by their own evil actions.

Scenes of terror, such as are found in this tragedy, stand alone; otherwise, says Schlegel, 'the tragic muse might exchange her mask for the head of Medusa.'

HISTORICAL SUMMARY OF 'KING JOHN.'

THE materials of the present play are to be found in the Chronicles of Holinshed; Shakespeare, however, has closely followed the incidents of a former drama, entitled 'The troublesome Raigne of John king of England, with the Discoverie of King Richard Cordelion's base Son, vulgarly named the Bastard Faulconbridge; also the Death of King John at Swinstead Abbey: as it was sundry times publikely acted by the Queenes Majesties Players in the honourable Cittie of London.' This piece was printed anonymously in the year 1591: on its republication in 1611, the bookseller, for whom it was printed, fraudulently inserted the letters 'W. Sh.' in the title-page; and in a third edition in 1622, the name of 'William Shakespeare' is inserted at full length. Pope attributes the composition of this crude performance to the joint pens of Shakespeare and Rowley, though without stating his authority.

This tragedy is supposed by Malone to have been written in 1596, though it was not printed till 1623. It is the only one of our poet's uncontested plays that is not entered in the books of the Stationers' Company.

'The tragedy of King John,' says Dr. Johnson, 'though not written with the utmost power of Shakespeare, is varied with a very pleasing interchange of incidents and characters. The lady's grief is very

KING JOHN. ACT III. SCENE I.

Lord Salisbury is sent to Constance to fetch her to the Kings.

affecting; and the character of the Bastard contains that mixture of greatness and levity, which this author delighted to exhibit.'

PERSONS REPRESENTED.

KING JOHN.
PRINCE HENRY, his son; afterwards King Henry III.
ARTHUR, duke of Bretagne, son of Geffrey, late duke of Bretagne, the elder brother of King John.
WILLIAM MARESHALL, earl of Pembroke.
GEFFREY FITZ-PETER, earl of Essex, chief justiciary of England.
WILLIAM LONGSWORD, earl of Salisbury.
ROBERT BIGOT, earl of Norfolk.
HUBERT DE BURGH, chamberlain to the king.
ROBERT FAULCONBRIDGE, son of Sir Robert Faulconbridge.
PHILIP FAULCONBRIDGE, his half-brother; bastard son to King Richard the First.
JAMES GURNEY, servant to Lady Faulconbridge.
PETER OF POMFRET, a prophet.

PHILIP, king of France.
LEWIS, the Dauphin.
ARCHDUKE OF AUSTRIA.
CARDINAL PANDULPH, the pope's legate.
MELUN, a French lord.
CHATILLON, ambassador from France to King John.

ELINOR, widow of King Henry II. and mother of King John.

CONSTANCE, mother to Arthur.
BLANCH, daughter to Alphonso, king of Castile, and niece to King John.
LADY FAULCONBRIDGE, mother to the Bastard and Robert Faulconbridge.

Lords, Ladies, Citizens of Angiers, Sheriff, Heralds, Officers, Soldiers, Messengers, and other Attendants.

SCENE, sometimes in England, and sometimes in France.

COMPENDIUM OF THE PLAY.

AT the death of Richard Cœur de Lion, the English crown is seized by John from the feeble hands of his nephew Arthur, the rightful heir, whose claims are supported by Philip, king of France: the prospect of uniting the English territories with his own kingdom, by the marriage of the Dauphin with a niece of John, induces the French monarch to withdraw his protection from Arthur, when the arrival of a legate from the Pope prevents the completion of the treaty, and rekindles the flames of war. Philip is defeated in a general engagement; and Arthur, now a captive, is committed by his uncle to the custody of one Hubert, with secret orders to put him to death. Softened by the innocence and entreaties of the youth, Hubert ventures to disobey the cruel mandate; Arthur loses his life in an endeavor to effect his escape from the castle in which he is confined, and his lifeless body is discovered by some discontented nobles, who are resolved to emancipate themselves from the thraldom of the tyrant John by the desperate measure of inviting the Dauphin to assume the crown, under the sanction of the papal court. On the arrival of the young prince, John is compelled to purchase a disgraceful peace by a pusillanimous surrender of his regal dignity into the hands of the cardinal legate, who now hastens to arrest the progress of the Dauphin. The mediation proves ineffectual, and hostilities are about to recommence, when the intelligence of the loss of a large supply of French troops on the Goodwin Sands, together with the defection of the English auxiliaries, damps the ardor of the French prince, and disposes him to terms of peace. In the meantime John is poisoned by a monk, and is succeeded in his government by his son, Henry the Third.

In considering this play without any reference to history, we must speak of it very highly; though destitute of the poetic halo which beautifies many of the bard's more imaginative dramas, it is still invested with a warlike and solemn grandeur. We feel that the theme is kingdoms and the chief actors princes. The air seems to resound with the brazen clang of trumpets and the clash of arms; the sunbeams gild the banners of rival armies, and dance upon the plumed crests of thousands of brave knights. The secret motives of monarchs are divined with the accuracy of a seer, and the hearts of kings laid bare in the sight of the people. The interest never flags for a moment; the play has several strongly marked characters, most effectively grouped together. The dark portrait of John is finely contrasted with the bold chivalrous bastard, Faulconbridge, 'the very spirit of Plantagenet,' who appears to be entirely a creation of the poet. He is the sunshine of the picture. His mirthful sallies relieve the oppressed spirits, after some of the painful tragic scenes, and chase away the gloomy shadows which seem rapidly closing around us. His fine natural spirits, shrewd worldly sense, undaunted courage, and witty, sparkling discourse, bespeak him a son of the lion-hearted Richard. The brave, reckless, but manly-tempered hero of Palestine seems to live again in him, somewhat modified by difference of station. Witnessing the interested motives of all around him, he exclaims, 'Gain, be my lord! for I will worship thee;' but he is an honest soldier, and serves the king with an undeviating integrity that was worthy of a nobler master. In this character the poet has shown that great talents and energy employed in a bad cause seldom enjoy a lengthened triumph; but, like an ill-manned vessel on an unexplored sea, drift about in uncertainty and peril. Faulconbridge becomes a serious man, and accumulated disasters wring from his iron nature a prayer to heaven not to tempt him above his power.

Lady Constance is an instance of maternal affection and dangerous ambition. These united feelings prompt her to claim the crown of England for her child, and thus to plunge the kingdom into a fearful war to gratify her feelings, and to advance her son. The title of John was at the least as good as that of Arthur, if not less liable to objection. But in the final anguish of the bereaved mother we forget the ambition of the woman; the intensity of her grief is painfully affecting, and few can listen to the passionate exclamations wrung from her breaking heart, when Arthur is captured by his uncle John, without a sympathizing tear. Her question to the cardinal, whether she shall know her child in heaven? and her rejoinder to the expostulation of King Philip—

> 'Grief fills up the room of my absent child,' etc.,

pierce every bosom, soften every heart. The character of Arthur is made sweetly touching from the helplessness of infancy, and the extreme gentleness of his nature. The poet, in deviating slightly from historic truth, gained, in this instance, a great dramatic advantage. The want of ambition and utter unobtrusiveness of the young prince endear him to us:

> 'So I were out of prison and kept sheep,
> I should be as merry as the day is long.'

That is his modest thought; happy had it been for him could it have been realized; but the grim red-handed fiend of murder dogs his guileless steps, and drives him to a blood-stained grave.

There are two scenes which stand prominently out from the rest: the one where the troubled tyrant works upon Hubert to undertake the death of Arthur, in which the fiendish character of John is shown without a veil; and the other where Hubert endeavors to execute his revolting commission of burning out the eyes of the young prince, but is diverted from his savage purpose by the poor boy's tears and entreaties. These two scenes deserve to be ranked with the grandest tragic efforts of the poet. The scene where John recriminates the guilt of Arthur's death upon Hubert and equivocates respecting the warrant for it, is also highly Shakespearian.

The closing scene is touched by a master hand; we pity the death-struck wretch writhing in anguish before us, who is described as singing in his agony. Painful is his reply to his son's inquiry as to his state, solemnly affecting from its profound and irredeemable misery:

'Poisoned: ill fare! dead, forsook, cast off!'

A terrible retribution has come upon the tyrant; body and soul seem perishing before us.

RICHARD II. ACT IV. SCENE I.

Richard resigns the crown to Bolingbroke.

HISTORICAL SUMMARY OF 'KING RICHARD II.'

This play comprises little more than the last two years of the reign of Richard II. The action of the drama commences with Bolingbroke's challenge to Mowbray, duke of Norfolk, on an accusation of high treason, which took place in 1398, and it concludes with the murder of King Richard at Pomfret castle towards the end of 1400, or the beginning of the following year. Holinshed furnished the facts which the poet dramatized: the speech of the bishop of Carlisle in favor of Richard's divine right, and exemption from human jurisdiction, is copied, almost *verbatim*, from that old historian.

The year 1593 is the date assigned by Malone to the production of this drama, which was printed four times during the lifetime of our author; the first two editions appearing in 1597 and 1598, without the scene of the deposition, which was first appended in 1608. The next impression was that of 1615.

PERSONS REPRESENTED.

King Richard the Second.
Edmund of Langley, duke of York, } uncles to the
John of Gaunt, duke of Lancaster, } king.

HENRY, surnamed Bolingbroke, duke of Hereford, son to John of Gaunt; afterwards King Henry IV.
DUKE OF AUMERLE, son to the duke of York.
MOWBRAY, duke of Norfolk.
DUKE OF SURREY.
EARL OF SALISBURY.
EARL BERKLEY.
BUSHY, BAGOT, GREEN, } creatures to King Richard.
EARL OF NORTHUMBERLAND.
HENRY PERCY, his son.
LORD ROSS. LORD WILLOUGHBY. LORD FITZWATER.
BISHOP OF CARLISLE. ABBOT OF WESTMINSTER.
LORD MARSHAL; and another Lord.
SIR PIERCE OF EXTON. SIR STEPHEN SCROOP.
Captain of a band of Welshmen.

QUEEN to King Richard.
DUCHESS OF GLOSTER.
DUCHESS OF YORK.
Lady attending on the Queen.

Lords, Heralds, Officers, Soldiers, two Gardeners, Keeper, Messenger, Groom, and other Attendants.

SCENE, dispersedly in England and Wales.

COMPENDIUM OF THE PLAY.

HENRY BOLINGBROKE, eldest son of John of Gaunt, duke of Lancaster, accuses Mowbray, duke of Norfolk, of high treason, and, in confirmation of his assertion, challenges him to single combat, which is eagerly accepted by his opponent. At the appointed time, the combatants enter the lists, and the conflict is about to commence, when the king interposes, and pronounces a sentence of perpetual banishment on Norfolk, while the exile of Bolingbroke is limited to the period of six years. Shortly after the departure of his son, John of Gaunt dies, and his property and estates are unjustly seized by the indigent monarch. Stung by this scandalous act of oppression, Bolingbroke takes advantage of the king's absence in Ireland, and arrives in England, where, by his artful professions of loyalty, together with solemn protestations of circumscribing his views within the reasonable demand of a repeal of his exile and a recovery of his patrimony, he insensibly acquires a power too formidable to be resisted; and the unfortunate Richard is compelled to resign his crown into the hands of his cousin; after which he is confined in Pomfret castle, where he is put to death by the connivance of Bolingbroke.

Between the death of John and the commencement of this play four kings had successively worn the crown of England, and a period of nearly two centuries had elapsed; but this and the seven plays which follow are one continuous history. A certain connection is kept up between them, and they may be termed one perfect historical romance, of which the different plays constitute the books, and the acts and scenes the chapters. Disagreeing with Schlegel as to the invariable historical fidelity of these productions, and condemning the adulatory spirit and eager 'hero-worship' which would call that history which the poet only intended as a romance, I still gladly avail myself of the happily expressed thought of the great German critic, and say that this series of dramas 'furnishes examples of the political course of the world, applicable to all times.' *This mirror of kings should be the manual of young princes*; from it they may learn the intrinsic dignity of their hereditary vocation, but they will also learn from it the difficulties of their situation, the dangers of usurpation, the inevitable fall of tyranny, which buries itself under its attempts to obtain a firmer foundation; lastly, the ruinous consequences of the weaknesses, errors, and crimes of kings, for whole nations and many subsequent generations.

These historic dramas must be regarded as lofty fictions, fictions teaching truth; great political parables based on facts, but rearing their high and graceful pinnacles into the realms of imagination. But if they are pronounced to be strict literal history, then must we say that much of history is merely what Napoleon declared it to be—'a fiction agreed upon.'

Schlegel says: "In 'King Richard the Second' the poet exhibits to us a noble kingly nature, at first obscured by levity and the errors of unbridled youth, and afterwards purified by misfortune, and rendered more highly splendid and illustrious. When he has lost the love and reverence of his subjects, and is on the point of losing also his throne, he then feels with painful inspiration the elevated vocation of the kingly dignity and its prerogatives over personal merit and changeable institutions. When the earthly crown has fallen from off his head he first appears as a king whose innate nobility no humiliation can annihilate. This is felt by a poor groom: he is shocked that his master's favorite horse should have carried the proud

Bolingbroke at his coronation; he visits the captive king in his prison and shames the desertion of the great. The political history of the deposition is represented with extraordinary knowledge of the world—the ebb of fortune on the one hand and the swelling tide on the other, which carries everything along with it; while Bolingbroke acts as a king, and his adherents behave towards him as if he really were so, he still continues to give out that he comes with an armed band merely for the sake of demanding his birthright and the removal of abuses. The usurpation has been long completed before the word is pronounced and the thing publicly avowed. John of Gaunt is a model of chivalrous truth: he stands there like a pillar of the olden time which he had outlived.

HISTORICAL SUMMARY OF 'KING HENRY IV.'—PART I.

THIS drama was first entered at Stationer's Hall February 25, 1597–8: its production is assigned by Malone to the year 1597, while Mr. Chalmers and Dr. Drake suppose it to have been written during the preceding year. No fewer than five quarto editions of this play were published during the lifetime of our author; in 1598, 1599, 1604, 1608 and 1613.

The action of the First Part of Henry the Fourth begins immediately after the defeat of the Scots at Holmedon in 1402, and terminates with the defeat and death of Hotspur at Shrewsbury about ten months afterwards.

Dr. Johnson observes, that 'Shakespeare has apparently designed a regular connection of these dramatic histories from Richard the Second to Henry the Fifth. King Henry, at the end of Richard the Second, declares his purpose to visit the Holy Land, which he resumes in the first speech of this play. The complaint made by King Henry, in the last act of Richard the Second, of the wildness of his son, prepares the reader for the frolics which are here to be recounted, and the characters which are now to be exhibited.'

It may be remarked, however, that the introduction of the prince at this early period of history is to be attributed solely to the desire of the poet to produce dramatic effect; since, at the time when the conspiracy

HENRY IV.—PART I. ACT II. SCENE IV.

Falstaff shows Prince Henry how he would play the part of the King.

of the duke of Aumerle was discovered, Prince Henry was but twelve years old; and, therefore, too young as yet to be a partaker in the debaucheries of London taverns. It is also extremely probable, that the licentious habits, attributed to him by the English chroniclers of the sixteenth century, have been greatly exaggerated.

PERSONS REPRESENTED.

KING HENRY THE FOURTH.
HENRY, prince of Wales, } sons to the king.
PRINCE JOHN OF LANCASTER, } sons to the king.
EARL OF WESTMORELAND, } friends to the king.
SIR WALTER BLUNT, } friends to the king.
THOMAS PERCY, earl of Worcester.
HENRY PERCY, earl of Northumberland.
HENRY PERCY, surnamed Hotspur, his son.
EDMUND MORTIMER, earl of March.
SCROOP, archbishop of York.
ARCHIBALD, earl of Douglas.
OWEN GLENDOWER.
SIR RICHARD VERNON.
SIR JOHN FALSTAFF.
SIR MICHAEL, a friend of the archbishop of York.
POINS.
GADSHILL.
PETO.
BARDOLPH.

LADY PERCY, wife to Hotspur, and sister to Mortimer.

LADY MORTIMER, daughter to Glendower, and wife to Mortimer.

MRS. QUICKLY, hostess of a tavern in Eastcheap.

Lords, Officers, Sheriff, Vintner, Chamberlain, Drawers, two Carriers, Travellers and Attendants.

SCENE, England.

COMPENDIUM OF THE PLAY.

THE chief characters in this play are Falstaff, Prince Henry, Percy and King Henry. After the deposition and death of the unfortunate Richard, the attention of King Henry is directed to the incursions of the Scots, who, under conduct of Douglas, advance to the borders of England, where they are totally routed by the celebrated Percy, surnamed Hotspur. The intelligence of this victory no sooner reaches the ears of the king, than, regardless of the debt of gratitude due to the powerful family of the Percies, he demands the prisoners taken in the late struggle, among whom was the renowned Douglas; contrary to the practice of those times, when the custody and destination of captives were determined at the discretion of the conquering general. Exasperated at this unexpected mandate, Hotspur dismisses all his prisoners without ransom, and with his relatives and dependents raises the standard of revolt against the sovereign, whose elevation they had so recently effected. Having formed a treaty of alliance with the Scottish and Welsh leaders, the insurgents arrive at Shrewsbury, where they are encountered by the king in person. A decisive battle ensues, in which Hotspur is slain, and the rebels sustain a signal defeat. The only two lady characters are Ladies Percy and Mortimer, the former a very pretty character. The remainder of this drama is occupied with the amusing detail of the frolics of the Prince of Wales and his merry companions, among whom Sir John Falstaff occupies the most conspicuous part. The meeting of Sir John, Poins and Prince Hal and their pranks at the Boar's Head Tavern in Eastcheap, and elsewhere with their attendants, Bardolph, Peto and Mrs. Quickly, hostess of the tavern, and their superb fooling of Sir John in the robbery at Gad's Hill, form one the of most jovial series of pictures ever presented in literature.

The transactions contained in the 'First Part of King Henry IV.' are comprised within the period of about ten months; for the action commences with the news brought of Hotspur having defeated the Scots under Archibald Earl of Douglas, at Holmedon (or Halidown Hall), which battle was fought on Holyrood day (the 14th of September), 1402; and it closes with the battle of Shrewsbury on Saturday, the 21st of July, 1403.

HISTORICAL SUMMARY OF 'KING HENRY IV.'—PART II.

THE composition of this play has been assigned by Malone to the year 1599, while Mr. Chalmers and Dr. Drake suppose it to have been written as early as 1596 or 1597. The play of 'Henry IV.' is mentioned in the list of Shakespeare's works, in Meres' 'Wits' Treasury,' 1598; and, by the Epilogue to this drama, it appears to have preceded 'King Henry V.,' which is fixed with some accuracy to 1599. It was entered at Stationers' Hall, August 23d, 1600, and the first two editions of it in quarto were published in the same year. Its action comprehends a period of nine years, commencing with Hotspur's death in 1403, and terminating with the coronation of King Henry V. in 1412–13. 'These two plays,' says Dr. Johnson, 'will appear to every reader, who shall peruse them without ambition of critical discoveries, to be so connected, that the second is merely a sequel to the first; to be two only because they are too long to be one.'

In reading Holinshed for these plays, our poet's eye was evidently eager in quest of scattered hints of personal character, and on these, whenever he was fortunate enough to meet with them, his exuberant imagination worked with boldness. The dismissal of Falstaff, as one of Henry's dissolute companions, is conformable to the old historian, but his committal to the

SECOND PART KING HENRY IV. ACT V. SCENE V.

King Henry V., returning from his coronation, is saluted by Falstaff, Pistol, etc., whom he banishes.

Fleet is an act of severity volunteered by Shakespeare. A reference to Stowe in this case would have been eminently useful to him: the prince's companions are there disposed of in a manner gratifying to the feelings of humanity and consistent with the claims of justice. 'After his coronation, King Henry called unto him all those young lords and gentlemen who were the followers of his young acts, to every one of whom he gave rich gifts; and then commanded, that as many as would change their manners, as he intended to do, should abide with him in his court; and to all that would persevere in their former like conversation, he gave express commandment, upon pain of their heads, never after that day to come in his presence.'

'None of Shakespeare's plays,' adds Dr. Johnson, 'are more read than the First and Second Parts of Henry the Fourth: perhaps no author has ever in two plays afforded so much delight. The great events are interesting, for the fate of kingdoms depends on them; the slighter occurrences are diverting, and, except one or two, sufficiently probable; the incidents are multiplied with wonderful fertility of invention; and the characters diversified with the utmost nicety of discernment, and the profoundest skill in the nature of man.

'The prince, who is the hero both of the comic and tragic part, is a young man of great abilities and violent passions; whose sentiments are right, though his actions are wrong; whose virtues are obscured by negligence, and whose understanding is dissipated by levity. In his idle hours he is rather loose than vicious, but when the responsibility of succession to the crown comes in his turn he proves himself a true king.'

PERSONS REPRESENTED.

KING HENRY THE FOURTH.

HENRY, prince of Wales, afterwards King Henry V.,
THOMAS, duke of Clarence,
PRINCE JOHN OF LANCASTER, afterwards (2 Henry V.) duke of Bedford,
PRINCE HUMPHREY OF GLOSTER, afterwards (2 Henry V.) duke of Gloster,
} his sons.

EARL OF WARWICK;
EARL OF WESTMORELAND,
GOWER, HARCOURT,
} of the king's party.

LORD CHIEF JUSTICE of the King's Bench.

A GENTLEMAN attending on the Chief Justice.

EARL OF NORTHUMBERLAND,
SCROOP, archbishop of York,
LORD MOWBRAY, LORD HASTINGS,
LORD BARDOLPH, SIR JOHN COLEVILLE,
} enemies to the king.

TRAVERS and MORTON, domestics of Northumberland.

FALSTAFF, BARDOLPH, PISTOL, and PAGE.

POINS and PETO, attendants on Prince Henry.

SHALLOW and SILENCE, country justices.

DAVY, servant to Shallow.

MOULDY, SHADOW, WART, FEEBLE, and BULLCALF, recruits.

FANG and SNARE, sheriff's officers.

RUMOR. A PORTER.

A DANCER, speaker of the Epilogue.

LADY NORTHUMBERLAND.

LADY PERCY.

HOSTESS QUICKLY.
DOLL TEAR-SHEET.

Lords and other Attendants; Officers, Soldiers, Messenger, Drawers, Beadles, Grooms, etc.

SCENE, England.

COMPENDIUM OF THE PLAY.

AFTER the defeat and death of Hotspur at Shrewsbury, the king despatches his son Prince John of Lancaster and the earl of Westmoreland, at the head of a large army, to encounter the northern insurgents, under the command of Scroop, archbishop of York. The two armies meet at Gualtree Forest in Yorkshire, where Prince John, unwilling to hazard a general engagement, invites the discontented chieftains to a conference, with whom he concludes a treaty, promising a full redress of their alleged grievances, and stipulating for a dismissal of the troops on either side. The royalist forces however receive secret instructions, and, by an unparalleled act of perfidy, are commanded to destroy the disbanded insurgents, while the archbishop and his coadjutors are led to immediate execution. In the meantime, Prince Henry is summoned from the society of his dissipated companions to attend the death-bed of his father, whom he finds in a swoon, with the crown on his pillow. Judging him to have breathed his last, the prince removes the diadem;—an act which incurs the bitter reproaches of the king when he awakes: his son justifies his conduct to the satisfaction of the dying monarch; and no sooner assumes the regal dignity, than he dismisses forever from his presence Sir John Falstaff and the companions of his youthful excesses, and resolves to signalize his reign by the splendor of his achievements and the virtues of his character. The success of Falstaff at the Battle of Shrewsbury set up the old knight in every way—in purse, in character and influence. The revels are continued and some new characters introduced: Doll Tear-sheet, Davy, Shallow's servant, and the scene of the recruits besides other mirthful scenes at the Boar's Head in Eastcheap.

J. W. Singer says: The historical dramas of Shakespeare have become the popular history. Vain attempts have been made by Walpole to vindicate the character of King Richard III., and in later times by Mr. Luders, to prove that the youthful dissipation ascribed to King Henry V. is without foundation. The arguments are probable and ingeniously urged, but we still cling to our early notions of 'that mad chap—that same sword and buckler, Prince of Wales.' No plays were ever more read, nor does the inimitable, all powerful genius of the poet ever shine out more than in the two parts of King Henry IV., which may be considered as one long drama divided.

It has been said that 'Falstaff is the summit of Shakespeare's comic invention,' and we may consequently add the most inimitable comic character ever delineated; for who could invent like Shakespeare? Falstaff is now to us hardly a creature of the imagination. He is so definitely and distinctly drawn that the mere reader of these dramas has the complete impression of a personal acquaintance. He is surrounded by a group of comic personages from time to time, each of which would have been sufficient to throw any ordinary creation into the shade, but they only serve to make the super-eminent humor of the knight doubly conspicuous. What can come nigher to truth and real individual nature than those admirable delineations, Shallow and Silence? How irresistibly comic are all the scenes in which Falstaff is made to humor the fatuity and vanity of this precious pair!

The historic characters are delineated with a felicity and individuality not inferior in any respect. Harry Percy is a creation of the first order; and our favorite hare-brained Prince of Wales, in whom mirthful pleasantry and midnight dissipation are mixed up with heroic dignity and generous feeling, is a rival worthy of him. Owen Glendower is another personification, managed with the most consummate skill; and the graver characters are sustained and opposed to each other in a manner peculiar to our great poet.

HISTORICAL SUMMARY OF 'KING HENRY V.'

From a passage in the chorus at the commencement of the fifth act, this drama appears to have been written during the absence of the earl of Essex in Ireland, between April and September, 1599, those being the dates of that nobleman's departure and return. It was entered at Stationers' Hall August 14, 1600, and three editions were published before the death of our author; namely, in 1600, 1602, and 1608. In all of these he choruses are omitted, and the play commences with the fourth speech of the second scene. The historical transactions occupy little more than the first six years of the reign of the illustrious monarch whose exploits are here commemorated, the materials of which have been derived from the Chronicles of Holinshed, and an older play, entitled 'The famous Victories of Henry the Fift, containing the honorable Battle of Agincourt,' which was entered at Stationers' Hall, May 2, 1594.

'This play,' says Dr. Johnson, 'has many scenes of high dignity, and many of easy merriment. The character of the king is well supported, except in his courtship, where he has neither the vivacity of Hal nor the grandeur of Henry. The humor of Pistol is very happily continued: his character has perhaps been the model of all the bullies that have yet appeared on the English stage. The lines given to the

HENRY V. ACT V. SCENE I.

Fluellen, the Welshman, compelling Pistol to swallow the leek.

Chorus have many admirers; but the truth is, that in them a little may be praised, and much must be forgiven: nor can it be easily discovered why the intelligence given by the Chorus is more necessary in this play than in many others where it is omitted. The great defect of this play is the emptiness and narrowness of the last act, which a very little diligence might have easily avoided.'

PERSONS REPRESENTED.

KING HENRY THE FIFTH.

DUKE OF GLOSTER, DUKE OF BEDFORD, brothers to the king.

DUKE OF EXETER, uncle to the king.

DUKE OF YORK, cousin to the king.

EARLS OF SALISBURY, WESTMORELAND, and WARWICK.

ARCHBISHOP OF CANTERBURY.

BISHOP OF ELY.

EARL OF CAMBRIDGE, LORD SCROOP, SIR THOMAS GREY, conspirators against the king.

SIR THOMAS ERPINGHAM, GOWER, FLUELLEN, MACMORRIS, JAMY, officers in King Henry's army.

BATES, COURT, WILLIAMS, soldiers in the same.

NYM, BARDOLPH, PISTOL, formerly servants to Falstaff, now soldiers in the same.

BOY, servant to them. A HERALD. CHORUS.

CHARLES THE SIXTH, king of France.

LEWIS, the Dauphin.
DUKES OF BURGUNDY, ORLEANS, and BOURBON.
THE CONSTABLE OF FRANCE.
RAMBURES and GRANDPREE, French lords.
GOVERNOR OF HARFLEUR.
MONTJOY, a French herald.
AMBASSADORS to the king of England.

ISABEL, queen of France.
KATHARINE, daughter of Charles and Isabel.
ALICE, a lady attending on the princess Katharine.
QUICKLY, Pistol's wife, an hostess.

Lords, Ladies, Officers, French and English Soldiers, Messengers, and Attendants.

The SCENE, at the beginning of the play, lies in England; but afterwards, wholly in France.

COMPENDIUM OF THE PLAY.

HENRY is no sooner in possession of the English crown, than he prepares to fulfil the injunctions of his dying father, and to efface from the minds of his subjects the defects in his title by the splendor of foreign conquest; in pursuance of which design he now revives an antiquated claim to the sceptre of France, which he prepares to advocate by assembling a powerful army. The French court, intimidated at these demonstrations of hostility, basely endeavor to procure the assassination of the English monarch by profusely bribing three powerful noblemen, Cambridge, Scroop and Grey. The conspiracy is brought to light and punished, and Henry safely arrives in France, and takes the town of Harfleur by capitulation. Sickness and want of provisions at length diminish his army, and compel him to retreat in the face of an enemy five times his superior in numbers, who force him to risk a general engagement near the village of Agincourt, where he obtains a complete victory, which renders further resistance unavailing. The French king is now reduced to the necessity of submitting to the hard terms imposed on him by his conqueror, who is publicly recognized as heir to the crown and united in marriage to the princess Katharine.

The poet has carefully elaborated the character of Henry; he introduces him into three dramas, carries him uncontaminated through scenes of riot and dissipation, represents him repenting his lost hours with tears of shame and affection, at the feet of his father, and, on his accession to the "golden rigol," after winning the good graces of prelates, nobility, and people, and passing undaunted through a fearful ordeal, such as would have overwhelmed many a stout heart, leaves him on a summit of military glory more brilliant than had been achieved even by his brave and illustrious ancestors. The fine description by the Archbishop of Canterbury of the King's reformation, and the sudden blaze of those virtues and accomplishments which he was not suspected to have possessed, has been aptly applied to Shakespeare himself. Like Henry, the wildness of his youth promised not the brilliant performances of his manhood. With the poet, as with the prince,

> 'Consideration like an angel came,
> And whipp'd the offending Adam out of him;
> Leaving his body as a paradise,
> To envelop and contain celestial spirits.'

The introductory dialogue between the two bishops, independent of its exquisite beauty, easily and naturally prepares us for the change of the frolicsome idle prince to the serious and majestic king.

As a monarch he is drawn with great spirit and power; he is sincere, magnanimous, eloquent, and pious, though it must be confessed his piety is often of a very convenient character. His address to his army before the walls of Harfleur is a model of military oratory, full of manly fire and enthusiasm. We can fancy the soldiers listening with set teeth, dilated nostrils, and flashing eyes, and then again following him with resistless fury to the breach in the walls of the besieged city. In his warning to the governor of Harfleur is contained the most terribly eloquent description of war in the English language.

The mirthful and early pranks of Henry are not forgotten in this play; his acceptance of the glove of the soldier as a challenge, and bestowal of it upon Fluellen, show that his sportive disposition is not extinguished, but tempered by rank and responsibility of station. Still he turns moralist in his extremity, and exclaims to his brother:

> 'There is some soul of goodness in things evil,
> Would men observingly distil it out.'

Henry's claim upon France was politic but ungenerous, for that unhappy country was distracted by internal broils, possessed a lunatic for a king, and was laid waste by the furious contentions of its own nobles. So far from his having any title to the crown of France, his right to the sovereignty of his own country would not bear examination; and it was to evade inquiry, and that his nobility might not have leisure to conspire against him in England, that he led them to war against France; and the archbishop encourages and justifies the design, that Henry may not pry too closely into the vast possessions of the church. Such are the secret springs of war and conquest.

In many of his historical plays, but chiefly in this, does Shakespeare evince a patriotic love of his native country; his language is well calculated to excite a natural pride in English bosoms, and we share the enthusiasm with which he paints the hardihood and prowess of his countrymen; but when we reflect upon the past conflicts with France, we should remember that an insular position is exceedingly advantageous. England, when governed by a powerful military king, always took advantage of any calamity in France, to make invasions which its temporary weakness and the sea prevented it from readily returning. The different occupations of the two armies and their leaders on the eve of battle are pointed out in a manner from which the poet intended us to infer the opposite character of the two nations. The French nobility are engaged in frivolous conversation respecting their horses and their armor, and in playing at dice for the prisoners whom they assume they shall capture the next day. The English are occupied in patient watching and serious meditation upon the fearfully unequal contest in which a few hours will involve them. This comparison is hardly just, but a little exultation was both natural and pardonable in a poet living at a period not more distant from the event than was the reign of Elizabeth.

In this play we hear the last of Falstaff; his death is related by Mrs. Quickly. We cannot help feeling sad for the poor old knight, dying in an inn, surrounded only by rude dependents, and the faithful hostess, whom we respect for her kind attachment to him to the last. No wife or child is near; no gentle kindred hand to do kind offices in the hour of weakness and despondency. In his half-delirious moments his last joke was made upon the flea on Bardolph's nose, which he said 'was a black soul burning in hell-fire.' The scene between the Welsh, Irish, and Scotch captains, each speaking in his peculiar *patois*, is very humorous, but these three do not amount to one Falstaff. The episode between Pistol and the French soldier, whom, by his fierce looks, he frightens into paying a good ransom for his life, is much richer; but the crown of mirth in this play is where the Welshman cudgels Pistol, and makes him eat his leek for having mocked him respecting it. All the group that surrounded Falstaff are here disposed of; Bardolph and Nym are hanged, the boy is killed by the flying French soldiers after the battle, Mrs. Quickly dies in the hospital, and Pistol sneaks home in disgrace and obscurity.

Although there is tragic matter enough in this play, it ends like a comedy—with a marriage of convenience. Henry espoused the princess Katharine on the 2d of June, 1418, in the church of St. John at Troyes. The next day, after he had given a splendid banquet, it was proposed by the French that the event should be honored by a series of tournaments and public rejoicings. This Henry would not sanction. 'I pray,' said he to the French monarch, 'my lord the king to permit, and I command his servants and mine to be all ready to-morrow morning to go and lay siege to Sens, wherein are our enemies: there every man may have jousting and tourneying enough, and may *give proof of his prowess; for there is no finer prowess than that of doing justice on the wicked, in order that the poor people may breathe and live.*' In the exhibition of this courage, activity, and feeling for the lower orders, lay the secret of Henry's popularity. He lived four years after his marriage, a period which Shakespeare has left unrecorded; but the death of this heroic king was a scene for the poet. Still only in his thirty-fourth year, a conqueror in the full blaze of military glory, a king beloved by his people almost to idolatry, the husband of a young, beautiful, and accomplished wife, and the father of an infant son, this world was to him a demi-paradise, an earthly Eden; still he breathed his last without one complaint, and was himself calm and resigned, though all around wept as they promised to protect his wife and child. The solemn pomp displayed at his funeral was extraordinary; no such procession had hitherto attended the remains of any English king. His funeral car was preceded and flanked by a crowd of heralds, banner-bearers, and it was followed by some hundreds of knights and esquires in black armor and plumes; while, far in the rear, travelled the young widow, with a gorgeous and numerous retinue. She, however, does not appear to have been inconsolable, for she was married again shortly after Henry's death to a Welsh gentleman, Sir Owen Tudor, one of the handsomest men of his time. She brought him two sons, of whom the eldest, Edmund, was created earl of Richmond, and his son afterwards ascended the English throne, under the title of Henry the Seventh.

HISTORICAL SUMMARY OF 'KING HENRY VI.'—PART I.

THIS piece is supposed by Malone to have made its appearance on the stage about the year 1588, and to have been formerly known by the appellation of 'The Historical Play of King Henry VI.' The learned commentator has endeavored to prove that it was written neither by Shakespeare nor by the author of the other two plays detailing the events of a subsequent period of the same reign; and these conjectures are confirmed by the manuscript accounts of Henslowe, proprietor of the Rose Tavern, Bankside, which have been since discovered at Dulwich College. The entry is dated the 3d of March, 1591; and the play being the property of Lord Strange's company, and performed at the Rose Theatre, with neither of which Shakespeare had at any time the smallest connection, the testimony of Malone's position as to the antiquity, priority, and insulated origin of this drama, is much corroborated.

At this distance of time it is impossible to ascertain on what principle our author's friends, Heminge and Condell, admitted The First Part of 'King Henry VI.' into their volume. Malone remarks, that they may have given it a place as a necessary introduction to the two other parts, and because Shakespeare had made some slight alterations, and written a few lines in it.

FIRST PART HENRY VI. ACT II. SCENE III.

Talbot astonishes the Countess of Auvergne.

The events contained in this dramatic history commence with the funeral of Henry V. in 1422, and concluded with the earl of Suffolk being sent to France for Margaret of Anjou, at the close of 1443. The author, however, has not been very precise as to the date and disposition of his facts, since Lord Talbot is killed at the end of the fourth act of this play, who did not really fall till July 13, 1453.

PERSONS REPRESENTED.

King Henry the Sixth.
Duke of Gloster, uncle to the king, and protector.
Duke of Bedford, uncle to the king, and regent of France.
Thomas Beaufort, duke of Exeter, great uncle to the king.
Henry Beaufort, great uncle to the king, bishop of Winchester, and afterwards cardinal.
John Beaufort, earl of Somerset; afterwards duke.
Richard Plantagenet, eldest son of Richard, late earl of Cambridge; afterwards duke of York.
Earl of Warwick. Earl of Salisbury. Earl of Suffolk.
Lord Talbot, afterwards earl of Shrewsbury.
John Talbot, his son.
Edmund Mortimer, earl of March.
Mortimer's Keeper, and a Lawyer.
Sir John Fastolfe. Sir William Lucy.
Sir William Glansdale. Sir Thomas Gargrave.

MAYOR OF LONDON. WOODVILLE, lieutenant of the Tower.

VERNON, of the white rose, or York faction.

BASSET, of the red rose, or Lancaster faction.

CHARLES, Dauphin, and afterwards king of France.

REIGNIER, duke of Anjou, and titular king of Naples.

DUKE OF BURGUNDY. DUKE OF ALENÇON.

GOVERNOR OF PARIS. BASTARD OF ORLEANS.

MASTER GUNNER OF ORLEANS, and his SON.

GENERAL of the French forces in Bourdeaux.

A FRENCH SERGEANT. A PORTER.

AN OLD SHEPHERD, father to Joan la Pucelle.

MARGARET, daughter to Reignier; afterwards married to King Henry.

COUNTESS OF AUVERGNE.

JOAN LA PUCELLE, commonly called Joan of Arc.

Fiends appearing to La Pucelle, Lords, Warders of the Tower, Heralds, Officers, Soldiers, Messengers and several Attendants both on the English and French.

SCENE, partly in England, and partly in France.

COMPENDIUM OF THE PLAY.

THE sceptre is no sooner transferred from the hands of the conqueror of France to the feeble grasp of his son, then an infant, than the favorable opportunity is seized by the French, who are enabled, by the courage and energy of a young woman named Joan of Arc, to recover their former possessions, and to swear allegiance to their native monarch. In the meantime the violent feuds of the dukes of York and Somerset, whose parties are distinguished by white and red roses, lay the foundation of that civil war which was ere long to deluge the whole kingdom with blood. The brave Talbot and his son, together with a small band of faithful followers, are overpowered at Bourdeaux by the united forces of the enemy, and sacrificed to the private jealousy of these hostile nobles, who neglect to send him the necessary reinforcements. The intrepid Joan is at length taken prisoner by the duke of York, and cruelly condemned to the stake; while King Henry is induced, by the artful suggestions of the earl of Suffolk, to solicit the hand of Margaret, daughter of the duke of Anjou: a treaty of alliance is speedily concluded with the father, and the earl despatched to accompany the princess to England.

The earlier scenes of this drama are most artistically adapted to introduce the misrule and dark and bloody struggles of the turbulent reign of Henry. The iron-hand of the hero of Agincourt being laid in the grave, and the enthusiastic patriotism, which was warmed into active existence by his gorgeous and triumphant career, having subsided into the calm stream of common life, the elements of discord break forth. The fierce contentions of Beaufort and Gloucester show the disordered state of the kingdom consequent upon the supremacy of a child, and are a natural prelude to the savage contests which afterwards took place under the name of the Wars of the Roses.

Talbot is a boldly drawn character; he resembles a grim armed giant, whose presence everywhere causes terror and flight, yet he is thoroughly English in his nature—that is, he possesses all those qualities which were prominent in the most just and patriotic warriors of his country in the fifteenth century. Terrible to his enemies, fierce and savage in war, he is yet mild and genial to his associates, while on his tenderness as a father the great interest of his character depends. The scene between him and the Countess of Auvergne is an admirable episode, full of life and vigor, and written by the pen of genius; if, according to the conjecture of Mr. Malone, either Greene or Peele was the author of this play, it is to be regretted that they have not left more such scenes for the admiration of posterity. The generosity of Talbot to the crafty but outwitted Frenchwoman is the result of a noble spirit; a meaner general would probably have razed her castle to its foundations, or left it in flames, as a punishment for her perfidious abuse of the sacred laws of hospitality.

The brave Talbot is at last sacrificed through the dissensions and treachery of York and Somerset: each blames the other for neglect, but stands aloof himself; the intrepid general is surrounded without the walls of Bordeaux by forces immeasurably superior to his own, and, after performing prodigies of valor, is slain. Just before his death he has an interview with his son, whom after an absence of seven years he had sent for, to tutor in the strategies of war. The meeting is a melancholy one; certain death awaits them both, unless avoided by flight—the elder Talbot, grown gray in peril and in honor, counsels his son to escape, but will himself remain to meet his fate; the young hero will not stir from the side of his father, who eventually dies with the dead body of his son in his arms.

In the scene in the Temple Garden, the great Earl

of Warwick is introduced—that Warwick whose after achievements gained for him the title of the 'King-maker,' and although he does not appear so prominently in this play, as in the two following ones, yet here we have the germs of his future character, and a very spirited and Shakespearian speech is uttered by him. Somerset and Plantagenet having disputed on some legal question, appeal to the earl, who at first declines to side with either party, exclaiming—

> Between two hawks, which flies the higher pitch,
> Between two dogs, which hath the deeper mouth,
> Between two blades, which bears the better temper,
> Between two horses, which doth bear him best,
> Between two girls, which hath the merriest eye,
> I have, perhaps, some shallow spirit of judgment:
> But in these nice sharp quillets of the law,
> Good faith, I am no wiser than a daw.

Something of the princely and chivalrous earl, whose hospitality was as royal and boundless as his wealth, and who kept so many retainers, that sometimes six oxen were eaten by them at a breakfast, is shadowed forth in this hearty and bounding speech. They who are conversant with the language of our poet will need no argument to induce them to believe that it was the work of his pen. In this scene we have detailed the supposed origin of the two badges, the white rose and the red, afterwards worn by the rival houses of York and Lancaster.

The character of Joan la Pucelle, though it has not the finish of Shakespeare's later works, yet partakes of their strength. It is only to be regretted that he has attributed to satanic agency what was doubtless the result of pure patriotism and vivid religious enthusiasm; but the era of the poet was one of intense and obstinate superstition, when to express a disbelief in witchcraft was frequently deemed an act of impiety, and it is not to be expected that in his youth he should be emancipated from the errors of his time. But this unjust picture has given Schlegel occasion to say that 'the wonderful saviour of her country, Joan of Arc, is portrayed by Shakespeare with an Englishman's prejudices.' History has since done justice to her memory, and time has found the solution of her supposed miraculous influence. The inhabitants of the little hamlet where she was born were remarkable for their simplicity and their superstition; and the poor peasant girl, whom a pious education had ripened into a religious enthusiast, was led, while tending her flocks in solitude among the hills and pastures of a wild and picturesque country, to occupy herself with day-dreams concerning the ascetic and miraculous lives of the saints, and the wonderful heroism of the virgin martyrs. This sort of life led to its natural result in a fervent and susceptible mind; after a short time she was haunted by visions, and listened in ecstasy to the voices of spirits; angelic faces appeared to her surrounded by a halo of light and glory; amongst them were St. Catherine and St. Margaret, wearing crowns which glittered with celestial jewels, and these heavenly visitants spoke to her in voices which were sweeter than the softest music. They commanded her to deliver her country, and told her that she would be endowed with strength from heaven. The devoted enthusiast went to the king, declared her mission, liberated France, and was finally, with a cruelty at which humanity recoils, burnt at the stake for sorcery. It is to be wished that Shakespeare had taken a more lofty and generous view of her character. The family of this unhappy woman was ennobled by the monarch to whom she had rendered such important services, but he made no effort whatever to rescue from the hands of the English a heroine 'to whom the more generous superstition of the ancients would have erected altars.'

Viewed historically, there are some slight apologies to be made for the conduct of York in attempting to supplant Henry on the throne; but in the drama he stands convicted of complicated treachery and constant perjury. The feeble but generous king restores him to his rank and estates, which had been forfeited by the treason of his father, who was beheaded for a plot to assassinate Henry the Fifth. He promises eternal gratitude and allegiance, exclaiming—

> And so thrive Richard as thy foes may fall!
> And as my duty springs, so perish they
> That grudge one thought against your majesty!

Yet this very man, perceiving the imbecility of Henry, casts an evil eye unto the crown, and eventually he and his sons, after shedding the blood of nearly a hundred thousand Englishmen, exterminate the house of Lancaster, and place the sensual, perjured Edward upon the throne.

In the early part of the play the young king does not appear, and when he does, it is only to make a miserable exhibition of his weakness and vacillation of mind; for, although contracted to another lady, he falls in love with Margaret merely from Suffolk's description of her personal charms, and thus becomes the dupe of that cunning courtier, who loves her him-

self. The play ends abruptly with Henry's dispatching Suffolk to France to woo Margaret for him, and the wily emissary speeds on his mission rejoicing in the probable success of his treachery.

HISTORICAL SUMMARY OF 'KING HENRY VI.'—PART II.

An old play in two parts, which appears to have been written about the year 1590, and which is ascribed by Malone to the pen of Christopher Marlowe, assisted by his friends Poole and Greene, is the foundation of this and the ensuing drama; the prototype of the present being called 'The First Part of the Contention of the two famous Houses of Yorke and Lancaster.' These two parts were published in quarto, the first in 1594, the second in the following year: both were reprinted in 1600, and seem to have been moulded by our author, with many alterations and additions, into the shape in which they at present appear.

The action of this drama comprises ten years, commencing with Henry's marriage with Margaret of Anjou, in May, 1445; and terminating with the first battle of Saint Albans, in favor of the house of York, May 22, 1455.

PERSONS REPRESENTED.

King Henry the Sixth.
Humphrey, duke of Gloster, his uncle.
Cardinal Beaufort, bishop of Winchester, great uncle to the king.

RICHARD PLANTAGENET, duke of York.

EDWARD and RICHARD, his sons.

DUKE OF SOMERSET, DUKE OF SUFFOLK, DUKE OF BUCKINGHAM, LORD CLIFFORD, YOUNG CLIFFORD, his son, } of the king's party.

EARL OF SALISBURY, EARL OF WARWICK, } of the York faction.

LORD SCALES, governor of the Tower. LORD SAY.

SIR HUMPHREY STAFFORD, and his brother. SIR JOHN STANLEY.

A SEA CAPTAIN, MASTER and MASTER'S MATE, and WALTER WHITMORE.

TWO GENTLEMEN, prisoners with Suffolk.

A HERALD. VAUX.

HUME and SOUTHWELL, two priests.

BOLINGBROKE, a conjurer. A Spirit raised by him.

THOMAS HORNER, an armorer. PETER, his man.

CLERK OF CHATHAM. MAYOR OF SAINT ALBANS.

SIMPCOX, an impostor. TWO MURDERERS.

JACK CADE, a rebel.

GEORGE, JOHN, DICK, SMITH the weaver, MICHAEL, etc., his followers.

ALEXANDER IDEN, a Kentish gentleman.

MARGARET, queen to King Henry.

ELEANOR, duchess of Gloster.

MARGERY JOURDAIN, a witch. WIFE TO SIMPCOX.

Lords, Ladies, and Attendants; Petitioners, Aldermen, a Beadle, Sheriff, and Officers; Citizens, Prentices, Falconers, Guards, Soldiers, Messengers, etc.

SCENE, dispersedly in various parts of England.

COMPENDIUM OF THE PLAY.

THE nuptials of King Henry VI. with Margaret of Anjou are scarcely celebrated, in the 24th year of the king, when the new queen resolves to exercise unlimited control over the councils of her imbecile husband, and with the assistance of a number of powerful nobles, to remove the duke of Gloster from his post of protector. Their purpose is at length effected, and the virtuous duke confined on a charge of high treason. His accusers, perceiving the evidence of his guilt insufficient to obtain the least credit, have recourse to assassination. The populace, driven to desperation at the murder of their patron, tumultuously insist on the immediate banishment of Suffolk, his avowed enemy, who, in his passage to France, is captured by pirates and beheaded. In the meantime the government of Ireland is intrusted to the duke of York, who previous to his departure induces a needy dependent, named Cade, to commence an insurrection in Kent, laying claim to the crown as a descendant of Edmund Mortimer, in order that he may thereby be enabled to judge of the probability of his own success. Cade and his party are at length dispersed by the king's forces, and the duke of York soon after arrives in England to support his pretensions to the throne by force of arms. The hostile parties come to a general engagement near Saint Albans, where the Lancastrians sustain a total defeat, and the victorious duke resolves to commence his march to the capital without delay.

In perusing this play we seem to be walking among covered pitfalls; the snares of treachery are spread in all directions; every noble is striving for supremacy, and each exclaiming on the ambition of the rest. The drama forms a dark and terrible picture of the wickedness of courts; for sophistry, perjury and murder stain nearly every character except the weak king and the 'good Duke Humphrey.' We recoil in disgust from this diabolical exhibition of state-craft: these wily courtiers play for the crown of the feeble Henry with all the recklessness of ruined gamblers; they stake body and soul upon the cast, or rather play as if they had no souls to lose. The poet, with all the ingenuity of youth, scourges hypocrisy with unsparing vehemence, treachery is made transparent, and the great struggle for self rendered obvious and disgusting; he tears aside the disguises of patriotism and religion, and shows us the human fiends concealed beneath them.

The character of the king is very weak, and the feebleness of infancy had not given way to the strength and vigor of manhood; and the son of that determined prince, who was regarded by the people with affectionate awe, was a gentle, weak, superstitious man. As a village priest he would have proved a valuable member of society; happy would it have been for him and England had he been born to such a station; but as a king who had to govern a powerful and insolent nobility, and a semi-barbarous people, his very virtues were his chief defects. In those times a strong bad man, so that he had judgment enough not to stretch his prerogative too far, made a better sovereign than a weak good man. Where much power attaches to the crown, a feeble king is worse than no king, for the powers of government are wielded by any hand that is bold enough to seize them and strong enough to guide them. Thus with Henry—Gloucester, Beaufort, Suffolk, Somerset, York, and Warwick, each in turn influence and coerce this phantom of a king. The mind of the unfortunate monarch was worse than feeble; it was diseased. He was several times seized with an extraordinary apathy and imbecility, which rendered him unfit for the commonest duties of life, and unconscious of the presence or inquiries of his friends; but Shakespeare has not alluded to this mental defect in his portraiture of the unhappy king.

Margaret of Anjou was selected by the cardinal and his compeers for Henry as a wife calculated to rouse him into greater activity, and to impart to him some of the decision of character and strength of mind that she possessed. Added to great personal beauty and remarkable vivacity, she had a courageous temper and masculine intellect, and was regarded as the most accomplished woman of her age. Her pride and vindictiveness of temper she had not yet revealed; no royal state or adverse fortune had called them into activity; the young beauty had lived in comparative seclusion, adding accomplishments to natural graces, and it was thought, with much probability, that when she shared the throne of Henry, she would increase its lustre and elevate the character of its occupant. Had her husband possessed a sounder judgment, and a royalty of nature, she would doubtless have fulfilled these hopes respecting her, but Margaret had no one whose influence could restrain in her those arbitrary doctrines which she had learnt in France and attempted to apply in England. She was distinguished by a haughtiness greater than had hitherto been assumed by any of their native kings, and she sank into unpopularity and dislike.

HISTORICAL SUMMARY OF 'KING HENRY VI.'—PART III.

THE second part of the old drama which supplied our author with materials for the present production is entitled 'The true Tragedie of Richarde Duke of Yorke, and the Death of good King Henrie the Sixt; with the whole Contention between the two Houses Lancaster and Yorke; as it was sundry times acted by the Right Honorable the Earle of Pembrooke his servants.' Both this and the preceding play were reprinted together in 1600, which Malone considers as a strong proof that they cannot be ascribed to the author of the first part of this sovereign's history.

The present historical drama was altered by Crowne, and brought on the stage in the year 1680, under the title of 'The Miseries of Civil War.' The works of Shakespeare could have been little read at that period; for the author, in his prologue, declares the play to be entirely his own composition; whereas the very first scene is that of Jack Cade, copied almost *verbatim* from the 'Second Part of King Henry VI.' and several others from his Third Part with as little variation.

The action of this play comprehends a period of sixteen years. It commences with the events immediately succeeding the first battle of Saint Albans in 1455, and concludes with the murder of King Henry VI. and the birth of Prince Edward, afterwards Edward V., in 1471.

'Of these three plays,' says Dr. Johnson, 'I think

THIRD PART HENRY VI. ACT I. SCENE I.

The Duke of York seated on the throne in Parliament House, backed by his sons and adherents with white roses in their helmets.

the second the best.' The truth is, that they have not sufficient variety of action, for the incidents are too often of the same kind; yet many of the characters are well discriminated. King Henry and his queen, King Edward, the duke of Gloster, and the earl of Warwick are very strongly and distinctly painted.

PERSONS REPRESENTED.

KING HENRY THE SIXTH.
EDWARD, prince of Wales, his son.
LEWIS XI., king of France.
DUKE OF SOMERSET,
DUKE OF EXETER,
EARL OF OXFORD,
EARL OF NORTHUMBERLAND,
EARL OF WESTMORELAND,
LORD CLIFFORD,
} lords on King Henry's side.
RICHARD PLANTAGENET, duke of York.
EDWARD, earl of March, afterwards King Edward IV.,
EDMUND, earl of Rutland,
GEORGE, afterwards duke of Clarence,
RICHARD, afterwards duke of Gloster,
} his sons.
DUKE OF NORFOLK,
MARQUIS OF MONTAGUE,
EARL OF WARWICK,
EARL OF PEMBROKE,
LORD HASTINGS,
LORD STAFFORD,
} of the duke of York's party.

SIR JOHN MORTIMER, } uncles to the duke of York.
SIR HUGH MORTIMER, }

HENRY, earl of Richmond, a youth.

LORD RIVERS, brother to lady Grey. SIR WILLIAM STANLEY. SIR JOHN MONTGOMERY. SIR JOHN SOMERVILLE. TUTOR to Rutland. MAYOR OF YORK. LIEUTENANT OF THE TOWER. A NOBLEMAN. TWO KEEPERS. A HUNTSMAN. A Son that has killed his father. A Father that has killed his son.

QUEEN MARGARET.

LADY GREY, afterwards queen to Edward IV.

BONA, sister to the French queen.

Soldiers and other Attendants on King Henry and King Edward, Messengers, Watchmen, etc.

SCENE, during part of the third act, in France; during all the rest of the play, in England.

COMPENDIUM OF THE PLAY.

THE duke of York enters London in triumph, and extorts from the imbecile Henry a recognition of his succession to the throne in return for an undisturbed possession of his regal dignity during life. The conflicting interests of each party soon lead to an infraction of this treaty: Richard is defeated and taken prisoner in a battle near Wakefield in Yorkshire, and soon after put to death; while the infant duke of Rutland, his son, is barbarously murdered in cold blood by Lord

Clifford. The powerful assistance of the earl of Warwick enables the depressed Yorkists in their turn to defeat their opponents at Towton in Yorkshire, and place Edward duke of York on the throne. King Henry escapes to Scotland, but is at length committed to the Tower, while his queen and son repair to Paris to implore the aid of the French king, whose sympathy is weakened by the presence of Warwick, who is commissioned by his master to solicit the hand of the princess Bona, the sister of Lewis; when a messenger from England suddenly arrives with the intelligence of Edward's marriage with Lady Elizabeth Grey. Exasperated at this insult, Warwick forms a treaty of alliance with Margaret and Lewis, and speedily dethrones his sovereign, who effects his escape to Burgundy, where he obtains a supply of troops, and soon after lands at Ravensburg: a great number of his adherents flock to his standard, and Warwick is routed and slain in a general engagement near Barnet. A still more decisive action at Tewkesbury destroys the relics of the Lancastrian forces: the prince of Wales is stabbed to the heart by the three royal brothers in the presence of his mother; while the captive monarch is himself assassinated in the Tower by Richard, duke of Gloster.

HISTORICAL SUMMARY OF 'KING RICHARD III.'

SHAKESPEARE'S historical authorities in the composition of this popular drama were the 'History of Richard the Third' by Sir Thomas More, and its continuation in the 'Chronicles of Holinshed.' The date of 1593 is the period assigned by Malone to its production, which however was not entered at Stationers' Hall till 1597.

The reign of Richard III. appears to have been a favorite subject of dramatists and other poets who preceded our author; but no sufficient evidence has been produced that Shakespeare borrowed from any of them. Mr. Boswell indeed supposed that an old play, published in 1594, 'An Enterlude, intitled the Tragedie of Richard the Third, wherein is showne the deathe of Edward the Fourthe, with the smotheringe of the two princes in the Tower, with the lamentable ende of Shore's wife, and the contention of the two houses of Lancaster and Yorke,'—had so great a resemblance to this play, that the author must have seen it before he composed his own. It is, notwithstanding, one of the worst of the ancient dramas, and bears but few traces of general likeness.

The historical events here recorded occupy a space of about fourteen years, but are frequently confused for the purposes of dramatic representation. The second scene of the first act commences with the fu-

RICHARD III. ACT I. SCENE II.

Gloster, interrupting the funeral of Henry VI., offers his sword to the Lady Anne.

neral of King Henry VI., who is said to have been murdered on the 21st of May, 1471, while the imprisonment of Clarence, which is represented previously in the first scene, did not take place till 1477–8.

In speaking of this play, Dr. Johnson remarks: 'This is one of the most celebrated of our author's performances, yet I know not whether it has not happened to him as to others, to be praised most when praise is not most deserved. That this play has scenes noble in themselves, and very well contrived to strike on the exhibition, cannot be denied; but some parts are trifling, others shocking, and some improbable.'

PERSONS REPRESENTED.

KING EDWARD THE FOURTH.
EDWARD, prince of Wales, afterwards King Edward V., } sons to the king.
RICHARD, duke of York, } sons to the king.
GEORGE, duke of Clarence, } brothers to the king.
RICHARD, duke of Gloster, afterwards King Richard III., } brothers to the king.
A young SON of Clarence.
HENRY, earl of Richmond, afterwards King Henry VII.
CARDINAL BOURCHIER, archbishop of Canterbury.
THOMAS ROTHERAM, archbishop of York.
JOHN MORTON, bishop of Ely.
DUKE OF BUCKINGHAM.
DUKE OF NORFOLK. EARL OF SURREY, his son.

EARL RIVERS, brother to King Edward's queen.
MARQUIS OF DORSET and LORD GREY, her sons.
EARL OF OXFORD. LORD HASTINGS. LORD STANLEY. LORD LOVEL.
SIR THOMAS VAUGHN. SIR RICHARD RATCLIFF.
SIR WILLIAM CATESBY. SIR JAMES TYRREL.
SIR JAMES BLOUNT. SIR WALTER HERBERT.
SIR ROBERT BRAKENBURY, lieutenant of the Tower.
CHRISTOPHER URSWICK, a Priest. Another Priest.
LORD MAYOR OF LONDON. SHERIFF OF WILTSHIRE.

ELIZABETH, queen of King Edward IV.
MARGARET, widow of King Henry VI.
DUCHESS OF YORK, mother to King Edward IV. Clarence and Gloster.
LADY ANNE, widow of Edward, prince of Wales, son to King Henry VI.; afterwards married to the duke of Gloster.
A young DAUGHTER of Clarence.

Lords, and other Attendants; two Gentlemen; a Pursuivant, Scrivener, Citizens, Murderers, Messengers, Ghosts, Soldiers, etc.

SCENE, England.

COMPENDIUM OF THE PLAY.

THE extinction of the house of Lancaster and the declining health of the king induce Richard, duke of Gloster, to commence his career of ambition with the removal of the duke of Clarence, who is privately assassinated in prison by his orders. Edward shortly after expires, leaving Richard protector of the realm, who immediately withdraws the two young princes from the superintendence of their maternal relatives: these unfortunate noblemen are executed on a pretended discovery of treason; a similar fate awaits Lord Hastings for his fidelity to the legitimate successor of his deceased master; while the innocent children are conveyed to the Tower. By the powerful assistance of the duke of Buckingham, Richard obtains the crown, which is followed by the murder of his nephews in the Tower, and the poisoning of his wife, in order to facilitate an alliance with his niece, which he hopes to accomplish by the aid of her mother. These events are succeeded by the defection and execution of the duke of Buckingham. In the meantime, Henry, earl of Richmond, having assembled a large army, embarks at Bretagne, and lands at Milford Haven: he resolves to proceed towards the capital without delay, and reaches the town of Bosworth in Leicestershire, where he is encountered by the forces of the usurper, who is defeated and slain; while the regal dignity devolves on his fortunate rival, who assumes the title of Henry VII. and puts a period to the long contention between the rival families by an immediate union with Elizabeth, the daughter of Edward IV.

The part of Richard is, perhaps beyond all others, variegated, and consequently favorable to a judicious performer. It comprehends, indeed, a trait of almost every character on the stage: the hero, the lover, the statesman, the buffoon, the hypocrite, the hardened and repenting sinner, etc., are to be found within its compass. No wonder, therefore, that the discriminating powers of a Burbage, a Garrick and a Henderson, Booth, Cook, Kean, Phelps and Irving should at different periods have given it a popularity beyond other dramas of the same author.

HENRY VIII. ACT III. SCENE II.

The Disgrace of Cardinal Wolsey.

HISTORICAL SUMMARY OF 'KING HENRY VIII.'

This drama is conjectured by Malone to have been written a short time previous to the death of Queen Elizabeth, which happened March 24, 1602–3, as well from the prophetic eulogium on that princess in the last scene, as from the imperfect manner in which the panegyric on her successor is connected with the foregoing and subsequent lines. After having been laid aside for several years, it is said to have been revived at the Globe Theatre, June 29, 1613, under the title of 'All is True,' with new decorations, and a prologue and epilogue. During this representation, the theatre accidentally caught fire, occasioned by the discharge of some small pieces, called chambers, on King Henry's arrival at Cardinal Wolsey's gate at Whitehall, one of which being injudiciously managed, set fire to the thatched roof of the building, which was entirely consumed.

Unlike the other English historical plays of Shakespeare, 'Henry the Eighth' had no predecessors on the stage. The pages of history alone furnish materials for its composition; and there are few passages throughout the play which cannot be traced to Fox's 'Acts and Monuments of Christian Martyrs,' or to Cavendish's 'Life of Wolsey,' as found in the 'Chronicles of Holinshed.' The action comprises a period of twelve years, commencing in 1521, the twelfth year of

King Henry's reign, and ending with the baptism of Elizabeth in 1533. It should be observed, however, that Queen Katharine did not die until January 8, 1536.

'This play,' says Dr. Johnson, 'is one of those which still keep possession of the stage by the splendor of its pageantry: yet pomp is not its only merit. The meek sorrows and virtuous distress of Katharine have furnished some scenes which may be justly numbered among the greatest efforts of tragedy: but the genius of Shakespeare comes in and goes out with Katharine. Every other part may be easily conceived and easily written.'

PERSONS REPRESENTED.

KING HENRY THE EIGHTH.
CARDINAL WOLSEY. CARDINAL CAMPEIUS.
CAPUCIUS, ambassador from the emperor, Charles V.
CRANMER, archbishop of Canterbury.
DUKE OF NORFOLK. DUKE OF BUCKINGHAM.
DUKE OF SUFFOLK. EARL OF SURREY.
LORD CHAMBERLAIN. LORD CHANCELLOR.
GARDINER, bishop of Winchester.
BISHOP OF LINCOLN. LORD ABERGAVENNY. LORD SANDS.
SIR HENRY GUILDFORD. SIR THOMAS LOVELL.
SIR ANTHONY DENNY. SIR NICHOLAS VAUX.
SECRETARIES to Wolsey.
CROMWELL, servant to Wolsey.
GRIFFITH, gentleman usher to Queen Katharine.

THREE OTHER GENTLEMEN.
DOCTOR BUTTS, physician to the king.
GARTER, king at arms.
SURVEYOR to the duke of Buckingham.
BRANDON, and a SERGEANT at arms.
DOORKEEPER of the council chamber. PORTER, and his MAN.
PAGE to Gardiner. A CRIER.

QUEEN KATHARINE, wife to King Henry: afterwards divorced.
ANNE BULLEN, her maid of honor; afterwards queen.
AN OLD LADY, friend to Anne Bullen.
PATIENCE, woman to Queen Katharine.

Several Lords and Ladies in the dumb shows; Women attending upon the queen; Spirits, which appear to her; Scribes, Officers, Guards and other Attendants.

SCENE, chiefly in London and Westminster; once, at Kimbolton.

COMPENDIUM OF THE PLAY.

THE duke of Buckingham imprudently involves himself in personal hostilities with Cardinal Wolsey, who finds means of seducing the confidential servants of his rival, and convicting him of high treason. The king shortly after becomes violently enamored of a young lady named Anne Bullen, the power of whose attractions contributes to increase the conscientious scruples which he had previously entertained of the legality of his marriage with Queen Katharine, the widow of his deceased brother. The cardinal, apprehensive of his master's union with one who is suspected to favor the principles of the Reformation, sends private instructions to the papal court, to whose decision Queen Katharine had appealed, that the sentence of divorce may be delayed. This letter, together with an inventory of his enormous wealth, falls by mistake into the hands of the enraged monarch, who immediately deprives Wolsey of all his civil offices; and the fallen favorite is only saved from a charge of high treason by the timely interposition of death. The new queen is now crowned with great magnificence, while her amiable predecessor dies of a broken heart. In the meantime a conspiracy is formed against Archbishop Cranmer, who is enabled to triumph over the malice of his powerful enemies by the favor of the king. The play concludes with the baptism of the infant Elizabeth, the glories of whose future reign, and those of her successor, are prophetically foretold by Cranmer, who is appointed by Henry as sponsor to the princess.

HISTORICAL SUMMARY OF 'TROILUS AND CRESSIDA.'

THE composition of this play is attributed by Malone to the date of 1602. That it was written and acted before the decease of Queen Elizabeth is evident from the manner in which it is entered on the Stationers' books; being registered on February 7, 1602-3, 'as acted by my lord chamberlein's men,' who, in the year of the accession of King James, obtained a license for their theatre, and were denominated 'his majesty's servants.'

Chaucer had celebrated the loves of Troilus and Cressida in a translation from a Latin poem of one Lollius, an old Lombard author: but Shakespeare is supposed to have received the greatest part of his materials for the structure of this drama from Guido of Columpna, a native of Messina in Sicily, who wrote his 'History of Troy' in Latin. This work appears to have been soon after translated by Raoul le Fevre into French, from whom Caxton rendered it into English in 1471, under the title of 'Recuyles, or Destruction of Troy.' Our author has in his story followed, for the greater part, the old book of Caxton, which was then very popular; but the character of Thersites, of which it makes no mention, is a proof that this play was written after Chapman had published his version of Homer in 1596.

PERSONS REPRESENTED.

PRIAM, king of Troy.
HECTOR, TROILUS, PARIS, DEIPHOBUS, HELENUS, } his sons.
ÆNEAS, ANTENOR, } Trojan commanders.
CALCHAS, a Trojan priest, taking part with the Greeks.
PANDARUS, uncle to Cressida.
MARGARELON, a bastard son of Priam.

AGAMEMNON, the Grecian general.
MENELAUS, his brother.
ACHILLES, AJAX, ULYSSES, NESTOR, DIOMEDES, PATROCLUS, } Grecian commanders.
THERSITES, a deformed and scurrilous Grecian.
ALEXANDER, servant to Cressida.
Servant to Troilus; Servant to Paris; Servant to Diomedes.

HELEN, wife to MENELAUS.
ANDROMACHE, wife to Hector.
CASSANDRA, daughter to Priam; a prophetess.
CRESSIDA, daughter to Calchas.

Trojan and Greek Soldiers and Attendants.

SCENE, Troy, and the Grecian camp before it.

COMPENDIUM OF THE PLAY.

CALCHAS, a Trojan priest of Apollo, deserts the cause of his country, and traitorously joins the camp of the Grecians, to whom he renders most important services, in recompense of which he intercedes for the ransom of a powerful Trojan captive named Antenor, in exchange for his daughter Cressida, who resides in Troy, under the protection of her uncle Pandarus, where her beauty and accomplishments make a deep impression on prince Troilus, the son of king Priam, whose addresses she is induced to accept, when their felicity is suspended by the arrival of Diomed, who is commissioned to effect the exchange and restore Cressida to her father. Vows of mutual fidelity are interchanged by the separated lovers, and Troilus soon finds an opportunity to repair secretly to the Grecian tents, where he has the mortification of witnessing the inconstancy of his mistress, who has transferred her affections to Diomed. In the meantime, Hector, disregarding the predictions of his sister Cassandra, and the entreaties of his wife Andromache, repairs to the field of battle, where he slays Patroclus, the friend of Achilles, who soon after revenges his death on his conqueror, whose dead body he cruelly attaches to his chariot, which he drives round the walls of the city.

The destruction of Troy would have been a theme worthy of the pen of Shakespeare, had he confined his overflowing and sometimes erratic genius to his subject; he had admirable materials in his hand, had he attempted less. The play abounds with characters, but they are introduced and then abandoned: before we are fairly acquainted with them they vanish. Cressida is little more than a sketch, and Cassandra, the mad prophetess, something less than one. The best developed character is Pandarus, and he is altogether contemptible. Thersites is probably the original of Apemantus; there is, at least, a resemblance between them, but the latter is the most finished character. Shakespeare apparently intended to create a sympathy and admiration for Troilus, for he makes 'that same dog-fox, Ulysses,' speak eloquently in his favor, comparing him with Hector, and declaring that he was—

'Not yet mature, yet matchless; firm of word;
Speaking in deeds, and deedless in his tongue;
Not soon provoked, nor, being provoked, soon calmed;
His heart and hand both open and both free.'

Still, a mere lover is generally an insipid creation, and Troilus is scarcely an exception to the rule; he wants purpose, decision, and moral courage. The conduct of Pandarus is mean and officious enough, but Troilus shares his shame by employing him. Cressida was open to be wooed, and easy to be won; she is sufficiently complying, in all conscience, and only retires when she is feebly pursued. Had Troilus won her in an open, manly manner, he would probably have preserved both her affection and her honor. Fanciful, giddy coquette as she is, she would have remained virtuous, had she not encountered temptation.

But the play is full of fine poetry and profound observations; if we are for a moment angry with Shakespeare for his wanderings or his inconsistency, he soon wins us back to him with bribes of thought and beauty. The play also has many fine scenes; for instance, that between Cressida and her uncle, in the first act, is remarkable for sparkling dialogue; the same may be said of the first scene of the second act, between the savage jester Thersites and the blunt Ajax. The short scene in the third act, where Helen is introduced, is exceedingly natural and lively; the equivocations of the servant whom Pandarus addresses are fully as humorous as the sayings of the licensed fools in other of our poet's plays. The scene in the garden of Pandarus, where the lovers meet and confess their affection, is exceedingly beautiful; we are reminded for a moment of a similar scene in 'Romeo and Juliet,' but the resemblance soon ceases—the passionate though chaste and womanly affection of Juliet, compared to the wanton appetite of Cressida, is as a pure bright star in heaven to the cold delusive fire which dances in darkness over the stagnant pool or trackless marsh. The dialogue between Achilles and Hector after the tournament is in Shakespeare's happiest style. The bulky Achilles, scanning the Trojan prince with his eyes, and soliciting the gods to tell him in what part of his body he should destroy great Hector, is the sublime of chivalry. Hector's passionate rejoinder,

> 'Henceforth, guard thee well;
> For I'll not kill thee there, nor there, nor there;
> But, by the forge that stithed Mars his helm,
> I'll kill thee everywhere, yea, o'er and o'er,'

is equally fine; while the whole of the fifth act is full of vigor and bustle, and exceedingly animated.

HISTORICAL SUMMARY OF 'TIMON OF ATHENS.'

No printed edition anterior to the folio of 1623 has yet been discovered of this tragedy, which abounds with perplexed, obscure and corrupt passages. The year 1610 is conjectured by Malone as the most probable date of its production, while Dr. Drake and Mr. Chalmers suppose it to have been written as early as 1601 or 1602.

Shakespeare is thought to have derived some of his materials for this drama from the perusal of a novel in Painter's 'Palace of Pleasure,' and from a very slight notice of Timon in Plutarch's 'Life of Antony,' translated by Sir Thomas North. The late celebrated engraver, Mr. Strutt, had, however, a manuscript play on this subject, which appeared to have been written or transcribed about the year 1600, in which was a scene resembling Timon's feast in the third act of this drama; though, instead of warm water, the guests are served with stones painted like artichokes, with which they are driven out of the room: which incident our author is supposed to have had in mind when he made his fourth lord say,

'One day he gives us diamonds, next day stones.'

In the old play Timon then retires to the woods, attended by his faithful steward Laches, who disguises himself that he may continue his services to his master;

TIMON OF ATHENS. ACT I. SCENE II.

Timon in his days of prosperity.

and in the last act the recluse is followed by his inconstant mistress, Callimela, and others, who had heard that he had discovered a treasure in digging; features likewise adopted in the present tragedy, in which, however, all these hints have been incomparably improved and expanded; the original being a very inferior production, though, from the Greek frequently introduced, apparently the work of a scholar.

PERSONS REPRESENTED.

TIMON, a noble Athenian.

LUCIUS, LUCULLUS, SEMPRONIUS, } lords, and flatterers of Timon.

VENTIDIUS, one of Timon's false friends.

APEMANTUS, a churlish philosopher.

ALCIBIADES, an Athenian general.

FLAVIUS, steward to Timon.

FLAMINIUS, LUCILIUS, SERVILIUS, } Timon's servants.

CAPHIS, PHILOTUS, TITUS, LUCIUS, HORTENSIUS, } servants to Timon's creditors.

TWO SERVANTS of Varro, and the SERVANT of Isidore; two of Timon's creditors.

CUPID and MASKERS. THREE STRANGERS.

POET, PAINTER, JEWELLER and MERCHANT.
OLD ATHENIAN. PAGE. FOOL.

PHRYNIA, } mistresses to Alcibiades.
TIMANDRA, }

Other Lords, Senators, Officers, Soldiers, Thieves and Attendants.

SCENE, Athens and the woods adjoining.

COMPENDIUM OF THE PLAY.

AN opulent citizen of Athens, named Timon, expends the whole of his possessions in the service of his country and pretended friends, who enrich themselves by encouraging the indiscriminate profusion of their patron. The approach of poverty and the desertion of his flatterers at length open the eyes of the deluded Timon; and he resolves to express his sense of their ingratitude at a repast, where nothing is provided but hot water, with which he besprinkles his affrighted guests. He now abjures all human intercourse, and seeks an asylum in the woods, where he subsists on the roots of the earth, in digging for which he discovers a large treasure in gold. This acquisition enables him to reward the fidelity of his steward Flavius, who adheres to the broken fortunes of his master; while a considerable sum is appropriated to the service of Alcibiades, who was at that period laying siege to Athens, with the intention of chastising the arrogance of the senate, which had ungratefully repaid his past services by a sentence of perpetual exile. The unfortunate misanthrope is soon after discovered in his cave dead, and the Athenians surrender their city, after procuring favorable terms from their appeased conqueror.

The tragedy includes two incidents, each arising from a similar cause, the flight of Timon and the banishment of Alcibiades; let us now turn our attention to the latter. Shakespeare also found his life in Plutarch, but the poet has not very fully elaborated the character of the Athenian general. Alcibiades was famous for his great personal beauty, his stubborn and ambitious temper, his eloquence, craftiness and dissipation. His resolution was strongly shown even in his boyhood; for it is related that on one occasion he was playing at dice with some other boys in the street, when a loaded wagon coming up interrupted the game; Alcibiades called to the driver to stop, as it was his turn to throw, but the man disregarded him and drove on; while the other boys got out of the way, Alcibiades, however, was not to be so readily overcome, for throwing himself flat upon his face directly before the wagon, he told the rustic to drive on if he pleased. Upon this the man was so startled that he instantly stopped his horses, and the resolute boy got up and had his throw with the dice. Brought up in luxury and universally courted he gave way to every dissipation, but was still exceedingly attached to the philosopher Socrates.

Shakespeare does not adhere to history respecting the cause of the banishment of Alcibiades. He was accused of sacrilege towards the goddesses Ceres and Proserpine and condemned to death, but he saved himself by taking refuge among the Spartans; to whose hospitality he made a vile return by seducing the wife of their king Agis. After a life spent in dissipation, war and political intrigue, he was at length assassinated by a secret order of the magistrates of Sparta. He was at that time living in a small village in Phrygia with his mistress Timandra. His murderers surrounded the house at night and set it on fire, and on his issuing out, sword in hand, they fled to a distance and slew him with their darts and arrows. He was buried by Timandra as honorably as her circumstances would permit.

CORIOLANUS. ACT I. SCENE I.

HISTORICAL SUMMARY OF 'CORIOLANUS.'

This play was neither entered in the books of the Stationers' Company, nor printed, till the year 1623, when it appeared in the folio edition of Heminge and Condell. From a slight resemblance between the language of the fable told by Menenius in the first scene, and that of the same apologue in 'Camden's Remains,' published in 1605, Malone supposes the passage to have been imitated from that volume. He assigns the production, however, to 1609 or 1610; partly because most of the other plays of Shakespeare have been reasonably referred to other years, and therefore the present might be most naturally ascribed to a time when he had not ceased to write, and was probably unemployed; and partly from the mention of the mulberry by Volumnia, the white species of which fruit was brought into England in great quantities in 1609, though possibly other sorts had been already planted here.

A rigid adherence to historical truth is preserved in the characters and events of this drama. Many of the principal speeches are copied from Plutarch's 'Life of Coriolanus,' as translated by Sir Thomas North. The time of action comprehends a period of about four years, commencing with the secession to the Mons Sacer in the year of Rome 262, and ending with the death of Coriolanus, A. U. C. 266.

PERSONS REPRESENTED.

Caius Marcius Coriolanus, a noble Roman.

Titus Lartius, } generals against the Volscians.
Cominius,

Menenius Agrippa, friend to Coriolanus.

Sicinius Velutus, } tribunes of the people.
Junius Brutus,

Young Marcius, son to Coriolanus.

Roman Herald.

Tullus Aufidius, general of the Volscians.

Lieutenant to Aufidius.

Conspirators with Aufidius.

Citizen of Antium.

Two Volscian Guards.

Volumnia, mother to Coriolanus.

Virgilia, wife to Coriolanus.

Valeria, friend to Virgilia.

Gentlewoman, attending Virgilia.

Roman and Volscian Senators, Patricians, Ediles, Lictors, Soldiers, Citizens, Messengers, Servants to Aufidius, and other Attendants.

Scene, partly in Rome, and partly in the territories of the Volscians and Antiates.

COMPENDIUM OF THE PLAY.

The expulsion of the Tarquins from Rome is succeeded by a famine, during which the plebeians extort from the weakness of the nobility a gratuitous distribution of corn, together with the appointment of two popular officers called tribunes to protect their interests from the alleged oppression of the patricians. The haughty Coriolanus, by his opposition to these concessions, renders himself highly unpopular: his civil defects are, however, soon after effaced by the splendor of his military achievements, which are rewarded by his appointment to the consulate by the senate, whose choice is about to be ratified by the suffrages of the people, when the powerful influence of the two tribunes procures his rejection. The violence of temper displayed by Coriolanus at this disappointment affords matter of triumph to his crafty adversaries, who condemn him to perpetual banishment by a decree of the people. Exasperated at this insult, the illustrious exile repairs to the capital of the Volscians, who gladly aid him in his schemes of revenge by investing him and their own general Aufidius with a joint command, which speedily overcomes all opposition; and the hostile occupation of Rome is expected with terror by its affrighted citizens. The conqueror, in the meantime, refuses to listen to the most solemn embassies of his countrymen, until his mother and wife, accompanied by a deputation of eminent Roman matrons, at length prevail on him to raise the siege. The Volscian army soon after returns home, where Coriolanus, while justifying his conduct to the senate, is assassinated by a band of conspirators in the interest of his colleague Aufidius.

Coleridge says: 'This play illustrates the wonderfully philosophic impartiality of Shakespeare's politics.' The poet, however, shows himself something of an aristocrat. He seems to entertain a contempt for the common order of people, and places them in a very ridiculous light. The citizens are made mere creatures of fear and contradiction, wafted about by every wind, and won by every suppliant. More stress is laid on the folly of the plebeii than on the vices of the patricians; and if history has recorded the former as fickle, it has not left the latter stainless. Their courage and self-denial sometimes made them regarded as demi-gods, but their vices sunk them below the brutes. The Roman satirists give pictures of life in the great city which fill modern readers with disgust and loathing. Shakespeare laughs at the people; but if he intended Coriolanus to represent the principle of aristocracy, he places that in no very attractive light.

Some apologists for the turbulent character of Coriolanus have been found who urge the prejudices he had derived from birth and education; from the fact that he was a spoiled child of fortune; and because that, in his day, there were no connecting links between the higher and lower classes, by which they might become known to and respect each other; but these excuses fall very short of a reasonable defence of his haughtiness.

Volumnia, also, has been much praised as a noble character; but she possesses too much of the pride and arrogance of her son, though his nature is certainly softened in her: she is an Amazonian scold, that holds the lives of the Roman citizens in less estimation than a mere whim of her son's; when they have irritated him, she wishes that they may all hang and burn too. She has more experience and wisdom than he; and though she despises and hates the people as much, she truly vaunts she has a brain 'that leads her use of anger to better advantage.' The softer character of Virgilia shows pale beside her, but it is far more pleasing; the sound of flutes is sweeter than the clang of trumpets, and the tender solicitude of the wife more interesting than the stately ambition of the mother.

Menenius is something between a patrician and a buffoon; his connexions are aristocratic, but his sympathies are with the people. Out of his love for Coriolanus he becomes his parasite, and is, in the end, treated by that proud and selfish man with insolence and ingratitude. His application of the fable of the belly and its members to the mutiny of the citizens is apt enough: but we see that, after all, he loves the poor rogues whom he traduces. His great objects of abuse are the tribunes; but they show far more sense than he: they were chosen guardians of the liberty of the people, and in opposing Coriolanus in his attempt at arbitrary power they but performed their duty. To have done less would have proved them unworthy of their great trust.

HISTORICAL SUMMARY OF 'JULIUS CÆSAR.'

THE adventures of Julius Cæsar and his untimely death had occupied the pens of several of our early dramatic authors previous to the composition of this tragedy, which is conjectured by Malone to have made its appearance in 1607; about which period, William Alexander, afterwards earl of Sterline, published a tragedy on the same subject, in which the assassination of Cæsar, which is not exhibited, but related to the audience, forms the catastrophe of his piece. To none of these sources, however, so far as we are acquainted with them, does Shakespeare appear to have been at all indebted; whilst every scene of his play proclaims his obligations to Plutarch's Lives, then recently translated by Sir Thomas North. This drama was neither entered at Stationers' Hall, nor printed before 1623; but a memorandum in the papers of the late Mr. George Vertue states that a play, called 'Cæsar's Tragedy,' was acted at court before April 10, 1613, which is supposed to have been the present piece; it being a frequent practice at that time to alter the name of our author's plays.

The events contained in this drama commence with the festival of the Lupercalia, in February, A. U. C. 709, and concludes with the defeat of Brutus and Cassius, about the end of October, A. U. C. 711.

JULIUS CÆSAR. ACT II. SCENE II.

Calphurnia endeavoring to prevent Cæsar's going to the capitol with the conspirators.

PERSONS REPRESENTED.

JULIUS CÆSAR.
OCTAVIUS CÆSAR,
MARCUS ANTONIUS,
M. ÆMIL. LEPIDUS,
} triumvires after the death of Julius Cæsar.
CICERO, PUBLIUS, POPILIUS LENA, senators.
MARCUS BRUTUS,
CASSIUS,
CASCA,
TREBONIUS,
LIGARIUS,
DECIUS BRUTUS,
METELLUS CIMBER,
CINNA,
} conspirators against Julius Cæsar.
FLAVIUS and MARULLUS, tribunes.
ARTEMIDORUS, a sophist of Cnidos.
A SOOTHSAYER.
CINNA, a poet. Another POET.
LUCILIUS, TITINIUS, MESSALA, YOUNG CATO and VOLUMNIUS, friends to Brutus and Cassius.
VARRO, CLITUS, CLAUDIUS, STRATO, LUCIUS, DARDANIUS, servants to Brutus.
PINDARUS, servant to Cassius.

CALPHURNIA, wife to Cæsar.
PORTIA, wife to Brutus.

Senators, Citizens, Guards, Attendants, etc.

SCENE, during a great part of the play, at Rome; afterwards at Sardis; and near Philippi.

COMPENDIUM OF THE PLAY.

The defeat of the two sons of Pompey in Spain having extinguished all opposition, Cæsar returns in triumph to the city, in order to prepare for his Parthian expedition, previous to which he is anxious to assume the crown, which is publicly presented to him by Mark Antony at the festival of the Lupercalia. Alarmed at this prospect of regal usurpation, a band of conspirators, with Brutus and Cassius at their head, resolve to emancipate their country from tyranny; and the conqueror is accordingly assassinated in the senate-house. The humane though mistaken policy of Brutus preserves the life of Antony, who soon finds means to excite the populace in his favor, and expel the conspirators from Rome. The endeavors of this profligate man to succeed to the despotism of his late master prove unsuccessful; and he is reluctantly compelled to admit Octavius Cæsar, and a powerful general named Lepidus, to a share of the government, with whom a triumvirate is at length formed. After issuing a sanguinary proscription, in which Cicero is included, and witnessing the destruction of their domestic enemies, Octavius and Antony embark for Macedonia, in pursuit of Brutus and Cassius, who risk a general engagement near Philippi, in which the republican army is totally routed; while their daring leaders are reduced to the melancholy necessity of resorting to a voluntary death to escape the vengeance of their victorious opponents.

Julius Cæsar was a character worthy of the closest analytical investigation by the master-mind of Shakespeare; his attainment of power, and his great influence with the Roman people, was entirely attributable to his lofty talents and indomitable courage; his patience under toil, his industry in the pursuit of success, his wise deliberation, and the unshaken steadiness with which he carried out his wonderful resolutions, were the terror of his adversaries and the astonishment of the world.

'Brutus,' says Mr. Drake, 'the favorite of the poet, is brought forward, not only adorned with all the virtues attributed to him by Plutarch, but in order to excite a deeper interest in his favor, and to prove that not jealousy, ambition, or revenge, but unalloyed patriotism was the sole director of his conduct. Our author has drawn him as possessing the utmost sweetness and gentleness of disposition, sympathizing with all that suffer, and unwilling to inflict pain, but from motives of the strongest moral necessity. He has most feelingly and beautifully painted him in the relations of a master, a friend and a husband; his kindness to his domestics, his attachment to his friends and his love to Portia, demonstrating that nothing but a high sense of public duty could have induced him to lift his hand against Cæsar. It is this struggle between the humanity of his temper, and his ardent and hereditary love of liberty, now threatened with extinction by the despotism of Cæsar, that gives to Brutus that grandeur of character, and that predominancy over his associates in purity of intention, which secured to him the admiration of his contemporaries, and to which posterity has done ample justice, through the medium of Shakespeare, who has placed the virtues of Brutus, and the contest in his bosom between private regard and patriotic duty, in the noblest light;

wringing, even from the lips of his bitterest enemy, the fullest eulogium on the rectitude of his principles and the goodness of his heart.'

Cassius is a man of more worldly wisdom than Brutus; his great tact and knowledge of human nature is displayed in his remark to Antony, to reconcile him to the murder of Cæsar:

> 'Your voice shall be as strong as any man's
> In the disposing of new dignities.'

Many touches of this worldliness appear in him; he is eminently fitted for a conspirator, but is still noble. We feel that Mark Antony, in his hour of triumph, slanders the memory of Cassius, in attributing his conspiring against Cæsar merely to envy. The scene in the streets of Rome, where Cassius walks through the storm at night, amid the prodigies that foretell the death of the ambitious dictator, and bares his 'bosom to the thunder-stone,' is the sublime of tragedy: it raises our expectations to the highest pitch, and is a fitting prelude to the approaching catastrophe; when Cæsar, surrounded by fierce looks and glittering swords, and gashed with three-and-twenty hideous wounds, falls dead on the base of his rival's statue, which is bespattered with his blood, and is supposed to look down, with grim satisfaction, on the death of his destroyer. The following scene, where Brutus in his orchard meditates the death of Cæsar, is finer still: his struggle between tenderness and duty, his love for his friend and his love for his country, his high bearing to his fellow-conspirators, where he deprecates the necessity of an oath to bind just men 'that have spoke the word and will not palter,' and his generous yielding of the secret to his heroic and noble wife, are all pregnant with the vivid fire of genius, all point to Shakespeare as the master-bard, who with exquisite and unerring coloring has filled up the spirited sketches of Plutarch.

HISTORICAL SUMMARY OF 'ANTONY AND CLEOPATRA.'

THE composition of this tragedy is assigned by Malone to the date of 1608, although no publication of it has been hitherto discovered anterior to the folio edition of 1623. Some of its incidents are supposed to have been borrowed from a production of Daniel, called 'The Tragedie of Cleopatra,' which was entered on the books of the Stationers' Company in the year 1593. The materials used by Shakespeare were derived from North's translation of Plutarch; and he appears to have been desirous of introducing every incident and person which he found recorded; for when the historian mentions his grandfather Lamprias as his authority for his account of the entertainments of Antony at Alexandria;—in the old copy of this play, in a stage direction, in act i., scene 2, Lamprias, Rannius and Lucilius enter with the rest, but sustain no share in the dialogue. Of the three plays founded by our author on the history of Plutarch this is the one in which he has least indulged his fancy. His adherence to his authority is minute, and he bestowed little pains in the adaptation of the history to the purposes of the drama, beyond an ingenious and frequently elegant metrical arrangement of the humble prose of North. The action comprises the events of ten years, commencing with the death of Fulvia, B. C. 40, and termi-

ANTONY AND CLEOPATRA. ACT III. SCENE VI.

The return of Octavia to Rome.

nating with the final overthrow of the Ptolemean dynasty, B. C. 30.

PERSONS REPRESENTED.

M. ANTONY,
OCTAVIUS CÆSAR,
M. ÆMIL. LEPIDUS, } triumvirs.
SEXTUS POMPEIUS.
DOMITIUS ENOBARBUS,
VENTIDIUS,
EROS,
SCARUS,
DERCETAS,
DEMETRIUS,
PHILO, } friends of Antony.
MECÆNAS,
AGRIPPA,
DOLABELLA,
PROCULEIUS,
THYREUS,
GALLUS, } friends to Cæsar.
MENAS,
MENECRATES,
VARRIUS, } friends of Pompey.
TAURUS, lieutenant-general to Cæsar.
CANIDIUS, lieutenant-general to Antony.
SILIUS, an officer in Ventidius's army.
EUPHRONIUS, an ambassador from Antony to Cæsar.
ALEXAS, MARDIAN, SELEUCUS and DIOMEDES, attendants on Cleopatra.
SOOTHSAYER. CLOWN.

CLEOPATRA, queen of Egypt.
OCTAVIA, sister to Cæsar, and wife to Antony.
CHARMIAN, } attendants to Cleopatra.
IRAS, }
Officers, Soldiers, Messengers and other Attendants.
SCENES in Alexandria and several parts of the Roman empire.

COMPENDIUM OF THE PLAY.

THE government of the eastern provinces, awarded to Antony in the threefold partition of the Roman empire, enables him to indulge without restraint his natural taste for prodigality and dissipation ; and the duties of his high office are sacrificed at the shrine of Cleopatra, whose influence is suspended by the maritime superiority of Sextus Pompeius, which recalls her admirer to the capital. A family alliance is here contracted with Octavia, the sister of Cæsar, who becomes the wife of Antony, and accompanies her husband to his seat of government, after the seeming restoration of public tranquility. The success of Cæsar, who soon after defeats the forces of Pompey, and deprives Lapidus of his share in the triumvirate, at length alarms the effeminate Antony, who provokes the resentment of his powerful rival by his desertion of the amiable Octavia, and his renewed subjugation to the charms of the Egyptian queen. The hostile fleets encounter near the promontory of Actium, where the fortunes of Cæsar prevail, in consequence of the perfidy of Cleopatra, who betakes herself to flight in the midst of the action ; and the infatuated

Antony, following her example, is compelled to avoid impending captivity by resorting to the alternative of a voluntary death; while Cleopatra is reserved to grace the triumph of her conqueror, whose vigilance she contrives to elude by depriving herself of life by the poison of asps, secretly conveyed to her in a basket of figs.

In the play there are four characters which stand out prominently from the canvas—Cleopatra, Antony, Cæsar and Enobarbus. Of Cleopatra, as painted by the pencil of history, what a soft glow of voluptuous languor is thrown around her, and with what irresistible fascinations she is invested, the reader of the tragedy can alone feel and appreciate. Great as her faults are, for her life is but a tissue of refined and poetical sensuality, such is her devotion to Antony, and so winning is the gigantic extravagance of her affection for him, that we not only forgive her errors, but admire and applaud the actor of them.

Antony and Cæsar are placed in strong contrast to each other; the one brave, reckless and prodigal, the other cool, prudent and avaricious. 'Cæsar gets money,' says Pompey, 'where he loses hearts.' Antony is a warrior and a prodigal, and Octavius a statesman, whose feelings are strictly under command. Something of predestination reigns through this play; everything tends towards the downfall of Antony and the advancement of Cæsar.

Enobarbus, although an historical character, and to be found in Plutarch, does not there appear very prominently, and may, to no small extent, be called a creation of the pen of Shakespeare. He found the name in history, but not the man he pictured. Enobarbus forms one of the rich sunlights of the picture;

his plain bluntness has all the cheering hilarity of comedy. But his jocularity would be out of place in the latter scenes of the tragedy; how admirably does Shakespeare obviate this. The dotage and ill-fortune of Antony transform Enobarbus to a serious man, and finally corrupt this hitherto faithful soldier; he deserts his master and flies to the service of Cæsar. The munificent Antony sends after him his chests and treasure, which, in the hurry of flight, he had left behind; this act of kindness strikes the penitent fugitive to the heart, and wasting in grief, he goes forth to die; and alone, without the camp, breathing his deep sorrow to the cold moon, does Enobarbus end his life in the bitterness of despair.

As his final ruin draws on, Antony is alternately 'valiant and dejected;' looking upon his high rank and qualities, his unbounded but dazzling dissipation, his imperial generosity, great personal courage, and his gorgeous career; when hearing of his death, we feel inclined to say with Cæsar:

'The death of Antony
Is not a single doom: in the name lay
A moiety of the world.'

That of Cleopatra follows; it is consistent with her brilliant and luxurious life; she robs death of its hideousness, and, enveloped in her royal robes and crown, still radiant in that seductive beauty which subdued Cæsar and ruined Antony, she applies to her bosom the envenomed instrument of death, and falls into an everlasting slumber 'as sweet as balm, as soft as air,' where she yet looks:

'As she would catch another Antony
In her strong toil of grace.'

CYMBELINE. ACT II. SCENE IV.

Iachimo produces the bracelet as proof of his having won his wager.

HISTORICAL SUMMARY OF 'CYMBELINE.'

THIS play is conjectured by Malone to have been written in the year 1609, although it was neither entered on the books of the Stationers' Company nor printed till 1623. The main incidents on which the plot rests occur in a novel of Boccace; but our author is supposed to have derived them from an old storybook popular in that age, entitled 'Westward for Smelts.' All he knew of 'Cymbeline' he acquired from Holinshed, who is sometimes closely followed, and sometimes strangely perverted. This king, according to the old historian, succeeded his father in the 19th year of the reign of Augustus; and the play commences about the 24th year of Cymbeline's reign, which was the 42d of the reign of Augustus and the 16th of the Christian era; notwithstanding which, Shakespeare has peopled Rome with modern Italians, Philario, Iachimo, etc. 'Cymbeline' is said to have reigned 35 years, leaving at his death two sons, Guiderius and Arviragus.

This drama, if not in the construction of its fable, one of the most perfect of our author's productions, is, in point of poetic beauty, of variety and truth of character, and in the display of sentiment and emotion, one of the most interesting.

PERSONS REPRESENTED.

CYMBELINE, king of Britain.
CLOTEN, son to the Queen by a former husband.
LEONATUS POSTHUMUS, a gentleman, husband to Imogen.
BELARIUS, a banished lord, disguised under the name of Morgan.
GUIDERIUS, ARVIRAGUS, } sons to Cymbeline, disguised under the names of Polydore and Cadwal, supposed sons to Belarius.
PHILARIO, friend to Posthumus, IACHIMO, friend to Philario, } Italians.
FRENCH GENTLEMAN, friend to Philario.
CAIUS LUCIUS, general of the Roman forces.
ROMAN CAPTAIN. TWO BRITISH CAPTAINS.
PISANIO, servant to Posthumus.
CORNELIUS, a physician.
TWO GENTLEMEN.
TWO JAILERS.

QUEEN, wife to Cymbeline.
IMOGEN, daughter to Cymbeline by a former queen.
HELEN, woman to Imogen.

Lords, Ladies, Roman Senators, Tribunes, Apparitions, a Soothsayer, a Dutch Gentleman, a Spanish Gentleman, Musicians, Officers, Captains, Soldiers, Messengers and other Attendants.

SCENE, sometimes in Britain, sometimes in Italy.

COMPENDIUM OF THE PLAY.

THE Princess Imogen, only daughter of Cymbeline, king of Britain, secretly marries an accomplished courtier, named Posthumus, whose presumption is punished by a sentence of perpetual exile by the angry monarch. Deprived of the society of his amiable wife, the banished Posthumus repairs to Rome, where his confidence in the unshaken attachment of his princess is unhappily exchanged into a conviction of her infidelity by the false intelligence which he receives from Iachimo, a perfidious Italian; and the misguided husband immediately despatches orders to Pisanio, a faithful attendant residing in Britain, to put his mistress to death. Disregarding these cruel injunctions, Pisanio induces the unhappy lady to avoid the malice of her stepmother, and the importunities of her son Cloten, by flight. Disguised in male attire, Imogen arrives near Milford-haven, where she procures hospitable entertainment in the cottage of Belarius, a banished nobleman in the garb of a peasant, who had revenged the injuries which he had formerly sustained at the hands of Cymbeline, by stealing his two infant sons, and educating them as his own in this retreat. Cloten shortly after arrives in pursuit of Imogen, and is slain by the eldest of the princes in single combat. In the meantime, Posthumus and Iachimo accompany a Roman army to Britain, where Imogen, under the assumed name of Fidele, becomes a page to the Roman general, who sustains a signal defeat, in which the intrepid valor of Belarius and the two princes, assisted by Posthumus in the disguise of a British soldier, is chiefly conspicuous. Iachimo is taken prisoner, and makes a confession of his guilt to Cymbeline; Imogen is restored to her husband, Belarius pardoned, and the two princes publicly recognized, while the queen dies in despair at the loss of her son and the disappointment of her ambitious projects.

Our poet's object in writing this play was a noble one; the vindication of the character of woman from the lewd aspersions of thoughtless and unprincipled men. It is not Imogen alone whom the Italian profligate, Iachimo, slanders—it is her whole sex; of his attempt upon her chastity, he says to her husband: 'I durst attempt it against any lady in the world.' Impossible as it may appear to pure and innocent minds, men still live who are ignorant and sensual enough to make the same vile boast. Among the pleasure-seeking gallants of that lascivious age, when seduction and duelling were by a large number of that class considered mere venial vices, if not graceful accomplishments, such unbelievers in the purity of woman were, perhaps, not uncommon; and in this play the bard read them a stern reproof from the stage.

Imogen is a personification of woman; woman enthroned in the holy temple of her pure and chaste affections, rejecting the tempter of her honor with the bitterest scorn and loathing, and enduring wrong and suffering with the most touching patience and sweetness. The gentler sex should be always grateful to the memory of our great Shakespeare, for his genius did sweet homage to their character; he invests his female creations with all that is most pure and generous in humanity, picturing them, indeed, as beautiful to the eye, but a thousand times more acceptable to the heart. There is a moral dignity about his women, a holy strength of affection, which neither suffering nor death can pervert, that elevates them above the sterner nature of man, placing them on an equality with angels. The adventures of Imogen are like a beautiful romance; her flight after her banished husband, her wretchedness and forlorn condition when informed that he believes her false and has given order for her death; her assumption of boy's attire, in which disguise she wanders among the mountains at point to perish from hunger; her meeting with her disguised brothers in the cave; her supposed death and recovery, and, finally, her discovery of her repentant husband, and throwing herself, without one reproach, upon his bosom—are all beautifully portrayed. Imogen is, indeed, a pattern of connubial love and chastity.

Posthumus is an irritable and impatient character; his love for Imogen is rather a selfish one, or he would not have been so easily persuaded that she was false; it undergoes some purification in his trouble, and we scarcely sympathize with him until his repentance of his rashness. He then doubts his own worthiness, and feeling that he has wickedly presumed to direct the wrath of Heaven and punish its offenders, exclaims:

> 'Gods! if you
> Should have ta'en vengeance on my faults, I never
> Had lived to put on this.'

A reflection we all might advantageously make, when contemplating revenge for any real or supposed injury.

Iachimo is an unconfirmed villain, as dishonest as Iago, but not so devilish, for he has the grace to repent of his treachery; he tries to compound with his conscience, and satisfy it with flimsey sophistries.

He is ready to attest the truth of his false assertions with an oath, and does absolutely swear to Posthumus that he had the jewel from the arm of Imogen, which is literally true, but morally a perjury, because he stole the bracelet, and led the husband to suspect that it was given him in the gratification of an infamous affection. Iachimo equivocates; Iago would have had no compunction about the matter, but have sworn to any falsehood, however injurious and diabolical, without mental reservation. Iachimo's confession in the last scene is too wordy and tediously prolonged, and the humility of it is scarcely in accordance with his character, as portrayed in the earlier scenes of the play.

These three characters are the principal ones of that group to which the attention is chiefly attracted; Cymbeline, himself, is represented as weak and vacillating—a mere tool of his wicked queen, who says: 'I never do him wrong, but he does buy my injuries;' rewards her for them, as if they were benefits: this woman is utterly villainous without any redeeming quality, unless affection for her foolish and unprincipled son be called one; it is seldom that Shakespeare draws such characters, for he loves rather to elevate than to depress humanity, and to paint in sunbeams, than to people twilight with forms of darkness. Perhaps she is introduced to bring the sweet character of the pure and loving Imogen into greater prominence by the power of contrast. The conduct of Cymbeline is unaccountable, save in a timid and wavering mind; having beaten the Romans by accident, he is amazed at his own temerity, and, in the very triumph of victory, makes a peace, and promises to pay to Cæsar the tribute which he had gone to war to avoid.

Cloten has been said to be so singular a character, and possessed of qualities so contradictory, that he has been supposed to form an exception to Shakespeare's usual integrity in copying from nature. We cannot see in what particular he is irreconcilable to humanity; he is a knave, a braggart, and a fool in most matters, but that is no reason why he should not possess some shrewd common sense ideas occasionally. Nothing can be happier than his defiance of the Roman ambassador:—'If Cæsar can hide the sun from us with a blanket, or put the moon in his pocket, we will pay him tribute for light; else, sir, no more tribute.' Quaintly expressed, certainly, but unanswerable as an argument, it is not Cloten's want of sense, but his outrageous vanity, that makes him ridiculous. He is not half so great a contradiction to himself as is Polonius in 'Hamlet,' and yet we can easily understand the peculiarities of that character; the weakness of age consuming the strength of maturity, folly encroaching on wisdom; in Cloten, it is folly consuming common sense. Shakespeare requires no justification to the observing mind; few men are either all wisdom or all folly; the writings of the wisest man of whom we have any record are bitter condemnations of his own actions, eloquent laments for time misspent in voluptuous abandonment. We doubt not that the poet drew Cloten from a living model; singularities, in works of fiction, are generally copied from life—they are flights too bold for most authors to take without precedent. Respecting the character of Cloten, Hazlitt has remarked 'that folly is as often owing to a want of proper sentiments as to a want of understanding.'

In the delineation of the two princes, Guiderius and Arviragus, Shakespeare propagates a doctrine which will find many opponents in the present day: he infers that there is an innate royalty of nature, a sovereignty in blood in those born of a kingly stock; and the young princes brought up as simple rustics, and born of a weak uxorious father, are represented as feeling their high birth so strongly that it impels them to acts of heroism. Belarius says:

> 'Their thoughts do hit
> The roofs of palaces; and nature prompts them,
> In simple and low things, to prince it much
> Beyond the trick of others.'

Their old protector is a courtier, turned hermit from an acute sense of wrong and a consequent disgust of civilized life, and his language is that of one who has seen the world to satiety: he is full of bitter reflections on princes and their courts, where oft a man gains ill report for doing well, and 'must court'sey at the censure.' He bears some resemblance to the moralizing Jaques; all natural objects suggest to him lofty and religious reflections, and the low-roofed cave which makes him bow as he issues from it to greet the rising sun, instructs him to adore its great Creator. Jaques had been a libertine in his youth, and Belarius is guilty of a dishonorable and wicked revenge by bringing up the sons of Cymbeline as rustics; the father had injured him, but he had robbed the children of their birthright.

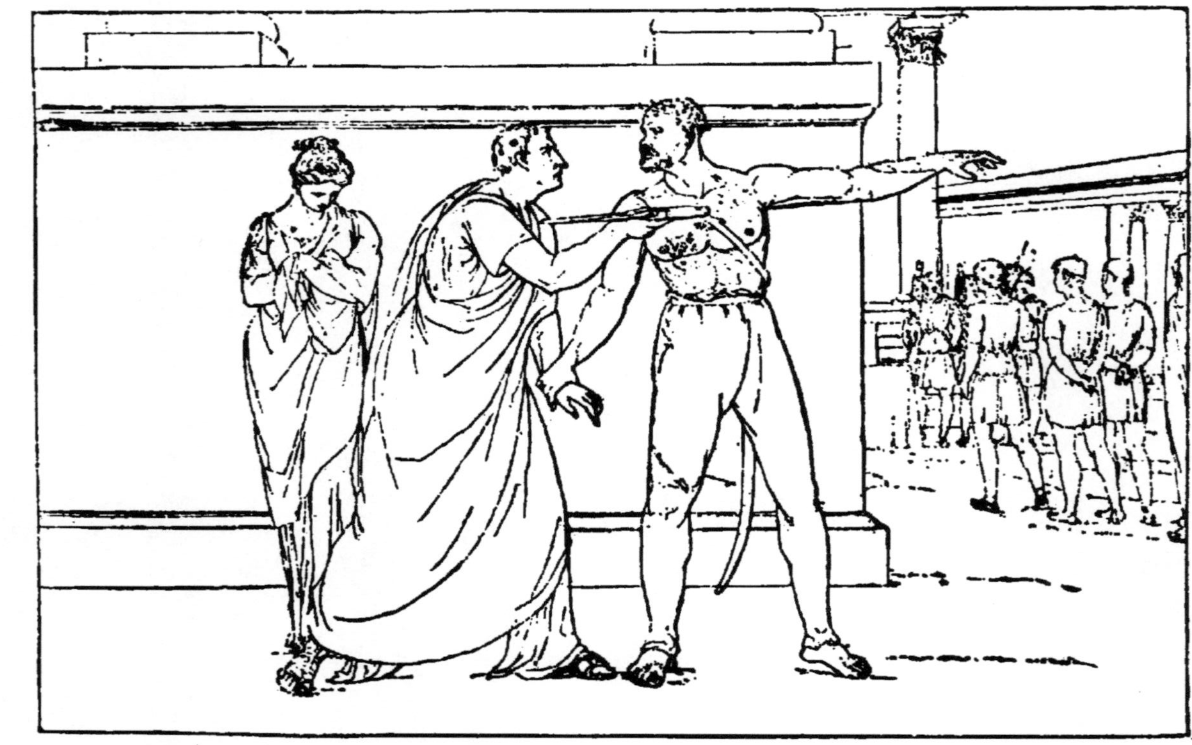

TITUS ANDRONICUS. ACT II. SCENE I.

Titus, Aaron and Lavinia. Martius and Quintus bound, passing to the place of execution.

HISTORICAL SUMMARY OF 'TITUS ANDRONICUS.'

THIS sanguinary and disgusting tragedy is still suffered to retain its place among the works of Shakespeare, although it is rejected by all the commentators and critics except Capell and Schlegel. The editors of the first folio edition, however, have included it in that volume, which implies that they considered the play as his production. George Meres enumerates it among his works in 1598, and this author was personally esteemed and consulted by our poet. It is now generally supposed that the present drama found admission into the original complete edition of Shakespeare's works only because he had written a few lines in it, assisted in its revisal, or produced it on the stage. A tradition to this effect is mentioned by Ravenscroft in the preface to his alteration of this tragedy, as acted at Drury Lane in 1687, where he says, 'I have been told by some anciently conversant with the stage, that it was not originally Shakespeare's, but was brought by a private author to be acted; and he gave only some master-touches to one or two of the principal parts.' The events of this drama are not of historical occurrence, but were probably borrowed from an old ballad on the same subject entered on the books of the Stationers' Company in 1593, about which period it appears to have been written. Mr.

Malone has marked with double inverted commas those passages in which he supposes the hand of Shakespeare may be traced.

It is recorded of the poet Robert Burns that, 'when in his fifteenth year, Mr. Murdoch, his school-teacher, sometimes visited the family at Mount Oliphant, and brought books with him. On one occasion he read 'Titus Andronicus' aloud, but Robert's pure taste rose in a passionate revolt and protest against its coarse cruelties and repugnant horrors.'

Alexander Smith's 'Life of Burns.'

PERSONS REPRESENTED.

SATURNINUS, son to the late emperor of Rome, and afterwards declared emperor himself.

BASSIANUS, brother to Saturninus; in love with Lavinia.

TITUS ANDRONICUS, a noble Roman, general against the Goths.

MARCUS ANDRONICUS, tribune of the people and brother to Titus.

LUCIUS,
QUINTUS,
MARTIUS,
MUTIUS, } sons to Titus Andronicus.

YOUNG LUCIUS, a boy, son to Lucius.

PUBLIUS, son to Marcus the tribune.

ÆMILIUS, a noble Roman.

ALARBUS,
CHIRON,
DEMETRIUS, } sons to Tamora.

AARON, a Moor, beloved by Tamora.
CAPTAIN, TRIBUNE, MESSENGER, and CLOWN; Romans.
Goths and Romans.

TAMORA, queen of the Goths.
LAVINIA, daughter to Titus Andronicus.
NURSE, and a black Child.

Kinsmen of Titus, Senators, Tribunes, Officers, Soldiers, and Attendants.

SCENE, Rome, and the country near it.

COMPENDIUM OF THE PLAY.

TITUS ANDRONICUS, a Roman general, in a successful campaign against the Goths, takes captive their queen Tamora with her three sons, and conveys them to Rome in triumph, where one of the youths is inhumanly sacrificed by the conqueror at the tomb of his children who had been slain in battle. Eager for revenge, the artful Tamora makes a favorable impression on the heart of the emperor Saturninus, and becomes the partner of his throne. By the contrivance of her two sons and a Moorish paramour named Aaron, she procures the assassination of Bassianus, the emperor's brother; while his wife Lavinia, the daughter of Titus, is deprived of her tongue and hands by the Gothic princess, in order to prevent a discovery of the ill usage which she had previously sustained. Two sons of Titus shortly after suffer death for their supposed participation in the murder of Bassianus: the real perpetrators are at length discovered; and the enraged father, having decoyed the young men to his house, puts a period to their existence, and serves up their mangled relics to their mother in a banquet. The unfortunate Lavinia falls by the hand of her father, who afterwards sacrifices the empress to his fury, for which he is slain by Saturninus, who in his turn loses his crown and life by the sword of Lucius, the only surviving son of Titus, who procures a repeal of his banishment by means of a Gothic army, and is proclaimed emperor by the senate and people.

We forbear comment on this tragedy.

PERICLES. ACT II. SCENE V.

Simonides giving Thaisa to Pericles.

HISTORICAL SUMMARY OF 'PERICLES.'

THE History of Apollonius, king of Tyre, contained in an old book of the fifteenth century entitled *Gesta Romanorum*, appears to have formed the groundwork of the present drama. Gower, in his *Confessio Amantis*, has related the same story, the incidents and antiquated expressions of which may here be distinctly traced; and hence, as Gower himself is introduced to perform the office of Chorus, it seems reasonable to conjecture that the work of the old poet has been chiefly followed.

That the greater part of this production was the composition of Shakespeare is rendered highly probable by the elaborate disquisitions of Steevens and Malone, who have decided, from the internal evidence, that he either improved some older imperfect work, or wrote in connection with some other author; that it contains more of his language than any of his doubted dramas; that many scenes throughout the whole piece are his, and especially the greater part of the last three acts; and that what he did compose was his earliest dramatic effort, being assigned to the year 1590. The external evidences are, that Edward Blount, one of the printers of the first folio Shakespeare, entered 'Pericles' at Stationers' Hall in 1608, though it appeared the next year from another publisher, with Shakespeare's name in the title-page; that it was acted at Shakespeare's own theatre, the Globe; and that it is ascribed to him by several authors near his time. This play is not to be found in the folio of 1623. the editors having probably forgotten it until the book was printed, as they did 'Troilus and Cressida,' which is inserted in the volume, but not in the Table of Contents.

The text of this play is so wretchedly corrupt, that it does not so much seem to want illustration as emendation, in which little assistance can be obtained from the inspection of the earliest printed copies, which appear in so imperfect a form that there is scarcely a single page undisfigured by the grossest errors.

'On the whole,' says Mr. Steevens, 'were the intrinsic merits of 'Pericles' yet less than they are, it would be entitled to respect among the curious in dramatic literature. As the engravings of Mark Antonio are valuable, not only on account of their beauty, but because they are supposed to have been executed under the eye of Rafaelle; so 'Pericles' will continue to owe some part of its reputation to the touches it is said to have received from the hand of Shakespeare.'

PERSONS REPRESENTED.

ANTIOCHUS, king of Antioch.
PERICLES, prince of Tyre.
HELICANUS, } two lords of Tyre.
ESCANES, }
SIMONIDES, king of Pentapolis.
CLEON, governor of Tharsus.

LYSIMACHUS, governor of Mitylene.
CERIMON, lord of Ephesus.
THALIARD, lord of Antioch.
PHILEMON, servant to Cerimon.
LEONINE, servant to Dionyza.
MARSHAL.
A PANDER, and his WIFE.
BOULT, their servant.
GOWER, as Chorus.

DAUGHTER OF ANTIOCHUS.
DIONYZA, wife to Cleon.
THAISA, daughter to Simonides.
MARINA, daughter to Pericles and Thaisa.
LYCHORIDA, nurse to Marina.
DIANA.

Lords, Ladies, Knights, Gentlemen, Sailors, Pirates, Fishermen, and Messengers, etc.

SCENE, dispersedly in various countries.

COMPENDIUM OF THE PLAY.

ANTIOCHUS, king of Antioch, in order to keep his daughter unmarried, subjects all suitors to the penalty of death who fail to expound a riddle which is recited to each : the beauty and accomplishments of the young princess overcome all their apprehensions, and prove fatal to many. At length, Pericles, prince of Tyre, explains the riddle to the monarch, who determines to reward his ingenuity by procuring his assassination.

To avoid the impending danger, which he is unable to resist, and to preserve his territories from invasion, Pericles quits his kingdom, and arrives at Tharsus, where his timely interposition preserves Cleon and his subjects from the horrors of famine. He is afterwards driven by a storm on the shore of Pentapolis, where he marries Thaisa, the daughter of king Simonides, who, in accompanying her husband to his kingdom, is delivered of a daughter at sea, named Marina. The body of Thaisa, who is supposed to be dead, is enclosed in a box by her disconsolate husband, and committed to the waves, which drive it towards the coast of Ephesus, where Cerimon, a compassionate and skilful nobleman, succeeds in restoring the vital functions of the lady, who afterwards becomes the priestess of Diana. In the meantime, Pericles commits his infant to the custody of Cleon and his wife, and embarks for Tyre. At the age of fourteen, Marina excites the jealousy of her guardians by the superiority of her attainments, which obscures the talents of their own daughter: a ruffian is accordingly hired to deprive her of life, who is about to execute his orders, when she is rescued from destruction by pirates, who hurry her to Mitylene; at which place she is recognized by her father, who, deceived by the representations of his perfidious friends, is bitterly lamenting her supposed death. By the directions of the goddess Diana, who appears to him in a dream, he repairs to Ephesus, where he recovers his long-lost Thaisa, and unites his daughter in marriage to Lysimachus, the governor of Mitylene; while Cleon and his wife fall victims to the fury of the enraged populace.

KING LEAR. ACT V. SCENE III.

The death of Cordelia.

HISTORICAL SUMMARY OF 'KING LEAR.'

THIS noble tragedy, the composition of which is assigned by Malone to the date of 1605, was entered on the books of the Stationers' Company Nov. 26, 1607, and is there mentioned to have been played the preceding Christmas before his majesty at Whitehall. The story was originally related by Geoffrey of Monmouth, and thence transcribed in Holinshed's Chronicle, which Shakespeare certainly consulted, though he appears to have been more indebted to an old drama on the same subject by an anonymous writer, which made its appearance in 1594. The episode of Gloster and his sons, which is blended by our author with such consummate skill in the development of his main design, was derived from the narrative of the blind king of Paphlagonia, in the Arcadia of Sir Philip Sidney.

Geoffrey of Monmouth informs us that Lear, who was the eldest son of Bladud, 'nobly governed his country for sixty years.' According to that historian, he died about eight hundred years before the Christian era.

PERSONS REPRESENTED.

LEAR, king of Britain.
KING OF FRANCE.

DUKE OF BURGUNDY.
DUKE OF CORNWALL.
DUKE OF ALBANY.
EARL OF KENT.
EARL OF GLOSTER.
EDGAR, son to Gloster.
EDMUND, bastard son to Gloster.
CURAN, a courtier.
OLD MAN, tenant to Gloster.
PHYSICIAN.
FOOL.
OSWALD, steward to Goneril.
OFFICER, employed by Edmund.
GENTLEMAN, attendant on Cordelia.
HERALD.
SERVANTS to Cornwall.

GONERIL, }
REGAN, } daughters to Lear.
CORDELIA, }

Knights attending on the king, Officers, Messengers, Soldiers, and Attendants.

SCENE, Britain, near Dover.

COMPENDIUM OF THE PLAY.

FATIGUED with the cares of royalty, Lear, king of Britain, determines to withdraw from public life, and to commit the government of his kingdom to his three daughters. The frank sincerity of Cordelia, his youngest child, so displeases the infatuated monarch that he resolves to disinherit her and divide her patrimony between Goneril and Regan, her more specious sisters, who are intrusted with the protection of their depôsed father. The two daughters no sooner find themselves emancipated from parental control than they subject the old king to a diminution of his retinue, and by their cruelty and ingratitude at length drive him, amidst the inclemencies of a midnight storm, to an adjoining heath, where he is met by Edgar in the disguise of a lunatic, assumed in order to elude the indignation of his father, the earl of Gloster, whose credulity has been imposed on by the villanous suggestions of Edmund, his natural son. The mental powers of Lear are overwhelmed by his accumulated sufferings, which are secretly relieved by Gloster, in defiance of the injunctions of the sisters; and his humanity is punished with the loss of his eyes, through the information communicated by the treacherous Edmund. In the meantime Cordelia bestows her hand on the French king, who despatches a large army under the conduct of his wife for the relief of Lear, whose intellects become partially restored by the tender assiduities of his affectionate daughter. A general engagement soon after ensues, in which Lear and Cordelia sustain a total defeat, and are committed to prison, where orders are received to hang Cordelia, and her unhappy father dies of a broken heart: Regan is poisoned by her sister Goneril, who stabs herself in despair at the discovery of her designs on the life of her husband, while Edmund falls by the hand of his injured brother.

The character of Lear is grand in the extreme; the choleric yet affectionate old king, jealous of his dignity, brooking no insult, rash and impetuous, blind to everything but momentary feeling, and heedless of all results—casts from his bosom his only affectionate child, and bestows his kingdom upon his two treacherous daughters, whose fiendish ingratitude robs him of the little which he had reserved to himself, and drives him forth to meet the midnight storm, and expose his white head to the 'oak-cleaving thunderbolts;' he wanders about in his pathless way until his mind is disturbed, and the impetuous, dishonored king and broken-hearted father becomes by degrees mad, from dwelling too intently on the monstrous ingratitude of his children. He is at length rescued from the frightful destitution and misery to which he had been abandoned; but it is too late; the blow has been inflicted; the shock was too great to permit of his recovery, and, as Schlegel eloquently observes, 'all that now remained to him of life is the capability of loving and suffering beyond measure.'

Some critics, amongst whom was Dr. Johnson, contended that the termination was too tragical for endurance, and that poetical justice was violated by the ultimate death of Lear and his daughter Cordelia; the sublime tragedy of Shakespeare was therefore banished from the stage, and Tate's corrupt version, in which the scenes are most unnecessarily transposed, altered, and interspersed with silly bombast and vapid puerility, was substituted in its stead; Lear was saved, and Cordelia retired with victory and happiness. A modern critic, in allusion to this, exclaims: 'a happy ending! as if the living martyrdom that he had gone through, the flaying of his feelings alive, did not make a fair dismissal from the stage of life the only decorous thing for him. If he is to live and be happy after, if he could sustain this world's burden after, why all this pudder and preparation? why torment us with all this unnecessary sympathy? As if the childish pleasure of getting his gilt robes and sceptre again could tempt him to act over again his misused station, as if at his years and with his experience, anything was left but to die.'

Tate also cut out of his adaptation of Shakespeare's tragedy the character of the Fool, which was much the same as if some modern dauber should paint out the sunlight from a landscape of Claude's. We feel more than a common interest for this jester on account of his strong attachment to Lear and his family; he is also a great favorite of the aged king, is a wise counsellor, and, though a bitter satirist, is faithful to the old man through all his persecutions, and is hanged at last for his adherence to the cause of his deposed master. He never forgets his character; reverse of fortune makes him satirical, but never serious; he talks with a purpose, and strives to arouse the old monarch to reassert his rank and condition, and enforce the respect due to it. The fourth scene in the third act is extremely grand, the real madness of Lear, the assumed madness of Edgar, and the quaint pithy sayings of the Fool, make a strange and almost startling picture; the very idea of bringing such characters together is a fine one, and would scarcely have occurred to any other author. The assumed insanity of Edgar is grandly contrasted with the real mental disorder of Lear. The latter never loses sight of the real causes of his misfortunes; when

Edgar first enters, personating the bedlamite, the aged king exclaims in tones of pity:

> 'What, have his *daughters* brought him to this pass?
> Could'st thou save nothing? Did'st thou give them all?'

And when the fool asks him whether a madman be a gentleman or a yeoman, with a vivid sense of his own rashness, he answers 'a king, a king!' But Edgar never alludes to the cause of his supposed madness, never forgets that he has a part to play, and the poet, with an exquisite observance of nature, makes him, in his anxiety to preserve his disguise, rather over-act the part; he is too learned; we see something of the gentleman through all the rags and mouthing of the assumed idiot. He is familiar with quaint traditions and odd tales of fiends and witches, which the real wandering idiot would never have thought of. Lear, in the disorder of his mind, is struck with the same disparity in human fortunes and sufferings; he had been somewhat despotic in his sanity, but he turns reformer in his madness and babbles about the abuses of authority.

Kent is a very noble character, in every respect faultless; his love for his royal master endears him to us, while his rough energy and bluntness of speech claim our admiration. He is a plain truth-teller either to king or peasant, a quaint humorist, a lover of justice and liberty, who sacrifices his rank and his estate rather than flatter the rash monarch in his course of angry injustice. His excuse for his boldness of speech also is admirable, 'To plainness honor's bound, when majesty stoops to folly.'

Of the bastard Edmund, the poet Coleridge says finely, 'it is a profound moral, that shame will naturally generate guilt, the oppressed will be vindictive.' Shakespeare seems not unfrequently to rough-hew a character in one play which he matures and perfects in another; thus Birón reappears as Benedick, and Edmund as Iago. Shakespeare, who has made Edmund a man of acute intellect, has no doubt through him expressed his own opinion of the follies of astrological studies.

Nowhere has Shakespeare drawn characters so alike as the two unnatural daughters of Lear; both selfish, ambitious, and overbearing, both guilty of the blackest ingratitude to their aged father, and even seeking his life; both, by a natural sequence, false to their husbands, both attached to the same paramour, and both dying by violence and in despair.

Shakespeare always vindicates the justice of God's providence; tyrants live hated and in fear, and die unpitied and in blood. The crafty perish by craft; the murderous and the treacherous live in a hell on earth; the wicked are heaven's instruments against themselves; and nature is eternally at war with sin. Thus with Regan and Goneril, they lead a life of conjunctive wickedness, carry on a partnership of devilry, and then growing jealous each of the other, Goneril poisons Regan, and then stabs herself.

Shakespeare's philosophy is a stern one; he is an impressive preacher of the doctrine of compensation—compensation to all, and for all deeds—evil for evil, good for good. Edgar, though a pagan, recognizes this in these lines:

> 'The gods are just, and of our pleasant vices
> Make instruments to scourge us.'

And the dying villain Edmund admits its truth, and exclaims:

> 'The wheel is come full circle; I am here.'

We can never escape this; it is a law of our being which we cannot evade or shake off; if in any we disturb another's peace we murder our own. It has been said, the dice of God are always loaded, there are no chance casts, and this doctrine Shakespeare never loses sight of. It is indeed wonderfully prominent in Lear, and the aged monarch himself, much as we sympathize with him, is but suffering the punishment, a dreadful one it is true, for his unjust partiality to his elder daughters and his passionate and cruel desertion of his youngest child.

ROMEO AND JULIET. ACT II. SCENE VI.

HISTORICAL SUMMARY OF 'ROMEO AND JULIET.'

THE story on which this play is founded is related as a true one in Girolamo de la Corte's 'History of Verona.' In 1562 Mr. Arthur Brooke published a poem on 'the Tragicall Historie of Romeus and Juliett;' the materials for which he chiefly obtained from a French translation, by Boisteau, of an Italian novel by Luigi da Porto, a gentleman of Vicenza, who died in 1529. A prose translation of Boisteau's work was also published in 1567, by Painter, in his 'Palace of Pleasure;' and on the incidents of these two works Shakespeare is supposed to have constructed this interesting tragedy. Malone imagines that the present piece was designed in 1591, and finished in 1596; but Chalmers refers it to 1592, and Dr. Drake to 1593. There are four early editions of it in quarto, namely those of 1597, 1599, 1609, and one without date; the first of which is less copious than the others; since each successive edition appears to have been revised, with additions to particular passages.

PERSONS REPRESENTED.

ESCALUS, prince of Verona.
PARIS, a young nobleman, kinsman to the prince.
MONTAGUE, } heads of two houses, at variance with
CAPULET, } each other.

OLD MAN, uncle to Capulet.

ROMEO, son to Montague.

MERCUTIO, kinsman to the prince, and a friend to Romeo.

BENVOLIO, nephew to Montague, and a friend to Romeo.

TYBALT, nephew to Lady Capulet.

FRIAR LAURENCE, a Franciscan.

FRIAR JOHN, of the same order.

BALTHASAR, servant to Romeo.

SAMPSON, } servants to Capulet.
GREGORY, }

ABRAM, servant to Montague.

APOTHECARY.

THREE MUSICIANS.

CHORUS. BOY; PAGE to Paris; PETER; an OFFICER.

LADY MONTAGUE, wife to Montague.

LADY CAPULET, wife to Capulet.

JULIET, daughter to Capulet.

NURSE to Juliet.

Citizens of Verona; several Men and Women, relations to both houses; Maskers, Guards, Watchmen, and Attendants.

SCENE, during the greater part of the play, in Verona; once in the fifth act, at Mantua.

COMPENDIUM OF THE PLAY.

THE violent feuds subsisting at Verona between the powerful families of the Capulets and Montagues form no obstruction to the establishment of a mutual attachment between Romeo, the only son of Montague, and Juliet, the heiress of the house of Capulet. A secret marriage appears to realize their fond anticipations of felicity, when Tybalt, a nephew of Capulet, rouses the indignation of the young bridegroom by the murder of his friend Mercutio, and falls a sacrifice to his resentment in single combat. This outrage subjects Romeo to a sentence of banishment by the prince; while the unsuspecting relatives of Juliet, attributing her grief to the loss of her cousin, resolve to divert her melancholy by an immediate marriage with Count Paris. Finding her parents inexorable to every entreaty of delay, the unfortunate lady repairs to the cell of Friar Laurence, who had married her; and receives from his hands a powerful soporific, causing a temporary suspension of the vital functions for two and forty hours. On the day appointed for the nuptials, Juliet is discovered stiff and cold, and is conveyed, amidst the tears of her family, to the cemetery of her ancestors. The good friar, in the meantime, despatches a messenger to the residence of Romeo at Mantua, arranging his secret return to his native city before the expiration of Juliet's sleep. But the destiny of the lovers is misfortune; the letter of Friar Laurence never reaches its destination; and the distracted husband, learning from another source the death of his mistress, hastens to Verona, forces an entrance in the obscurity of night to the monument of the Capulets, takes poison, and expires; soon after which the friar arrives to await the recovery of Juliet from her trance, who, reviving to a sense of her hopeless woe, and seeing the dead body of Romeo stretched before her, finds means to terminate her existence by plunging the dagger of her husband into her heart. The rival families now too late bewail their miserable infatuation and, at the intercession of the prince, bury their animosities in a treaty of peace and alliance.

No one can fail to admire the admirable construction of this tragedy of our poet; had it been merely a love story, it would have run the risk of becoming tedious; how artfully this is obviated! The broils of the rival factions of Capulet and Montague, extending even to their humblest retainers; the high spirits of Mercutio, with his lively wit and florid imagination; the unconquerable pugnaciousness of Tybalt, 'the very butcher of a silk button;' the garrulous coarseness of the Nurse, and the peevishness of old Capulet; all these give a briskness and rapidity to the early scenes of the play, while the latter ones are, as they should be, almost confined to the afflictions of the two lovers.

Romeo is an idealization of the early youth of genius; he is, in truth, a poet in his love. We fancy that Shakespeare wrote it with a vivid recollection of some early attachment of his own; and that Romeo utters the intense and extravagant passion which a gifted, but affectionate nature, such as Shakespeare might have given way to, before the judgment of maturer years had calmed down this frantic tyranny of love.

The poet has been censured for making Juliet Romeo's second love, and Garrick, in his adaptation of the play, cut out all allusion to Rosaline, whom Romeo first loves, with as much earnestness, and even more extravagance than that which he displays in his subsequent passion for Juliet. But his love for Rosaline was a mere creation of fancy, the feverish excitement of a nature, to which love was a necessity; in her he worshipped an ideal of his own warm imagination, which painted her as an angel amongst women. Shakespeare also indulges a gentle satire on the too positive convictions of youth. Romeo declares his unalterable fidelity to Rosaline, and trusts that when his eyes admit that they have seen her equal, his tears will turn to fire, and burn the 'transparent heretics;' and yet, in one brief hour from this time, even at the first glance, he transfers his love to Juliet. But we can easily forgive this fickleness; we feel angry at the haughty Rosaline, who 'hath forsworn to love,' for her cold rejection of the passionate affection of Romeo, and pleased that he has found one who receives and returns his passion. His poetic and fervent affection deserves the love which the generous Juliet bestows upon him; and how tender, how devoted, how utterly unselfish is her passion; how modestly beautiful and delicate is her apology for the immediate confession of it.

> Thou know'st the mask of night is on my face;
> Else would a maiden blush bepaint my cheek,
> For that which thou hast heard me speak to-night.
> Fain would I dwell on form; fain, fain deny
> What I have spoke. But farewell compliment!

There is no affected coyness, no frigid conventionality in her demeanor; she is a child of nature yielding to the sweet impulses of a first love, and proclaiming her passion to the object of it with the unrestrained sincerity of an innocent and confiding spirit. Her impatience for the arrival of her husband on the evening of their nuptials has been censured as inconsistent with a becoming modesty, and not to be reconciled with the natural timidity of a young maiden, even of Juliet's warm and impetuous nature. Mr. Hazlitt has finely answered this objection; he says—'Such critics do not perceive that the feelings of the heart sanctify, without disguising, the impulses of nature. Without refinement themselves, they confound modesty with hypocrisy.' How admirably also does Shakespeare provide for every improbable circumstance, and not only takes away their improbability, but renders them highly consistent and natural; thus when Juliet drinks the potion which is to consign her, a living woman, to a loathsome tomb, she is made to work upon her own imagination by a vivid picture of the horrors of her incarceration in the vault where the festering remains of all her 'buried ancestors are packed,' and at length swallows the potion in a paroxysm of terror.

The naturalness of the incident is also heightened by the first introduction of the Friar gathering medicinal herbs, and descanting upon their nature and properties. It is likely that he who was so well acquainted with the uses of 'baleful weeds and precious juic'd flowers' would employ them to carry out a difficult and dangerous stratagem. Shakespeare seldom omits an opportunity for the utterance of any instructive truth or moral maxim; he was the educator of his audiences, and it gives us a higher opinion of the playgoers of his time to know that they were pleased with the introduction of severe moral truths into their amusements. The language of this Friar is full of them; how fine is the reflection which crosses his mind when going forth in the early dawn to gather his medicinal herbs, and how naturally it arises out of the situation:

For nought so vile that on the earth doth live,
But to the earth some special good doth give;
Nor aught so good, but, strained from that fair use,
Revolts from true birth, stumbling on abuse.

Mercutio is one of Shakespeare's peculiarities, one of the favorite children of his sportive fancy, bred in the sunshine of his finely balanced mind. The mercurial and brilliant nature of the Veronese gentleman is full of that natural gladness, that 'overflow of youthful life, wafted on over the laughing waves of pleasure and prosperity,' which few authors besides Shakespeare impart to their creations. Well might Dr. Johnson say that his comedy seems to be instinct.

It may certainly be wished that the language given to Mercutio was less coarse and sensual than it frequently is, but this licentiousness of conversation is consistent with the probable humor of a man in the summer of life, in perfect health, and devoid of all anxiety; and, however repugnant to modern ideas of delicacy and gentlemanly breeding, is perhaps a picture of the discourse of the young nobles and gallants of Shakespeare's own time.

An instance of our poet's power of strongly delineating a character in a few lines, is to be seen in his introduction of the poor apothecary, who is as original a conception, and during his brief scene, wins upon the sympathy of the audience, as much as the hero of the story himself.

This, like most of our poet's tragedies, preaches a stern moral, it shows like a beacon-fire, to warn the young from unsanctioned love and idolatrous passion. Shakespeare probably intended to punish the lovers for the deception they both practised upon indulgent parents, while the parents are, through their children, scourged for their vain feuds and unreasonable hatred. The young die after the first brief hour of joy, the old live on, childless and desolate, to repent the blind malignity which has wrecked the happiness of them all.

HAMLET. ACT III. SCENE II.

The players' scene in Hamlet. Pouring poison in the ear of the sleeping king.

HISTORICAL SUMMARY OF 'HAMLET.'

THE French novelist Belleforest extracted from Saxo Grammaticus, the Danish historian, the history of 'Amleth,' and inserted it in the collection of novels published by him in the latter part of the sixteenth century; whence it was translated into English under the title of 'The Historie of Hamblett,' a small quarto volume printed in black letter, which formed the subject of a play previous to 1589; and on these materials our author is supposed to have constructed this noble tragedy, the composition of which is assigned by Malone to the date of 1600, while Mr. Chalmers and Dr. Drake contend that it was written as early as 1597, on the authority of Dr. Percy's copy of Speght's edition of 'Chaucer,' which once belonged to Gabriel Harvey, who had written his name at both the commencement and conclusion, with several notes between; among which was the following: The younger sort take much delight in Shakespeare's 'Venus and Adonis;' but his 'Lucrece,' and his tragedy of 'Hamlet, Prince of Denmarke,' have it in them to please the wiser sort, 1598. The original composition of this play may, therefore, be placed in 1597; and its revision, with additions, in 1600. The earliest entry of it at Stationers' Hall is July 26, 1602; and a copy of the play in its imperfect state, dated 1603, and supposed to have been printed from a spurious original, was first discovered in the beginning of 1825. Another edition appeared in 1604, 'newly imprinted, and enlarged to almost as much again as it was;' the variations in which are both numerous and striking.

PERSONS REPRESENTED.

CLAUDIUS, king of Denmark.
HAMLET, son to the former, and nephew to the present king.
POLONIUS, lord chamberlain.
HORATIO, friend to Hamlet.
LAERTES, son to Polonius.
VOLTIMAND, CORNELIUS, ROSENCRANTZ, GUILDENSTERN, courtiers.
OSRIC, a courtier.
ANOTHER COURTIER.
A PRIEST.
MARCELLUS, BERNARDO, officers.
FRANCISCO, a soldier.
REYNALDO, servant to Polonius.
CAPTAIN. AMBASSADOR.
GHOST of HAMLET'S FATHER.
FORTINBRAS, prince of Norway.

GERTRUDE, queen of Denmark, and mother of Hamlet.
OPHELIA, daughter of Polonius.

Lords, Ladies, Officers, Soldiers, Players, Grave-diggers, Sailors, Messengers, and other Attendants.

SCENE, Elsinore.

COMPENDIUM OF THE PLAY.

THE sudden death of Hamlet king of Denmark, and the hurried and indecent nuptials of his widow with his brother and successor, fill the mind of the young prince Hamlet with grief and shame, which is speedily exchanged into a desire of revenge because of the appearance of his father's spirit, which informs the astonished youth that his end has been effected by the operation of poison, administered to him in his sleep by his perfidious brother. Doubtful of the truth of this supernatural communication, Hamlet counterfeits madness in order to conceal his designs, and invites the king and his court to witness the performance of a play which bears a striking similarity to the murder detailed by the Ghost. Struck by the reproaches of a wounded conscience, the guilty monarch betrays the emotions of his mind to the vigilance of Hamlet, who is prevented from the prosecution of his revenge by the death of Polonius, the father of Ophelia, who is commissioned by the king to lie in ambush during an interview between the prince and his mother: Hamlet, hearing a noise, and conjecturing that it proceeds from his concealed uncle behind the arras, stabs the old man to the heart; a mistake, which deprives Ophelia of reason, and causes her self-destruction; while the unfortunate prince is banished to England by the king, who sends thither secret orders for his death on his arrival. The accomplishment of this cruel mandate is prevented by his captivity by pirates, who land him on the Danish coast. In the meantime, Laertes, the son of Polonius, in his anxiety to revenge the deaths of his father and sister, tarnishes the natural generosity of his character by listening to the insidious suggestions of the king, who accomplishes the destruction of his nephew by means of a poisoned weapon, with which he is wounded in a trial of skill in fencing with Laertes, to which the unsuspecting youth is invited; and in which his antagonist also becomes the victim of his own fraud. Finding his end fast approaching, Hamlet inflicts on his uncle the just punishment of his atrocities; and soon after expires, after witnessing the untimely death of his mother by poison.

Mr. Steevens estimates the character of Hamlet very sternly, and considers him not only unamiable but criminal; though he admits that the prince assassinated Polonius by accident, yet he states that he deliberately procures the execution of his two schoolfellows, who appear to have been ignorant of the treacherous nature of the mandate they were employed to carry; his conduct to Ophelia deprives her both of her reason and her life, and he then interrupts her funeral, and insults her brother by boasting of an affection for his sister which he had denied to her face, and that he kills the king at last to revenge himself, and not his father.

This summary of the character of Hamlet, though strongly stated, is not a false one; his conduct is certainly indefensible unless we regard him as a man whose mind was to some extent overthrown by the peculiarity of the circumstances in which he was placed. This brings us to the oft disputed question, whether the madness of Hamlet was real or feigned—an attentive perusal of the tragedy will, we think, lead us to the conclusion that it was both one and the other. His mind at times trembled on the brink of madness, shaken but not overthrown. Not utterly perverted by mental disease, but very far from the exercise of its healthy functions, at times enjoying the perfect use of reason, and at others clouded and confused. Hamlet exaggerates his mental defects, and feeling his mind disordered, plays the downright madman.

He, however, nowhere admits his insanity; and his soliloquies certainly bear no appearance of wildness. So far from believing himself mad, he has great faith in his own intellectual resources: he feels that he is surrounded by spies—by men whom he will trust as he will 'adders fanged;' but, he adds—

It shall go hard,
But I will delve one yard below their mines,
And blow them at the moon.

This implies great confidence in his own acuteness; and, to his mother, he most emphatically denies that he labors under mental disorder: he is, he says, 'not in madness, but mad in craft.' But we should not take the word of a madman for evidence respecting his own malady. Hamlet is rather cunning than wise—a quality not unfrequently found in men suffering from a partial mental alienation. It should be recollected, also, that he has no reason for assuming insanity to his friend Horatio, whom he had trusted with his secret, and informed that he might think fit 'to put an antic disposition on.' Still, when discoursing very gravely with him in the church-yard, he suddenly breaks off from his subject, and asks, abruptly—'Is not parchment made of sheep-skins?' A mind so flighty cannot be justly called sound.

Dr. Johnson says, 'of the feigned madness of Hamlet there appears no adequate cause, for he does nothing which he might not have done with the reputation of sanity. He plays the madman most when he treats Ophelia with so much rudeness, which seems to be useless and wanton cruelty.' This is true enough; Hamlet's assumed madness in no way assists in working out his revenge, but, on the contrary, nearly prevents its execution, for had the king succeeded in his design in sending him to England, the pretended lunacy would have brought him to his death; or it might very likely have led to his close confinement in Denmark. This absence, then, of a sufficient cause for feigning madness implies that some seeds of absolute insanity were the origin of it.

Hamlet's conduct to Polonius is very unjustifiable, only to be accounted for by supposing that his mind is somewhat disturbed, though he may also dislike the old courtier because he is the counsellor and companion of the king; but there is no treachery in the talkative old man. Polonius is very just and open; when he discovers Hamlet's love for his daughter, he lays no plot to induce him to marry her, he will not play 'the desk or table-book,' but discountenances the attachment, and informs the king and queen of it. Foolishly talkative, he is still a very shrewd man, and though his wisdom is fast falling into the weakness and childishness of age, he has been a very acute observer.

Dr. Johnson, who has given an admirable delineation of this character, says: 'Such a man is positive and confident, because he knows that his mind was once strong, and he knows not that it has become weak. Such a man excels in general principles, but fails in the particular application. He is knowing in retrospect, and ignorant in foresight. While he depends upon his memory, and can draw from his repositories of knowledge, he utters weighty sentences and gives useful counsel; but as the mind, in its enfeebled state, cannot be kept long busy and intent, the old man is subject to sudden dereliction of his faculties, he loses the order of his ideas, and entangles himself in his own thoughts, till he recovers the leading principle and falls again into his former train. This idea of dotage encroaching upon wisdom will solve all the phenomena of the character of Polonius.'

Ophelia is a gentle, affectionate character, drawn in and sucked down by the whirlpool of tragic events which surround her. Hamlet treats her very harshly, but, although this probably proceeds partly from his aberration of intellect, he is also influenced by a suspicion that she is acting treacherously towards him, and is an instrument in the hands of the king and her father for some unworthy purpose.

It has puzzled many of the critics to account for the circumstance, that although Ophelia is so modest in her sanity that she never even confesses her love for Hamlet, we only gather from her actions that she loves him; that when she becomes insane she sings snatches of obscene songs. Some have thought Shakespeare erred in this, but in the expression of human passions he never errs. It has been well suggested, that in madness people frequently manifest a disposition the very opposite of that which they possessed while in a state of sanity—the timid become bold, the tender cruel—and that Ophelia, in like manner, forsook her modesty of demeanor, and became the reverse of her natural character. Mr. G. Dawson thinks Ophelia, in her sanity, to be warm in her passions—not a coarse sensualist, like the queen; but what he calls *sensuous*—that way disposed, yet keeping a strict guard upon herself; and that when she becomes mad that restraint is removed, and her character appears in its natural colors.

Much controversy also has been expended upon the question whether the queen was an accessory to the murder of her husband; her surprise on Hamlet's exclamation in her chamber, 'As kill a king,' has been quoted to exonerate her. This supposition is strengthened by the fact, that she exhibits no uneasiness or remorse at the play, as the king does, and that no remark ever takes place between her and her husband in relation to it. Her agony of mind when her son compares her two husbands, and so severely censures her, arises from the recollection of her adulterous intercourse with Claudius during the life of the late king, and her hasty and incestuous marriage.

OTHELLO. ACT II. SCENE II.

Cassio's drunken squabble with Roderigo, contrived by Iago.

HISTORICAL SUMMARY OF 'OTHELLO.'

A STORY in Cynthio's novels is the prototype whence our author derived his materials for this sublime and instructive tragedy, which is assigned by Malone, after considerable hesitation, to the date of 1604; while Dr. Drake and Mr. Chalmers conjecture it to be the production of a period as late as 1612 or 1614. This play was first entered at Stationers' Hall Oct. 6, 1621, and appeared in quarto in the course of the following year; between which edition and the folio of 1623 many minute differences exist.

'The beauties of this play,' says Dr. Johnson, 'impress themselves so strongly on the attention of the reader, that they can draw no aid from critical illustration. The fiery openness of Othello, magnanimous, artless, and credulous, boundless in his confidence, ardent in his affection, inflexible in his resolution, and obdurate in his revenge; the cool malignity of Iago, silent in his resentment, subtle in his designs, and studious at once of his interest and his vengeance; the soft simplicity of Desdemona, confident of merit and conscious of innocence, her artless perseverance in her suit, and her slowness to suspect that she can be suspected, are such proofs of Shakespeare's skill in human nature, as, I suppose, it is vain to seek in any modern writer. The gradual progress which Iago makes in the Moor's conviction, and the circumstances which he employs to inflame him, are so artfully natural, that, though it will perhaps not be said of him as he says of himself, that he is 'a man not easily jealous,' yet we cannot but pity him, when at last we find him 'perplex'd in the extreme.'

PERSONS REPRESENTED.

DUKE OF VENICE.
BRABANTIO, a senator.
TWO OTHER SENATORS.
GRATIANO, brother to Brabantio.
LODOVICO, kinsman to Brabantio.
OTHELLO, the Moor.
CASSIO, his lieutenant.
IAGO, his ancient.
RODERIGO, a Venetian gentleman.
MONTANO, Othello's predecessor in the government of Cyprus.
CLOWN, servant to Othello.
HERALD.

DESDEMONA, daughter to Brabantio, and wife to Othello.
EMILIA, wife to Iago.
BIANCA, a courtesan, mistress to Cassio.

Officers, Gentlemen, Messengers, Musicians, Sailors, Attendants, etc.

SCENE, for the first act, in Venice; during the rest of the play, at a seaport in Cyprus.

COMPENDIUM OF THE PLAY.

A Moorish general in the service of the Venetians, named Othello, by his valor and mental accomplishments, captivates the affections of Desdemona, the only daughter of an eminent senator, who exposes herself to the resentment of an incensed father by eloping with her lover and becoming his wife. These nuptials are no sooner solemnized than Othello is required by the senate to assume the command of Cyprus, whither he is followed by Desdemona, whose influence over her husband is exerted in behalf of Cassio, who has been deprived of his lieutenancy for an act of indiscretion, into which he has been betrayed by the devices of Iago, in order that he may at once gratify his diabolical malignity and promote his personal advancement by instilling groundless suspicions into the ear of his commander of a criminal attachment subsisting between his wife and Cassio; which he substantiates by so much seeming honesty of purpose and the production of such strong external testimony, that the fierce desire of revenge in the bosom of the Moor stifles the generous sympathies of his nature, and he smothers his innocent wife, leaving the assassination of Cassio to be effected by the agency of his supposed friend, who however fails to accomplish his deadly purpose. The villany of Iago is at length brought to light by his wife Emilia, who is stabbed by her enraged husband; while the unfortunate Othello finds means to elude the vigilance of his attendants, and deprive himself of life by a concealed dagger. In the meantime, Cassio is advanced to the government of Cyprus, and Iago is sentenced to expiate his crimes by a painful and protracted death.

The Moor is amiable, brave, generous, and firm; with him, what should be, must be: he will not permit his feelings to interfere with what he deems his duty. This feature of his character contributes materially to the catastrophe of the tragedy: had he possessed the irresolution of Hamlet, Iago's villany would have been discovered and Desdemona saved; for Hamlet would always have been desiring more evidence, and even, when convinced of her falseness, would have remained undecided how to act, and probably would have ultimately divorced her. But Iago calculates on the hot Moorish blood which runs in Othello's veins; he knows the impetuous fierce passions which lie latent in the soul of the victim of his fiendish deception, and practises upon them accordingly. Othello is very philosophical until his mind is poisoned by the insinuations of Iago; he keeps a sort of military guard over his passions; remember his calm even conduct when Brabantio approaches him in the street at night, followed by armed servants and public officers, whom he bids to seize the Moor; he himself addressing him as 'vile thief,' and with other violent language. And before the duke he conducts his own cause with the subtilty and readiness of an advocate. What a touch of effective oratorical artifice is that where he tells the assembled senate that he had been bred in a camp, knew but little of the world, and therefore could not grace his cause by the arts of eloquence; thus leading them to the belief that he was incapable of defending himself, and then delivering the most effective oration that could have been uttered in his behalf.

But when the maddening conviction of his wife's treachery and shame is forced upon him, he breaks out into a paroxysm of frantic passion; his habit of self-government is for a time annihilated, and the hot blood of the savage triumphs over the judgment of the man. He tries to escape from this dreadful conviction:

> 'By heaven, I would most gladly have forgot it.'

But Iago draws the web gradually closer and more closely around him, and, with fiendish sagacity, keeps the subject in all its most hideous colors perpetually in his mind until the final perpetration of the terrible catastrophe of the drama. How painfully affecting is the anguish of soul with which he exclaims: 'But yet the pity of it, Iago!—O, Iago, the pity of it, Iago!' Well might Coleridge, with the true feeling of a poet, ask, as the curtain drops, which do we pity most, Desdemona, or the heart-broken Moor?

Iago is an utter villain, with no redeeming circumstances—love, benevolence, sympathy for his race, every holy and exalted feeling have, in him, no existence; their place is occupied by a satanic selfishness and an absolute love of malice; it is the fertile activity of his intellect, and the ingenuity of his wickedness, that alone make him endurable, otherwise we should shrink from him with loathing and disgust. He is the most villanous character ever drawn by Shakespeare, for Richard III. is cruel, to serve his ambition; but Iago is cruel and fraudulent, because he finds a pleasure in fraud and cruelty; he has no belief in honesty—does not think there is any such thing in the world; he entertains an obdurate incredulity as to the virtue of women, and has a perfect faith that Desdemona will be seduced by Cassio, if he tempts her. He looks upon everything only in a gross and sensual light, and delights in painting the purest feelings in the most repulsive colors. This will explain why Shakespeare has put so many coarse and revolting speeches in his mouth. No character the great poet ever drew utters so many offensive expressions, and this was, doubtless, intended to exhibit the intense depravity of his mind. He has a natural turn for dishonesty and trickery, and would rather gain his ends by deception than by straightforward conduct. He is proud of his cunning, and witty also, full of that ill-natured sarcasm which delights in giving pain to others.

The character of Cassio is admirably delineated—he is every way calculated to become an object of suspicion to the Moor—he is young, handsome and courteous, a scholar, and something of a poet, as his beautiful description of Desdemona will evidence. Even Iago admits, 'That he hath all those requisites in him that folly and green minds look after.'

Poor Desdemona is the perfection of womanly gentleness and tenderness—a generous, romantic girl, full of kindness to every one, and by the very liberality of her nature, laying herself open to the aroused suspicions of her husband. If she has a fault, it is that she is too passive. Observe the wide contrast between her character and that of Emilia, as finely portrayed in the third scene of the fourth act. Othello has desired his wife to retire and dismiss her attendant, and the two women are conversing before they separate for the night. Desdemona, in her simple purity, asks:

'Dost thou in conscience think,—tell me, Emilia,—
That there be women do abuse their husbands
In such gross kind.'

Note the worldliness of the other's reply; she would not do 'such a thing for a joint-ring,' *but*, etc.; and Desdemona's sceptical rejoinder, 'I do not think there is any such woman.' The absolute purity of her mind will not permit her to believe in evil. How sweetly touching is her character compared with that of Iago—a seraph and a demon.

CONCORDANCE

OF

FAMILIAR GEMS FROM SHAKESPEARE.

FAMILIAR in their mouths as Household WORDS.

King Henry V, act iv. sc. 3.

CONCORDANCE OF FAMILIAR GEMS.

A

Absolute—How *absolute* the knave is! We must speak by the card, or equivocation will undo us.
Hamlet, act v. sc. 1.

Abstract—They are the *abstract* and brief chronicles of the time. *Hamlet*, act ii. sc. 2.

Abuse—Nor aught so good but, strain'd from that fair use,
Revolts from true birth, stumbling on *abuse*.
Romeo and Juliet, act ii. sc. 3.

Accidents—Wherein I spake of most disastrous chances,
Of moving *accidents* by flood and field,
Of hair-breadth scapes i' the imminent deadly breach. *Othello*, act i. sc. 3.

Accommodated—*Accommodated*; that is, when a man is, as they say, accommodated; or when a man is, being, whereby a' may be thought to be accommodated; which is an excellent thing.
King Henry IV, part ii. act iii. sc. 2.

Accoutred—Cæsar said to me, 'Darest thou, Cassius, now
Leap in with me into this angry flood,
And swim to yonder point?' Upon the word,
Accoutred as I was, I plunged in,
And bade him follow. *Julius Cæsar*, act i. sc. 2.

Acres— In those holy fields,
Over whose *acres* walk'd those blessed feet,

Which, fourteen hundred years ago, were nail'd
For our advantage on the bitter cross.
King Henry IV, part i. act i. sc. 1.

Acting—Between the *acting* of a dreadful thing
And the first motion, all the interim is
Like a phantasma, or a hideous dream.
Julius Cæsar, act ii. sc. 1.

Action— With devotion's visage
And pious *action* we do sugar o'er
The devil himself. *Hamlet*, act iii. sc. 1.

Action—Suit the *action* to the word, the word to the action. *Hamlet*, act iii. sc. 2.

Actor—As in a theatre the eyes of men,
After a well-graced *actor* leaves the stage,
Are idly bent on him that follows next.
Richard II, act v. sc. 2.

Adam—Consideration, like an angel, came
And whipp'd the offending *Adam* out of him.
King Henry V, act i. sc. 1.

Admired—You have displaced the mirth, broke the good meeting,
With most *admired* disorder. *Macbeth*, act iii. sc. 4.

Adorned—She came adorned hither like sweet May.
King Richard II, act v. sc. 1.

Adversity—Sweet are the uses of *adversity*,
Which, like the toad, ugly and venomous,
Wears yet a precious jewel in his head;
And this our life, exempt from public haunt,
Finds tongues in trees, books in the running brooks,
Sermons in stones, and good in everything.
As You Like It, act ii. sc. 1.

Adversity—A man I am, cross'd with *adversity*.
Two Gentlemen of Verona, act iv. sc. 1.

Adversity—A wretched soul bruised with *adversity*.
Comedy of Errors, act ii, sc. 1.

Adversity—*Adversity's* sweet milk, philosophy.
Romeo and Juliet, act iii. sc. 3.

Affliction—Had it pleased Heaven
To try me with *affliction*; had he rain'd
All kinds of sores and shames on my bare head.
Othello, act iv. sc. 2.

Affliction— 'Tis a physic
That's bitter to sweet end.
Measure for Measure, act iv. sc. 6.

Africa—A foutra for the world and worldling's base!
I speak of *Africa* and golden joys.
Henry IV, part ii. act v. sc. 3.

After— Duncan is in his grave!
After life's fitful fever he sleeps well.
Macbeth, act iii. sc. 2.

Agate-stone—O, then, I see, Queen Mab hath been with you.
She is the fairies' midwife; and she comes
In shape no bigger than an *agate-stone*
On the forefinger of an alderman,
Drawn with a team of little atomies
Athwart men's noses as they lie asleep.
Romeo and Juliet, act i. sc. 4.

Age—The weariest and most loathed worldly life
That *age*, ache, penury, and imprisonment
Can lay on nature is a paradise
To what we fear of death.
Measure for Measure, act iii. sc. 1.

Age— And He that doth the ravens feed,
Yea, providently caters for the sparrow,
Be comfort to my *age!*
As You Like It, act ii. sc. 3.

Age—You see me here,—a poor old man,
As full of grief as *age;* wretched in both!
King Lear, act ii. sc. 4.

Age—*Age* cannot wither her, nor custom stale
Her infinite variety.
Antony and Cleopatra, act ii. sc. 2.

Age—Therefore my *age* is as a lusty winter,
Frosty, but kindly. *As You Like It*, act ii. sc. 3.

Age—The *age* is grown so picked, that the toe of the peasant comes so near the heel of the courtier, he galls his kibe. *Hamlet*, act v. sc. 1.

Age—The choice and master spirits of this *age*.
Julius Cæsar, act iii. sc. 1.

Age—Some smack of *age* in you, some relish of the saltness of Time. *Henry IV*, part ii. act i. sc. 2.

Ages— One man in his time plays many parts,
His acts being seven *ages*. At first the infant,
Mewling and puking in the nurse's arms:
And then the whining school-boy, with his satchel,
And shining morning face, creeping like snail
Unwillingly to school. And then the lover,
Sighing like furnace, with a woeful ballad
Made to his mistress' eyebrow. Then a soldier,
Full of strange oaths, and bearded like the pard;
Jealous in honor, sudden and quick in quarrel,
Seeking the bubble reputation
Even in the cannon's mouth. And then the justice;
In fair round belly, with good capon lined,
With eyes severe, and beard of formal cut,
Full of wise saws and modern instances;
And so he plays his part. The sixth age shifts
Into the lean and slipper'd pantaloon;
With spectacles on nose, and pouch on side;
His youthful hose well saved, a world too wide
For his shrunk shank; and his big manly voice,
Turning again toward childish treble, pipes
And whistles in his sound. Last scene of all,
That ends this strange, eventful history,
Is second childishness and mere oblivion;
Sans teeth, sans eyes, sans taste, sans everything.
As You Like It, act ii. sc. 7.

Air— When he speaks;
The *air*, a charter'd libertine, is still.
King Henry V, act i. sc. 1.

Air—And, like a dew-drop from the lion's mane,
Be shook to *air*. *Troilus and Cressida*, act iii. sc. 3.

Air—Nor do not saw the *air* too much with your hand, thus. *Hamlet*, act iii. sc. 2.

Air—Ere he can spread his sweet leaves to the *air*,
Or dedicate his beauty to the sun.
Romeo and Juliet, act i. sc. 1.

Air—Our revels now are ended: these our actors,
As I foretold you, were all spirits, and
Are melted into *air*, into thin *air*:
And, like the baseless fabric of this vision,
The cloud-capp'd towers, the gorgeous palaces,
The solemn temples, the great globe itself,
Yea, all which it inherit, shall dissolve,
And, like this insubstantial pageant faded,
Leave not a rack* behind. We are such stuff
As dreams are made on, and our little life
Is rounded with a sleep. *Tempest*, act iv. sc. 1.

Air—Mocking the *air* with colors idly spread.
King John, act v. sc. 1.

Airy— The lover, all as frantic,
Sees Helen's beauty in a brow of Egypt:
The poetic eye, in a fine frenzy rolling.
Doth glance from heaven to earth, from earth to heaven,
And, as imagination bodies forth
The forms of things unknown, the poet's pen
Turns them to shapes, and gives to *airy* nothing
A local habitation and a name.
Midsummer-Night's Dream, act v. sc. 1.

* So in the original, but Mr. Dyce reads "wreck."

Alabaster—Why should a man, whose blood is warm within,
Sit like his grandsire cut in *alabaster?*
Merchant of Venice, act i. sc. 1.

Alabaster—Nor scar that whiter skin of hers than snow,
And smooth as monumental *alabaster*.
Othello, act v. sc. 2.

Alacrity—I have a kind of *alacrity* in sinking.
Merry Wives of Windsor, act iii. sc. 5.

Ale—A quart of *ale* is a dish for a king.
Winter's Tale, act iv. sc. 2.

All— *All* things that are
Are with more spirit chased than enjoy'd.
Merchant of Venice, act ii. sc. 6.

All—Still in thy right hand carry gentle peace,
To silence envious tongues. Be just, and fear not;
Let *all* the ends thou aim'st at be thy country's,
Thy God's, and truth's.
King Henry VIII, act iii. sc. 2.

Alone—I, measuring his affections by my own,
That most are busied when they're most *alone*.
Romeo and Juliet, act i. sc. 1.

Alteration—Let me not to the marriage of true minds
Admit impediments. Love is not love
Which alters when it *alteration* finds. *Sonnet* cxvi.

Ambition—When that the poor have cried, Cæsar hath wept:
Ambition should be made of sterner stuff.
Julius Cæsar, act iii. sc. 2.

Ambition— I have no spur
To prick the sides of my intent, but only
Vaulting *ambition*, which o'erleaps itself
And falls on the other side. *Macbeth*, act i. sc. 7.

Ambition— Fling away *ambition;*
By that sin fell the angels.
King Henry VIII, act iii. sc. 2.

Amen—I had most need of blessing, and *Amen*
Stuck in my throat. *Macbeth*, act ii. sc. 2.

Ancestors—All his successors, gone before him, hath done't; and all his *ancestors* that come after him may. *Merry Wives of Windsor*, act i. sc. 1.

Ancient—A very *ancient* and fish-like smell.
Tempest, act ii. sc. 2.

Ancient—I will feed fat the *ancient* grudge I bear him.
Merchant of Venice, act i. sc. 3.

Ancient—My *Ancient.* *Othello*, act i. sc. 3.

Angels—*Angels* are bright still, though the brightest fell. *Macbeth*, act iv. sc. 3.

Angels—*Angels* and ministers of grace, defend us!
Hamlet, act i. sc. 4.

Angels— But man, proud man,
Dress'd in a little brief authority,
Most ignorant of what he's most assured,
His glassy essence, like an angry ape,
Plays such fantastic tricks before high Heaven
As make the *angels* weep.
Measure for Measure, act ii. sc. 2.

Angels— Besides, this Duncan
Hath borne his faculties so meek, hath been
So clear in his great office, that his virtues
Will plead like *angels*, trumpet-tongued, against
The deep damnation of his taking-off.
Macbeth, act i. sc. 7.

Anger— A countenance more
In sorrow than in *anger.* *Hamlet*, act i. sc. 2.

Anger—O, what a deal of scorn looks beautiful
In the contempt and *anger* of his lip!
Twelfth Night, act iii. sc. 1.

Anger— *Anger* is like
A full hot horse; who, being allow'd his way,
Self-mettle tires him. *King Henry VIII*, act i. sc. 1.

Anguish— One fire burns out another's burning,
One pain is lessen'd by another's *anguish*.
Romeo and Juliet, act i. sc. 2.

Anointed—Let not the heavens hear these tell-tale women
Rail on the Lord's *anointed*.
King Richard III, act iv. sc. 4.

Anthems—For my voice, I have lost it with holloaing and singing of *anthems*.
King Henry IV, part. ii. act i. sc. 2.

Anthropophagi—The *Anthropophagi*, and men whose heads
Do grow beneath their shoulders. This to hear
Would Desdemona seriously incline.
Othello, act i. sc. 3.

Antres—*Antres* vast, and desarts idle.
Othello, act i. sc. 3.

Apothecary—I do remember an *apothecary*, and hereabouts he dwells. *Romeo and Juliet*, act v. sc. 1.

Apparel—Every true man's *apparel* fits your thief.
Measure for Measure, act iv. sc. 2.

Apparel—Costly thy habit as thy purse can buy,
But not express'd in fancy; rich, not gaudy:
For the *apparel* oft proclaims the man.
Hamlet, act i. sc. 3.

Apparitions— I have mark'd
A thousand blushing *apparitions* start

Into her face; a thousand innocent shames
In angel whiteness bear away those blushes.
Much Ado about Nothing, act iv. sc. 1.

Appetite—Doth not the *appetite* alter? A man loves the meat in his youth that he cannot endure in his age. *Much Ado about Nothing*, act ii. sc. 3.

Appetite— And then to breakfast, with
What *appetite* you have.
King Henry VIII, act iii. sc. 2.

Appetite—Now, good digestion wait on *appetite*,
And health on both! *Macbeth*, act iii. sc. 4.

Appetite— Why, she would hang on him
As if increase of *appetite* had grown
By what it fed on. *Hamlet*, act i. sc. 2.

Appetite—O, who can hold a fire in his hand
By thinking on the frosty Caucasus?
Or cloy the hungry edge of *appetite*
By bare imagination of a feast?
King Richard II, act i. sc. 3.

Applaud—I would *applaud* thee to the very echo,
That should applaud again. *Macbeth*, act v. sc. 3.

Apple—A goodly *apple* rotten at the heart;
O, what a goodly outside falsehood hath!
Merchant of Venice, act i. sc. 3.

Apples—There's small choice in rotten *apples*.
Taming of the Shrew, act i. sc. 1.

Appliance— Diseases, desperate grown,
By desperate *appliance* are reliev'd,
Or not at all. *Hamlet*, act iv. sc. 3.

Appliances—With all *appliances* and means to boot.
King Henry IV, part ii. act iii. sc. 1.

Apprehension— The *apprehension* of the good
Gives but the greater feeling to the worse.
King Richard II, act i. sc. 3.

Apprehension—The sense of death is most in *apprehension;*
And the poor beetle that we tread upon
In corporal sufferance finds a pang as great
As when a giant dies.
Measure for Measure, act iii. sc. 1.

April—O, how this spring of love resembleth
The uncertain glory of an *April* day!
Two Gentlemen of Verona, act i. sc. 3.

Arabia—All the perfumes of *Arabia* will not sweeten this little hand. *Macbeth*, act v. sc. 1.

Argument—He draweth out the thread of his verbosity finer than the staple of his *argument.*
Love's Labor's Lost, act v. sc. 1.

Armorers—The hum of either army stilly sounds,
That the fix'd sentinels almost receive
The secret whispers of each other's watch:
Fire answers fire; and through their paly flames
Each battle sees the other's umber'd face:
Steed threatens steed, in high and boastful neighs
Piercing the night's dull ear; and, from the tents,
The *armorers*, accomplishing the knights,
With busy hammers closing rivets up,
Give dreadful note of preparation
King Henry V, act iv. chorus.

Arms— Eyes, look your last!
Arms, take your last embrace!
Romeo and Juliet, act v. sc. 3.

Arrow— I have shot mine *arrow* o'er the house,
And hurt my brother. *Hamlet*, act v. sc. 2.

Arrows—Some Cupid kills with *arrows*, some with traps.
Much Ado about Nothing, act iii. sc. 1.

Aspick's tongues— Swell, bosom, with thy fraught,
For 'tis of *aspick's tongues!* *Othello*, act iii. sc. 3.

Aspiring—What! will the *aspiring* blood of Lancaster
Sink in the ground?
King Henry VI, part iii. act v. sc. 6.

Ass—Cudgel thy brains no more about it, for your dull *ass* will not mend his pace with beating.
Hamlet, act v, sc. 1.

Ass—Egregiously an *ass*. *Othello*, act ii. sc. 1.

Ass—O, that he were here to write me down an *ass!*—
O, that I had been writ down an ass!
Much Ado about Nothing, act iv. sc. 2.

Assassination—If it were done when 'tis done, then 'twere well
It were done quickly: if the *assassination*
Could trammel up the consequence, and catch,
With his surcease, success; that but this blow
Might be the be-all and the end-all here.
Macbeth, act i. sc. 7.

Assembly—Is our whole diss(ass)embly appeared?
Much Ado about Nothing, act iv.

Assume—*Assume* a virtue if you have it not.
Hamlet, act iii. sc. 4.

Assurance- I'll make *assurance* double sure,
And take a bond of fate. *Macbeth*, act iv. sc. 1.

Assurance—A combination, and a form, indeed,
Where every god did seem to set his seal,
To give the world *assurance* of a man.
Hamlet, act iii. sc. 4.

Attempt— The *attempt*, and not the deed,
Confounds us. *Macbeth*, act ii. sc. 2.

Attendance—To dance *attendance* on their lordships' pleasures.
King Henry VIII, act v. sc. 2.

Augury—We defy *augury*. *Hamlet*, act v. sc. 2.

Avoided—Of all men else I have *avoided* thee:
But get thee back. *Macbeth*, act v. sc. 7.

Awe—I cannot tell what you and other men
Think of this life; but, for my single self,
I had as lief not be as live to be
In *awe* of such a thing as I myself.
Julius Cæsar, act i. sc. 2.

B

Babbled—*Babbled* of green fields.
King Henry V, act ii. sc. 3.

Bachelor—When I said I would die a *bachelor*, I did not think I should live till I were married.
Much Ado about Nothing, act ii. sc. 3.

Backing—Call you that *backing* of your friends? A plague upon such backing!
King Henry IV, part i. act ii. sc. 4.

Badge—Sufferance is the *badge* of all our tribe.
Merchant of Venice, act i. sc. 3.

Baggage—It will let in and out the enemy
With bag and *baggage*. *Winter's Tale*, act i. sc. 2.

Bag and baggage—Come, shepherd, let us make an honorable retreat, though not with *bag and baggage*, yet with scrip and scrippage.
As You Like It, act iii. sc. 2.

Bait—Your *bait* of falsehood takes the carp of truth.
Hamlet, act ii. sc. 1.

Ballad—I had rather be a kitten, and cry mew,
Than one of these same metre *ballad-mongers*.
King Henry IV, part i. act iii. sc. 1.

Balm—Methought I heard a voice cry, 'Sleep no more!
Macbeth does murder sleep,' the innocent sleep,
Sleep that knits up the ravelled sleave of care,
The death of each day's life, sore labor's bath,
Balm of hurt minds, great nature's second course,
Chief nourisher in life's feast.
Macbeth, act ii. sc. 2.

Bank—I know a *bank* where the wild thyme blows,
Where oxlips and the nodding violet grows.
Midsummer-Night's Dream, act ii. sc. 2.

Banish—*Banish* plump Jack, and banish all the world. *King Henry IV*, part i. act ii. sc. 4.

Bankrupt—A *bankrout*, a prodigal, who dare scarce show his head on the Rialto.
Merchant of Venice, act iii. sc. 1.

Banners—Hang out our *banners* on the outward walls;
The cry is still 'They come!' Our castle's strength
Will laugh a siege to scorn. *Macbeth*, act v. sc. 5.

Barks—The fox *barks* not when he would steal the lamb.
King Henry VI, part ii. act iii. sc. 1.

Barren—Upon my head they placed a fruitless crown,
And put a *barren* sceptre in my gripe;
Thence to be wrenched with an unlineal hand,
No son of mine succeeding. *Macbeth*, act iii. sc. 1.

Base—*Base* is the slave that pays.
King Henry V, act ii. sc. 1.

Base—To what *base* uses we may return, Horatio!
Hamlet, act v. sc. 1.

Basilisk—It is a *basilisk* unto mine eye;
Kills me to look on't. *Cymbeline*, act ii. sc. 4.

Battery—Let him alone, I'll go another way to work with him; I'll have an action of *battery* against him, if there be any law in Illyria; though I struck him first, yet it's no matter for that.
Twelfth Night, act iv. sc. 1.

Battery—Prove this, thou wicked Hannibal, or I'll have mine action of *battery* on thee.
Measure for Measure, act ii.

Bastard— He is but a *bastard* to the time
That doth not smack of observation.
King John, act i. sc. 1.

Bated— In a bondman's key,
With *bated* breath, and whispering humbleness.
Merchant of Venice, act i. sc. 3.

Battalions—When sorrows come, they come not single spies,
But in *battalions*. *Hamlet*, act iv. sc. 5.

Battles—The *battles*, sieges, fortunes,
That I have passed. *Othello*, act i. sc. 3.

Bay—I had rather be a dog, and *bay* the moon,
Than such a Roman. *Julius Cæsar*, act iv. sc. 3.

Be—*Be* thou familiar, but by no means vulgar.
The friends thou hast, and their adoption tried,
Grapple them to thy soul with hoops of steel.
Hamlet, act i. sc. 3.

Be—*To be, or not to be:* that is the question:—
Whether 'tis nobler in the mind to suffer
The slings and arrows of outrageous fortune,
Or to take arms against a sea of troubles,
And, by opposing, end them? To die: to sleep;
No more;—and, by a sleep, to say we end
The heart-ache, and the thousand natural shocks
That flesh is heir to; 'tis a consummation
Devoutly to be wished. To die, to sleep;
To sleep: perchance to dream;—ay, there's the rub;
For in that sleep of death what dreams may come,
When we have shuffled off this mortal coil,
Must give us pause. *Hamlet*, act iii. sc. 1.

Beadle—A very *beadle* to a humorous sigh.
Love's Labor's Lost, act iii. sc. 1.

Bear— Ye Gods, it doth amaze me,
A man of such a feeble temper should
So get the start of the majestic world
And *bear* the palm alone.
Julius Cæsar, act i. sc. 2.

Beard—What a *beard* hast thou got! thou hast got more hair on thy chin than Dobbin my phill-horse has on his tail. *Merchant of Venice*, act ii. sc. 2.

Beast—It is a familiar *beast* to man, and signifies—love.
Merry Wives of Windsor, act i. sc. 1.

Beast—A *beast*, that wants discourse of reason.
Hamlet, act i. sc. 2.

Beautiful—She's *beautiful*; and therefore to be wooed.
She is a woman; therefore to be won.
King Henry VI, part i. act v. sc. 3.

Beautiful—*Beautiful* tyrant! fiend angelical!
Romeo and Juliet, act iii. sc. 2.

Beauty—He hath a daily *beauty* in his life.
Othello, act v. sc. 1.

Beauty—For where is any author in the world
Teaches such *beauty* as a woman's eye?
Learning is but an adjunct to ourself.
Love's Labor's Lost, act iv. sc. 3.

Beauty—'Tis *beauty* truly blent, whose red and white
Nature's own sweet and cunning hand laid on.
Twelfth Night, act i. sc. 5.

Beauty's ensign— *Beauty's ensign* yet
Is crimson in thy lips and in thy cheeks,
And death's pale flag is not advanced there.
Romeo and Juliet, act v. sc. 3.

Bedfellows—Misery acquaints a man with strange *bedfellows*. *Tempest*, act ii. sc. 2.

Bee—Where the *bee* sucks, there suck I;
In a cowslip's bell I lie. *Tempest*, act v. sc. 1.

Beer—To suckle fools, and chronicle small *beer*.
Othello, act ii. sc. 1.

Bees—So work the honey *bees;*
Creatures that, by a rule in nature, teach
The act of order to a peopled kingdom.
King Henry V., act i. sc. 2.

Beggar—When King Cophetua loved the *beggar* maid.
Romeo and Juliet, act ii. sc. 1.

Beggar—A *beggar* begs that never begged before.
Richard II, act v. sc. 1.

Beggared— For her own person,
It *beggared* all description.
Antony and Cleopatra, act ii. sc. 2.

Beggarly—A *beggarly* account of empty boxes.
Romeo and Juliet, act v. sc. 1.

Beggars—When *beggars* die, there are no comets seen;
The heavens themselves blaze forth the death of princes. *Julius Cæsar*, act ii. sc. 2.

Beggary—There's *beggary* in the love that can be reckoned.
Antony and Cleopatra, act i. sc. 1.

Beginning—That is the true *beginning* of our end,
Midsummer-Night's Dream, prologue.

Beguile—And often did *beguile* her of her tears.
Othello, act i. sc. 3.

Belief—Stands not within the prospect of *belief*.
Macbeth, act i. sc. 3.

Believ'd—This would not be *believ'd* in Venice, though I should sware I saw't. *Othello*, act iv. sc. 1.

Bell—Silence that dreadful *bell:* it frights the isle
From her propriety. *Othello*, act ii. sc. 3.

Bell—Yet the first bringer of unwelcome news
Hath but a losing office ; and his tongue
Sounds ever after as a sullen *bell*,
Remember'd tolling a departing friend.
King Henry IV, part ii. act i. sc. 1.

Bells—Now see that noble and most sovereign reason,
Like sweet *bells* jangled, out of tune and harsh.
Hamlet, act iii. sc. 1.

Belly-full—Every Jack-slave hath his *belly-full* of fighting. *Cymbeline*, act ii. sc. 1.

Benedick—How dost thou, *Benedick* the married man ?
Much Ado about Nothing, act v. sc. 4.

Bent—They fool me to the top of my *bent*.
Hamlet, act iii. sc. 2.

Bermoothes—From the still-vexed *Bermoothes*.
Tempest, act i. sc. 2.

Berries—Two lovely *berries* moulded on one stem.
Midsummer-Night's Dream, act iii. sc. 2.

Best—The *best* in this kind are but shadows,
Midsummer-Night's Dream, act v. sc. 1.

Best—They say, *best* men are moulded out of faults.
Measure for Measure, act v. sc. 1.

Better—I could have *better* spared a better man.
King Henry IV, part i. act v. sc. 4.

Better— Verily
I swear 'tis *better* to be lowly born,
And range with humble livers in content,
Than to be perked up in a glistering grief,
And wear a golden sorrow.
King Henry VIII, act ii. sc. 3.

Betwixt—And as the soldiers bore dead bodies by,
He called them untaught knaves, unmannerly,
To bring a slovenly, unhandsome corse
Betwixt the wind and his nobility.
King Henry IV, part i. act i. sc. 3.

Beware— *Beware*
Of entrance to a quarrel; but, being in,
Bear't that th' opposed may beware of thee.
Give every man thy ear, but few thy voice:
Take each man's censure, but reserve thy judgment.
Hamlet, act i. sc. 3.

Bezonian—Under which king, *Bezonian?* Speak, or die.
King Henry IV, part ii. act v. sc. 3.

Bird—Some say that ever 'gainst that season comes
Wherein our Saviour's birth is celebrated,
The *bird* of dawning singeth all night long.
Hamlet, act i. sc. 1.

Biscuit— One that hath been a courtier,
And says, if ladies be but young and fair,
They have the gift to know it; and in his brain,
Which is as dry as the remainder *biscuit*
After a voyage, he hath strange places cramm'd
With observation. *As You Like It*, act ii. sc. 7.

Blackberries—Give you a reason on compulsion? If reasons were as plentiful as *blackberries*, I would give no man a reason upon compulsion.
King Henry IV, part i. act ii. sc. 4.

Bladder—A plague of sighing and grief! it blows a man up like a *bladder*.
King Henry IV, part i. act ii. sc. 4.

Blank—*Duke.* And what's her history?
Viola. A *blank*, my lord.
Twelfth Night, act ii. sc. 4.

Blast—Once more unto the breach, dear friends, once more;
Or close the wall up with our English dead!
In peace there's nothing so becomes a man
As modest stillness and humility;
But when the *blast* of war blows in our ears,
Then imitate the action of the tiger:
Stiffen the sinews, summon up the blood.
King Henry V, act iii. sc. 1.

Blood—For in my youth I never did apply
Hot and rebellious liquors in my *blood.*
As You Like It, act ii. sc. 3.

Blood—Thoughts that would thick my *blood.*
Winter's Tale, act i. sc. 3.

Blood— The *blood* more stirs
To rouse a lion than to start a hare.
King Henry IV, part i. act i. sc. 3.

Bloody—*Bloody* instructions, which, being taught, return
To plague the inventor: this even-handed justice
Commends the ingredients of our poisoned chalice
To our own lips. *Macbeth*, act i. sc. 7.

Blow—*Blow*, winds, and crack your cheeks! rage! blow! *King Lear*, act iii. sc. 2.

Blow—*Blow*, *blow*, thou winter wind,
Thou art not so unkind
As man's ingratitude.
As You Like It, act ii. sc. 7.

Blushing—Farewell, a long farewell, to all my greatness!
This is the state of man. To-day he puts forth
The tender leaves of hopes, to-morrow blossoms,
And bears his *blushing* honors thick upon him:
The third day comes a frost, a killing frost.
King Henry VIII, act iii. sc. 2.

Bodkin— There's the respect
That makes calamity of so long life;
For who would bear the whips and scorns of time,
The oppressor's wrong, the proud man's contumely,
The pangs of despised love, the law's delay,
The insolence of office, and the spurns
That patient merit of the unworthy takes,
When he himself might his quietus make
With a bare *bodkin?* who would fardels bear,
To grunt and sweat under a weary life,
But that the dread of something after death—

The undiscovered country, from whose bourn
No traveller returns—puzzles the will
And makes us rather bear those ills we have
Than fly to others that we know not of?
Thus conscience does make cowards of us all:
And thus the native hue of resolution
Is sicklied o'er with the pale cast of thought,
And enterprises of great pith and moment,
With this regard, their currents turn awry,
And lose the name of action. *Hamlet*, act iii. sc. 1.

Bond—I'll have my *bond;* I will not hear thee speak;
I'll have my bond; and therefore speak no more.
Merchant of Venice, act iii. sc. 3.

Bond—Is it so nominated in the *bond?*
Merchant of Venice, act iv. sc. 1.

Bondman—Who is here so base that would be a *bondman?* If any, speak; for him have I offended.
Julius Cæsar, act iii. sc. 2.

Bones—Full fathom five thy father lies;
Of his *bones* are coral made;
Those are pearls that were his eyes;
Nothing of him that doth fade
But doth suffer a sea-change
Into something rich and strange.
Tempest, act i. sc. 2.

Bones—The evil that men do lives after them;
The good is oft interred with their *bones.*
Julius Cæsar, act iii. sc. 2.

Bones—An old man, broken with the storms of state,
Is come to lay his weary *bones* among ye;
Give him a little earth for charity!
King Henry VIII, act iv. sc. 2.

Book—He hath never fed of the dainties that are bred in a *book.* *Love's Labor's Lost*, act iv. sc. 2.

Book—Your face, my thane, is as a *book*, where men
May read strange matters. *Macbeth*, act i. sc. 5.

Book—The painful warrior, famousëd for fight,
After a thousand victories once foiled,
Is from the *book* of honor razed quite,
And all the rest forgot for which he toiled.
Sonnets, son. xxv.

Born—I was not *born* under a rhyming planet.
Much Ado about Nothing, act v. sc. 2.

Borrow'd—The *borrow'd* Majesty of England.
King John, act i. sc. 1.

Borrower—Neither a *borrower* nor a lender be;
For loan oft loses both itself and friend,
And borrowing dulls the edge of husbandry.
This above all: to thine own self be true;
And it must follow, as the night the day,
Thou canst not then be false to any man.
Hamlet, act i. sc. 3.

Bosom— O *bosom*, black as death!
O limed soul, that, struggling to be free,
Art more engaged! Help, angels! Make assay!
Bow, stubborn knees! and, heart with strings of steel,
Be soft as sinews of the new-born babe!
Hamlet, act iii. sc. 3.

Bosom—My *bosom's* lord sits lightly in his throne.
Romeo and Juliet, act v. sc. 1.

Bottom—Bless thee, *Bottom!* bless thee! thou art translated.
Midsummer-Night's Dream, act iii. sc. 1.

Bounds—Not stepping o'er the *bounds* of modesty.
Romeo and Juliet, act iv. sc. 2.

Bowels—And that it was great pity, so it was,
That villanous saltpetre should be digged
Out of the *bowels* of the harmless earth,
Which many a good tall fellow had destroyed
So cowardly; and, but for these vile guns,
He would himself have been a soldier.
King Henry IV, part i. act i. sc. 3.

Bowels—Thus far into the *bowels* of the land
Have we marched on without impediment.
King Richard III, act v. sc. 2.

Braggart—O, I could play the woman with mine eyes,
And *braggart* with my tongue!
Macbeth, act iv. sc. 3.

Brain—Thy commandment all alone shall live
Within the book and volume of my *brain*,
Unmix'd with baser matter. *Hamlet*, act i. sc. 5.

Brain—Is this a dagger which I see before me,
The handle toward my hand? * * *
Art thou not, fatal vision, sensible
To feeling as to sight? or art thou but
A dagger of the mind, a false creation
Proceeding from the heat-oppressed *brain?*
Macbeth, act ii. sc. 1.

Brain—Shall quips. and sentences, and these paper bullets of the *brain* awe a man from the career of his humor? *Much Ado about Nothing*, act ii. sc. 3.

Brain—*Brain* him with his lady's fan.
King Henry IV, part i. act ii. sc. 3.

Brain—Memory, the warder of the *brain*.
Macbeth, act i. sc. 7.

Brain—This is the very coinage of your *brain*.
Hamlet, act iii. sc. 4.

Brain—Within the book and volume of my *brain*.
Hamlet, act i. sc. 5.

Brains—Cudgel thy *brains* no more about it.
Hamlet, act v. sc. 1.

Brains—O God, that men should put an enemy in their mouths, to steal away their *brains*.
Othello, act ii. sc. 3.

Brains— The times have been
That, when the *brains* were out, the man would die,
And there an end; but now they rise again,
With twenty mortal murders on their crowns,
And push us from our stools.
Macbeth, act iii. sc. 4.

Brass—Men's evil manners live in *brass*; their virtues
We write in water. *King Henry VIII*, act iv. sc. 2.

Brave'd—*Brav'd* in mine own house with a skein of thread! *Taming of the Shrew*, act iv. sc. 3.

Breach—But, to my mind,—though I am a native here,
And to the manner born,—it is a custom
More honor'd in the *breach* than the observance.
Hamlet, act i. sc. 4.

Bread—Gets him to rest, crammed with distressful *bread*. *King Henry V*, act iv. sc. i.

Breakfast—You may as well say that's a valiant flea that dare eat his *breakfast* on the lip of a lion.
King Henry V, act iii. sc. 7.

Breastplate—What stronger *breastplate* than a heart untainted?
Thrice is he armed that hath his quarrel just;
And he but naked, though locked up in steel,
Whose conscience with injustice is corrupted.
King Henry VI, part ii. act iii. sc. 2.

Breeches—King Stephen was a worthy peer,
His *breeches* cost him but a crown;
He held them sixpence all too dear,
With that he called the tailor lown.
Othello, act ii. sc. 3.

Breed—Rome, thou hast lost the *breed* of noble bloods.
Julius Cæsar, act i. sc. 2.

Brevity—*Brevity* is the soul of wit.
Hamlet, act ii. sc. 2.

Bricks—Sir, he made a chimney in my father's house, and the *bricks* are alive at this day to testify it.
King Henry VI, part ii. act iv. sc. 2.

Brief—*Hamlet.* Is this the prologue, or the poesy of a ring?
Ophelia. 'Tis *brief*, my lord.
Hamlet. As woman's love. *Hamlet*, act iii. sc. 2.

Brief—*Brief* as the lightning in the collied night,
That, in a spleen, unfolds both heaven and earth
And, ere a man hath power to say, Behold!
The jaws of darkness do devour it up:
So quick bright things come to confusion.
Midsummer-Night's Dream, act i. sc. 1.

Brief—We must be *brief* when traitors brave the field.
King Richard III, act iv. sc. 3.

Briers—O, how full of *briers* is this working-day world!
As You Like It, act i. sc. 3.

Bright—By Heaven, methinks it were an easy leap
To pluck *bright* honor from the pale-faced moon;
Or dive into the bottom of the deep,
Where fathom-line could never touch the ground,
And pluck up drowned honor by the locks.
King Henry IV, part i. act i. sc. 3.

Bright—*Bright* Apollo's lute strung with his hair.
Love's Labor's Lost, act iv. sc. 3

Bright— 'Twere all one
That I should love a *bright* particular star
And think to wed it; he is so above me.
All's Well that Ends Well, act i. sc. 1.

Brutus—For *Brutus* is an honorable man;
So are they all, all honorable men.
Julius Cæsar, act iii. sc. 2.

Bubbles—The earth hath *bubbles*, as the water has,
And these are of them. *Macbeth*, act i. sc. 3.

Buck—A *buck* of the first head.
Love's Labor's Lost, act iv. sc. 2.

Buckram—Thou knowest my old ward; here I lay, and thus I bore my point. Four rogues in *buckram* let drive at me.
King Henry IV, part i. act ii. sc. 4.

Burglary—Flat *burglary* as ever was committed!
Much Ado about Nothing, act iv. sc. 2.

Burnished—Mislike me not for my complexion,
The shadowed livery of the *burnish'd* sun.
Merchant of Venice, act ii. sc. 1.

Burst—Let me not *burst* in ignorance!
Hamlet, act i. sc. 4.

Bush—Good wine needs no *bush*.
As You Like It, epilogue.

Bush—Suspicion always haunts the guilty mind;
The thief doth fear each *bush* an officer.
King Henry VI, part iii. act v. sc. 6.

Butter'd—'Twas her brother that in pure kindness to his horse *butter'd* his hay. *King Lear*, act ii. sc. 4.

Button—On Fortune's cap we're not the very *button*.
Hamlet, act ii. sc. 2.

C

Cabined—*Cabined*, cribbed, confined, bound in
To saucy doubts and fears. *Macbeth*, act iii. sc. 4.

Cæsar—Imperious *Cæsar*, dead, and turned to clay,
Might stop a hole to keep the wind away.
Hamlet, act v. sc. 1.

Cæsar— Put a tongue
In every wound of *Cæsar* that should move
The stones of Rome to rise and mutiny.
Julius Cæsar, act iii. sc. 2.

Cæsar—Not that I loved *Cæsar* less, but that I loved Rome more. *Julius Cæsar*, act iii. sc. 2.

Cæsar—But yesterday, the word of *Cæsar* might
Have stood against the world; now lies he there,
And none so poor to do him reverence.
Julius Cæsar, act iii. sc. 2.

Cæsar—What tributaries follow him to Rome,
To grace in captive bonds his chariot wheels?
Julius Cæsar, act i. sc. 1.

Cæsar—How like a deer stricken by many princes,
Dost thou here lie. *Julius Cæsar*, act iii. sc. 1.

Cakes—Sir Toby. Dost thou think, because thou art virtuous, there shall be no more *cakes* and ale?

Clown. Yes, by Saint Anne! and ginger shall be hot i'the mouth, too. *Twelfth Night*, act ii. sc. 3.

Calf—Thou wear a lion's hide! doff it for shame,
And hang a *calf's* skin on those recreant limbs.
King John, act iii. sc. 1.

Calumny—Be thou as chaste as ice, as pure as snow, thou shalt not escape *calumny*.
Hamlet, act iii. sc. 1.

Can— *Can* such things be,
And overcome us like a summer's cloud,
Without our special wonder? *Macbeth*, act iii. sc. 4.

Candied—No, let the *candied* tongue lick absurb pomp;
And crook the pregnant hinges of the knee,
Where thrift may follow fawning.
Hamlet, act iii. sc. 2.

Candle—1. How far that little *candle* throws its beams!
So shines a good deed in a naughty world.
2. When the moon shone we did not see the *candle;*
So doth the greater glory dim the less.
Merchant of Venice, act v. sc. 1.

Candle—To-morrow, and to-morrow, and to-morrow,
Creeps in this petty pace from day to day,
To the last syllable of recorded time;
And all our yesterdays have lighted fools
The way to dusty death. Out, out, brief *candle!*
Life's but a walking shadow, a poor player
That struts and frets his hour upon the stage,
And then is heard no more; it is a tale
Told by an idiot, full of sound and fury,
Signifying nothing. *Macbeth*, act v. sc. 5.

Canker— In the sweetest bud
The eating *canker* dwells.
Two Gentlemen of Verona, act i. sc. 1.

Canker—I had rather be a *canker* in a hedge than a rose in his grace.
Much Ado about Nothing, act i. sc. 3.

Canker—Now will *canker* sorrow eat my bud.
King John, act iii. sc. 4.

Cankers—The *cankers* of a calm world and a long peace. *King Henry IV*, part i. act iv. sc. 2.

Cannot—I *cannot* but remember such things were
That were most precious to me.
Macbeth, act iv. sc. 3.

Canon—O that this too, too-solid flesh would melt,
Thaw, and resolve itself into a dew!
Or that the Everlasting had not fixed
His *canon* 'gainst self-slaughter! O God! O God!
How weary, stale, flat, and unprofitable
Seem to me all the uses of this world!
Hamlet, act i. sc. 2.

Canopied—I know a bank——
Quite *over-canopied* with luscious woodbine.
Midsummer-Night's Dream, act ii. sc. 2.

Cap—A very riband in the *cap* of youth.
Hamlet, act iv. sc. 7.

Captain—And simple truth miscalled simplicity,
And captive good attending *captain* ill.
Sonnets, son. lxvi.

Captain—That in the *captain's* but a choleric word
Which in the soldier is flat blasphemy.
Measure for Measure, act ii. sc. 2.

Care—*Care* keeps his watch in every old man's eye.
Romeo and Juliet, act ii. sc. 3.

Care—I am sure *care's* an enemy to life.
Twelfth Night, act i. sc. 3.

Casca—See, what a rent the envious *Casca* made!
Julius Cæsar, act iii. sc. 2.

Cassius—Let me have men about me that are fat;
Sleek-headed men, and such as sleep o'nights;
Yond' *Cassius* has a lean and hungry look:
He thinks too much: such men are dangerous.
Julius Cæsar, act i. sc. 2.

Cast— I have set my life upon a *cast*,
And I will stand the hazard of the die.
King Richard III, act v. sc. 4.

Cat—Letting "I dare not" wait upon "I would,"
Like the poor *cat* i' the adage. *Macbeth*, act i. sc. 7.

Cat—Let Hercules himself do what he may,
The *cat* will mew, and dog will have his day.
Hamlet, act v. sc. 1.

Catalogue—*Mur*. We are men, my liege.
Mac. Ay, in the *catalogue* ye go for men.
Macbeth, act iii. sc. 1.

Catastrophe—I'll tickle your *catastrophe.*
King Henry IV, part ii. act ii. sc. 1.

Catch— The play's the thing
Wherein I'll *catch* the conscience of the king.
Hamlet, act ii. sc. 2.

Cause—Romans, countrymen, and lovers! hear me for my *cause;* and be silent that you may hear.
Julius Cæsar, act iii. sc. 2.

Ceremony—No *ceremony* that to great ones 'longs,
Not the king's crown, nor the deputed sword,
The marshal's truncheon, nor the judge's robe,
Become them with one-half so good a grace
As mercy does. *Measure for Measure*, act ii. sc. 2.

Chaff—Gratiano speaks an infinite deal of nothing; more than any man in all Venice. His reasons are as two grains of wheat hid in two bushels of *chaff:* you shall seek all day ere you find them; and when you have them, they are not worth the search.
Merchant of Venice, act i. sc. 1.

Chanticleer—My lungs began to crow like *chanticleer.*
As You Like It, act ii. sc. 7.

Chamber—Sitting in my *dolphin-chamber*, at the round table, by a sea-cole fire.
King Henry IV, part ii. act ii. sc. 1.

Chaos—For he being dead, with him is beauty slain,
And beauty dead, black *chaos* comes again.
Venus and Adonis, stanza 170.

Chaos— Perdition catch my soul,
But I do love thee! and when I love thee not
Chaos is come again. *Othello*, act iii. sc. 3.

Chariest—The *chariest* maid is prodigal enough
If she unmask her beauty to the moon.
Hamlet, act i. sc. 3.

Charity—He hath a tear for pity, and a hand
Open as day for melting *charity.*
King Henry IV, part ii. act iv. sc. 4.

Charmed—I bear a *charmed* life.
Macbeth, act v. sc. 7.

Charybdis—Thus when I shun Scylla, your father, I fall into *Charybdis*, your mother.
Merchant of Venice, act iii. sc. 5.

Cheek— She never told her love,
But let concealment, like a worm i' the bud,
Feed on her damask *cheek:* she pined in thought,
And, with a green and yellow melancholy,
She sat, like Patience on a monument,
Smiling at grief. *Twelfth Night*, act ii. sc. 4.

Cheek—It seems she hangs upon the *cheek* of Night
Like a rich jewel in an Ethiop's ear.
Romeo and Juliet, act i. sc. 5.

Cheek—See, how she leans her *cheek* upon her hand!
O that I were a glove upon that hand,
That I might touch that *cheek!*
Romeo and Juliet, act ii. sc. 2.

Cherry— So we grew together,
Like to a double *cherry*, seeming parted.
Midsummer-Night's Dream, act iii. sc. 2.

Cherubins— Look how the floor of heaven
Is thick inlaid with patines of bright gold.
There's not the smallest orb which thou behold'st
But in his motion like an angel sings,
Still quiring to the young-eyed *cherubins;*
Such harmony is in immortal souls;
But, whilst this muddy vesture of decay
Doth grossly close it in, we cannot hear it.
Merchant of Venice, act v. sc. 1.

Chewing— Pacing through the forest,
Chewing the food of sweet and bitter fancy.
As You Like It, act iv. sc. 3.

Chickens—What! all my pretty *chickens*, and their dam,
At one fell swoop? *Macbeth*, act iv. sc. 3.

Child—Grief fills the room up of my absent *child*,
Lies in his bed, walks up and down with me,
Puts on his pretty looks, repeats his words,
Remembers me of all his gracious parts,
Stuffs out his vacant garments with his form.
King John, act iii. sc. 4.

Child—It is a wise father that knows his own *child*.
Merchant of Venice, act ii. sc. 2.

Child—How sharper than a serpent's tooth it is
To have a thankless *child!* *King Lear*, act i. sc. 4.

Children— True, I talk of dreams,
Which are the *children* of an idle brain,
Begot of nothing but vain fantasy.
Romeo and Juliet, act i. sc. 4.

Chimes—We have heard the *chimes* at midnight.
King Henry IV, part ii. act iii. sc. 2.

Chrysolite—One entire and perfect *chrysolite*.
Othello, act v. sc. 2.

Church-door—*Rom.* Courage, man! the hurt cannot be much.

Mer. No, 'tis not so deep as a well, nor so wide as a *church-door;* but 'tis enough.
Romeo and Juliet, act iii. sc. 1.

Churlish—My master is of *churlish* disposition,
And little recks to find the way to heaven
By doing deeds of hospitality.
As You Like It, act ii. sc. 4.

Churlish— I tell thee, *churlish* priest,
A minist'ring angel shall my sister be,
When thou liest howling. *Hamlet*, act v. sc. 1.

Civet—Give me an ounce of *civet*, good apothecary, to sweeten my imagination. *King Lear*, act iv. sc. 6.

Civil—*Civil* dissension is a viperous worm
That gnaws the bowels of the commonwealth.
King Henry VI, part i. act v. sc. 1.

Cloaks—When clouds are seen wise men put on their *cloaks*. *King Richard III*, act ii. sc. 3.

Clock—The iron tongue of midnight hath told twelve.
Midsummer-Night's Dream, act v. sc. 1.

Clod—Ay, but to die, and go we know not where;
To lie in cold obstruction, and to rot:
This sensible warm motion to become
A kneaded *clod;* and the delighted spirit
To bathe in fiery floods, or to reside
In thrilling region of thick-ribbed ice;
To be imprison'd in the viewless winds,
And blown with restless violence round about
The pendent world.
Measure for Measure, act iii. sc. 1.

Clouds—Now is the winter of our discontent
Made glorious summer by this sun of York,
And all the *clouds* that lowered upon our house
In the deep bosom of the ocean buried.
King Richard III, act i. sc. 1.

Cock-crowing— The early village *cock*
Hath twice done salutation to the morn.
King Richard III, act v. sc. 3.

Coil—I would that I were low laid in my grave;
I am not worth this *coil* that's made for me.
King John, act ii. sc. 1.

Coin— *Coin* heaven's image
In stamps that are forbid.
Measure for Measure, act ii. sc. 4.

Cold—The air bites shrewdly. *Hamlet*, act i. sc. 4.

Colossus—Why, man, he doth bestride the narrow world
Like a *Colossus;* and we petty men
Walk under his huge legs, and peep about
To find ourselves dishonorable graves.
Julius Cæsar, act i. sc. 2.

Come—Show his eyes, and grieve his heart!
Come like shadows, so depart.
Macbeth, act iv. sc. 1.

Come— *Come* what *come* may,
Time and the hour runs through the roughest day.
Macbeth, act i. sc. 3.

Common—Like a barber's chair, that fits all buttocks.
All's Well that Ends Well, act ii. sc. 2.

Company—I thank you for yonr *company;* but, good faith, I had as lief have been myself alone.
As You Like It, act iii. sc. 2.

Company—*Company*, villanous *company*, hath been the spoil of me.
King Henry IV, part i. act iii. sc. 3.

Comparisons—*Comparisons* are odorous.
Much Ado about Nothing, act iii. sc. 5.

Complete— In *complete* steel
Revisit'st thus the glimpses of the moon,
Making night hideous. *Hamlet*, act i. sc. 4.

Composture— I'll example you with thievery:
The sun's a thief, and with his great attraction
Robs the vast sea: the moon's an arrant thief,
And her pale fire she snatches from the sun:
The sea's a thief, whose liquid surge resolves
The moon into salt tears: the earth's a thief,
That feeds and breeds by a *composture* stolen
From general excrement: each thing's a thief.
Timon of Athens, act iv. sc. 3.

Compunctious—That no *compunctious* visitings of nature
Shake my fell purpose. *Macbeth*, act i. sc. 5.

Conclusion—But this denoted a foregone *conclusion.*
Othello, act iii. sc. 3.

Condemn—*Condemn* the fault, and not the actor of it.
Measure for Measure, act ii. sc. 2.

Confirmations— Trifles, light as air,
Are, to the jealous, *confirmations* strong
As proofs of holy writ. *Othello*, act iii. sc. 3.

Confusion—*Confusion* now hath made his masterpiece!
Most sacrilegious murder hath broke ope
The Lord's anointed temple, and stole thence
The life o' the building. *Macbeth*, act ii. sc. 3.

Congregate—Even there where merchants most do *congregate.*
Merchant of Venice, act i. sc. 3.

Constant—But I am *constant* as the northern star,
Of whose true-fixed and resting quality
There is no fellow in the firmament.
Julius Cæsar, act iii. sc. 1.

Contagious—And in the morn and liquid dew of youth
Contagious blastments are most imminent.
Hamlet, act i. sc. 3.

Content— O now forever,
Farewell the tranquil mind! farewell *content!*
Farewell the plumed troop, and the big wars,
That make ambition virtue! O farewell!
Farewell the neighing steed, and the shrill trump,
The spirit-stirring drum, the ear-piercing fife!
Othello, act iii. sc. 3.

Continual—Small have *continual* plodders ever won,
Save base authority from others' books.
Love's Labor's Lost, act i. sc. 1.

Convey—*Convey*, the wise it call. Steal! foh! a fico for the phrase!
Merry Wives of Windsor, act i. sc. 3.

Copy—You are the cruel'st she alive,
If you will lead these graces to the grave,
And leave the world no *copy.*
Twelfth Night, act i. sc. 5.

Correspondent—I will be *correspondent* to command,
And do my sp'riting gently. *Tempest*, act i. sc. 2.

Costard—The rational hind, *Costard*.
Love's Labor's Lost, act i. sc. 2.

Counterfeit—Look here, upon this picture, and on this:
The *counterfeit* presentment of two brothers.
See what a grace was seated on this brow!
Hyperion's curls; the front of Jove himself;
An eye like Mars, to threaten and command.
Hamlet, act iii. sc. 4.

Courage—For *courage* mounteth with occasion.
King John, act ii. sc. 1.

Courage—Screw your *courage* to the sticking-place.
Macbeth, act i. sc. 7.

Course—For aught that I could ever read,
Could ever hear by tale or history,
The *course* of true love never did run smooth.
Midsummer-Night's Dream, act i. sc. 1.

Court—I will make a star-chamber matter of it.
Merry Wives of Windsor, act i. sc. 1.

Courtesy—I am the very pink of *courtesy*.
Romeo and Juliet, act ii. sc. 4.

Coventry—A mad fellow met me on the way, and told me I had unloaded all the gibbets, and pressed the dead bodies. No eye hath seen such scare-crows. I'll not march through *Coventry* with them, that's flat! Nay, and the villains march wide betwixt the legs, as if they had gyves on; for, indeed, I had the most of them out of prison.
King Henry IV, part i. act iv. sc. 2.

Coward— Thou slave, thou wretch, thou *coward*,
Thou little valiant, great in villany!
Thou ever strong upon the stronger side!
Thou Fortune's champion, that dost never fight
But when her humorous ladyship is by
To teach thee safety! *King John*, act iii. sc. 1.

Coward—I was a *coward* on instinct.
King Henry IV, part i. act ii. sc. 4.

Cowards—*Cowards* die many times before their deaths:
The valiant never taste of death but once.
Julius Cæsar, act ii. sc. 2.

Cowards—A plague of all *cowards!* I say.
King Henry IV, part i. act ii. sc. 4.

Crack—What! will the line stretch out to the *crack* of doom? *Macbeth*, act iv. sc. 1.

Creatures—That we can call these delicate *creatures* ours,
And not their appetites. *Othello*, act iii. sc. 3.

Creditor— Spirits are not finely touched,
But the fine issues; nor Nature never lends
The smallest scruple of her excellence,
But, like a thrifty goddess, she determines
Herself the glory of a *creditor*
Both thanks and use.
Measure for Measure, act i. sc. 1.

Crimes— Tremble, thou wretch,
Thou hast within thee undivulged *crimes*,
Unwhipped of justice! *King Lear*, act iii. sc. 2.

Crispian—This day is called the feast of *Crispian*:
He that outlives this day, and comes safe home,
Will stand a tiptoe when this day is named,
And rouse him at the name of *Crispian*.
King Henry V, act iv. sc. 3.

Critical—For I am nothing, if not *critical*.
Othello, act ii. sc. 1.

Crotchets—Faith, thou hast some *crotchets* in thy head now. *Merry Wives of Windsor*, act ii. sc. 1.

Crown—Uneasy lies the head that wears a *crown*.
King Henry IV, part ii. act iii. sc. 1.

Crown—Within the hollow *crown*
That rounds the mortal temples of a king,

Keeps death his court; and there the antick sits,
Scoffing his state, and grinning at his pomp.
King Richard II, act iii. sc. 2.

Cruel—I must be *cruel* only to be kind.
Hamlet, act iii. sc. 4.

Cunning—An I thought he had been valiant, and so *cunning* in fence, I'd have seen him damn'd ere I'd have challenged him. *Twelfth Night*, act iii. sc. 4.

Cupid—Love looks not with the eyes, but with the mind,
And therefore is winged *Cupid* painted blind.
Midsummer-Night's Dream, act i. sc. 1.

Cur—O 'tis a foul thing when a *cur* cannot keep himself in all companies!
Two Gentlemen of Verona, act iv. sc. 4.

Curb—*Curb* this cruel devil of his will.
Merchant of Venice, act iv. sc. 1.

Curled—The wealthy *curled* darlings of our nation.
Othello, act i. sc. 2.

Curses— My way of life
Is fallen into the sere, the yellow leaf;
And that which should accompany old age,
As honor, love, obedience, troops of friends,
I must not look to have; but in their stead,
Curses, not loud, but deep, mouth-honor, breath,
Which the poor heart would fain deny and dare not.
Macbeth, act v. sc. 3.

Custom—But soft! methinks I scent the morning air;
Brief let me be: sleeping within mine orchard,
My *custom* always in the afternoon.
Hamlet, act i. sc. 5.

Cut—This was the most unkindest *cut* of all.
Julius Cæsar, act iii. sc. 2.

Cutpurse—A *cutpurse* of the empire and the rule,
That from a shelf the precious diadem stole
And put it in his pocket. *Hamlet*, act iii. sc. 4.

D

Daffodils—*Daffodils* that come before the swallow dares, and take
The winds of March with beauty; violets dim,
But sweeter than the lids of Juno's eyes,
Or Cytherea's breath. *Winter's Tale*, act iv. sc. 3.

Daggers—I will speak *daggers* to her, but use none.
Hamlet, act iii. sc. 2.

Daisies—When *daisies* pied, and violets blue,
And lady-smocks all silver-white,
And cuckoo buds of yellow hue,
Do paint the meadows with delight.
Love's Labor's Lost, act v. sc. 2.

Dalliance—Do not, as some ungracious pastors do,
Show me the steep and thorny way to heaven,
Whilst, like a puffed and reckless libertine,
Himself the primrose path of *dalliance* treads,
And recks not his own rede. *Hamlet*, act i. sc. 3.

Damnable—Thou hast *damnable* iteration.
King Henry IV, part i. act i. sc. 2.

Dan—This senior-junior, giant-dwarf, *Dan Cupid:*
Regent of love-rhymes, lord of folded arms,
The anointed sovereign of sighs and groans,
Liege of all loiterers and malcontents.
Love's Labor's Lost, act iii. sc. 1.

Danger—Out of this nettle, *danger*, we pluck this flower, safety. *King Henry IV*, part i. act ii. sc. 3.

Dangers— Upon this hint I spake:
She loved me for the *dangers* I had passed,
And I loved her that she did pity them.
Othello, act i. sc. 3.

Daniel—A *Daniel* come to judgment! Yea, a *Daniel!*
Merchant of Venice, act iv. sc. 1.

Dare—What man *dare*, I *dare*. *Macbeth*, act iii. sc. 1.

Dared—What! am I *dar'd* and bearded to my face?
King Henry VI, part i. act i. sc. 3.

Daughter—Still harping on my *daughter*.
Hamlet, act ii. sc. 2.

Daughters—I am all the *daughters* of my father's house,
And all the brothers too.
Twelfth Night, act ii. sc. 4.

Daws—But I will wear my heart upon my sleeve
For *daws* to peck at. *Othello*, act i. sc. 1.

Day—Night's candles are burnt out, and jocund *day*
Stands tiptoe on the misty mountain-tops.
Romeo and Juliet, act iii. sc. 5.

Day—As merry as the *day* is long.
Much Ado about Nothing, act ii. sc. 1.

Day—In the posteriors of this *day*, which the rude multitude call the afternoon.
Love's Labor's Lost, act v. sc. 1.

Dead—*Fal.* What! is the old king *dead?*
Pistol. As nail in door.
King Henry IV, part ii. act v. sc. 3.

Dearest— Nothing in his life
Became him like the leaving it; he died
As one that had been studied in his death
To throw away the *dearest* thing he owed
As 'twere a careless trifle. *Macbeth*, act i. sc. 4.

Death—Done to *death* by slanderous tongues.
Much Ado about Nothing, act v. sc. 3.

Death—The rest is silence. *Hamlet*, act v, sc. 2.

Death—*Death* will have his day.
King Richard II, act iii. sc. 2.

Death—*Death* lies on her, like an untimely frost,
Upon the sweetest flower of all the field.
Romeo and Juliet, act iv. sc. 5.

Death— All that lives must *die*,
Passing through nature to eternity.
Hamlet, act i. sc. 2.

Deceit— O that *deceit* should dwell
In such a gorgeous palace!
Romeo and Juliet, act iii. sc. 2.

Decree—It must not be; there is no power in Venice
Can alter a *decree* established:
'Twill be recorded for a precedent;
And many an error by the same example
Will rush into the state.
Merchant of Venice, act iv. sc. 1.

Deed—A little water clears us of this *deed*.
Macbeth, act ii. sc. 2.

Deed—The flighty purpose never is o'ertook,
Unless the *deed* go with it. *Macbeth*, act iv. sc. 1.

Deed—From lowest place when virtuous things proceed,
The place is dignified by the doer's *deed*.
All's Well that Ends Well, act ii. sc. 3.

Deed—A bloody *deed*: almost as bad, good mother,
As kill a king, and marry with his brother.
Hamlet, act iii. sc. 4.

Deed—A *deed* without a name. *Macbeth*, act iv. sc. 1.

Deeds—How oft the sight of means to do ill *deeds*
Makes ill *deeds* done! *King John*, act iv. sc. 2.

Deep— *Glen.* I can call spirits from the vasty *deep*.
Hot. Why, so can I, or so can any man;
But will they come when you do call for them?
King Henry IV, part i. act iii. sc. 1.

Deeper—*Deeper* than e'er plummet sounded.
Tempest, act iii. sc. 3.

Deer—Why, let the stricken *deer* go weep,
The hart ungalled play;
For some must watch, while some must sleep:
So runs the world away. *Hamlet*, act iii. sc. 2.

Deer—But mice, and rats, and such small *deer*,
Have been Tom's food for seven long year.
King Lear, act iii. sc. 4.

Denmark—Something is rotten in the state of *Denmark*. *Hamlet*, act i. sc. 4.

Desert—O, your *desert* speaks loud; and I should wrong it to lock it in the wards of covert bosom.
Measure for Measure, act v. sc. 1.

Desert—Use every man after his *desert*, and who should 'scape whipping? *Hamlet*, act ii. sc. 2.

Destiny—Hanging and wiving goes by *destiny*.
Merchant of Venice, act ii. sc. 9.

Detraction—An you had any eye behind you, you might see more *detraction* at your heels than fortunes before you. *Twelfth Night*, act ii. sc. 5.

Devil— The *devil* hath power
To assume a pleasing shape. *Hamlet*, act ii. sc. 2.

Devil—The *devil* can cite Scripture for his purpose.
Merchant of Venice, act i. sc. 3.

Devil—He will give the *devil* his due.
King Henry IV, part i. act i. sc. 2.

Devil—O, while you live, tell truth, and shame the *devil*. *King Henry IV*, part i. act iii. sc. 1.

Devil—Nay, then, let the *devil* wear black.
Hamlet, act iii. sc. 2.

Diana's foresters—*Diana's foresters*, gentlemen of the shade, minions of the moon.
King Henry IV, part i. act i. sc. 2.

Dictynna—*Dictynna*, good man Dull.
Love's Labor's Lost, act iv. sc. 2.

Die—
Blow, wind! come, wrack!
At least we'll *die* with harness on our back.
Macbeth, act v. sc. 5.

Dies—He that *dies*, pays all debts.
Tempest, act iii. sc. 2.

Dies—He *dies* and makes no sign.
King Henry VI, part ii. act iii. sc. 3.

Digestions—Unquiet meals make ill *digestions*.
Comedy of Errors, act v. sc. 1.

Discourse—It will *discourse* most eloquent music.
Hamlet, act iii. sc. 2.

Discourse—Sure, He that made us with such large *discourse*,
Looking before and after, gave us not
That capability and godlike reason
To fust in us unused. *Hamlet*, act iv. sc. 4.

Discourse—So sweet and voluble is his *discourse*.
Love's Labor's Lost, act ii. sc. 1.

Discourse—She'd come again, and with a greedy ear
Devour up my *discourse*. *Othello*, act i. sc. 3.

Discretion—The better part of valor is *discretion*.
King Henry IV, part i. act v. sc. 4.

Divided—I do perceive here a *divided* duty.
Othello, act i. sc. 3.

Divinity—There's such *divinity* doth hedge a king,
That treason can but peep to what it would.
Hamlet, act iv. sc. 5.

Divinity—They say there is *divinity* in odd numbers, either in nativity, chance, or death.
Merry Wives of Windsor, act v. sc. 1.

Divinity—There's a *divinity* that shapes our ends,
Rough hew them how we will. *Hamlet*, act v. sc. 2.

Division—That never set a squadron in the field,
Nor the *division* of a battle knows.
Othello, act i. sc. 1.

Dog—I had rather be a *dog*, and bay the moon,
Than such a Roman. *Julius Cæsar*, act iv. sc. 3.

Dog— I am Sir Oracle,
And when I ope my lips, let no *dog* bark!
Merchant of Venice, act i. sc. 1.

Dog—*Cel.* Not a word?
Ros. Not one to throw at a *dog*.
As You Like It, act i. sc. 3.

Dogs— The little *dogs* and all,
Tray, Blanch, and Sweetheart, see, they bark at me.
King Lear, act iii. sc. 6.

Dogs—Throw physic to the *dogs*: I'll none of it.
Macbeth, act v. sc. 3.

Dotes—But oh! what damned minutes tells he o'er,
Who *dotes*, yet doubts; suspects, yet strongly loves!
Othello, act iii. sc. 3.

Double—*Double, double* toil and trouble.
Macbeth, act iv. sc. 1.

Doubt— To be once in *doubt*
Is once to be resolved. *Othello*, act iii. sc. 3.

Doubt—*Doubt* thou the stars are fire;
Doubt that the sun doth move;
Doubt truth to be a liar;
But never *doubt* I love. *Hamlet*, act ii. sc. 2.

Doubts— Our *doubts* are traitors,

And make us lose the good we oft might win,
By fearing to attempt.
Measure for Measure, act i. sc. 5.

Dove—I will roar you as gently as any sucking *dove;*
I will roar you an 'twere any nightingale.
Midsummer-Night's Dream, act i. sc. 2.

Dreams—O, I have passed a miserable night,
So full of fearful *dreams*, of ugly sights,
That, as I am a Christian, faithful man,
I would not spend another such a night
Though 'twere to buy a world of happy days.
King Richard III, act i. sc. 4.

Drops—You are my true and honorable wife,
As dear to me as are the ruddy *drops*
That visit my sad heart. *Julius Cæsar*, act ii. sc. 1.

Dukedom—For me, poor man, my library
Was *dukedom* large enough. *Tempest*, act i. sc. 2.

Dust—What is pomp, rule, reign, but earth and *dust?*
And, live we how we can, yet die we must.
King Henry VI, part iii. act v. sc. 2.

E

Each—*Each* particular hair to stand on end,
Like quills upon the fretful porcupine.
Hamlet, act i. sc. 5.

Ear—That palter with us in a double sense;
That keep the word of promise to our *ear*,
And break it to our hope. *Macbeth*, act v. sc. 7.

Ear—Give every man thine *ear*, but few thy voice:
Take each man's censure, but reserve thy judgment.
Hamlet, act i. sc. 3.

Early—My only love sprung from my only hate!
Too *early* seen unknown, and known too late!
Romeo and Juliet, act i. sc. 5.

Earn—I *earn* that I eat, get that I wear; owe no man hate; envy no man's happiness; glad of other men's good, content with my harm.
As You Like It, act iii. sc. 2.

Ears—Thy old groans ring yet in my ancient *ears*.
Romeo and Juliet, act ii. sc. 3.

Ears—Tear a passion to tatters, to very rags, to split the *ears* of the groundlings. *Hamlet*, act iii. sc. 2.

Ears—Whose words all *ears* took captive.
All's Well that Ends Well, act v. sc. 3.

Earth—Lay her i' the *earth*;
And from her fair and unpolluted flesh
My violets spring. *Hamlet*, act v. sc. 1.

Earth—There are more things in heaven and *earth*, Horatio,
Than are dreamt of in my philosophy.
Hamlet, act i. sc. 5.

Earth—I'll put a girdle round about the *earth*
In forty minutes.
Midsummer-Night's Dream, act ii. sc. 1.

Earth— . Thou sure and firm-set *earth*,
Hear not my steps, which way they walk, for fear
Thy very stones prate of my whereabout.
Macbeth, act ii. sc. 1.

Earthlier—But *earthlier* happy is the rose distilled
Than that which, withering on the virgin thorn,
Grows, lives, and dies, in single blessedness.
Midsummer-Night's Dream, act i. sc. 1.

Ease—Shall I not take mine *ease* in mine inn?
King Henry IV, part i. act iii. sc. 3.

Easy—'Tis as *easy* as lying. *Hamlet*, act iii. sc. 2.

Eaten—He hath *eaten* me out of house and home.
King Henry IV, part ii. act ii. sc. 1.

Eaves-dropper—I'll play the *eaves-dropper.*
King Richard III, act v. sc. 3.

Ecstasy—This is the very *ecstasy* of love.
Hamlet, act ii. sc. 1.

Elder— Let still the woman take
An *elder* than herself; so wears she to him,
So sways she level in her husband's heart;
For, boy, however we do praise ourselves,
Our fancies are more giddy and unfirm,
More longing, wavering, sooner lost and won,
Than women's are. *Twelfth Night*, act ii. sc. 4.

Elements—His life was gentle, and the *elements*
So mixed in him that Nature might stand up
And say to all the world, This was a man!
Julius Cæsar, act v. sc. 5.

Embraced—What cannot be eschew'd, must be *embraced.* *Merry Wives of Windsor*, act v. sc. 5.

Enamell'd—He makes sweet music with th' *enamell'd* stones,
Giving a gentle kiss to every sedge
He overtaketh in his pilgrimage.
Two Gentlemen of Verona, act ii. sc. 7.

Encounter—To leave this keen *encounter* of our wits.
King Richard III, act i. sc. 2.

End— The *end* crowns all;
And that old common arbitrator, Time,
Will one day *end* it.
Troilus and Cressida, act iv. sc. 5.

Endured—Is most tolerable, and not to be *endured.*
Much Ado about Nothing, act iii. sc. 3.

Enemies—Had I but served my God with half the zeal

I served my king, he would not in mine age
Have left me naked to mine *enemies*.
King Henry VIII, act iii. sc. 2.

Enemy—A thing devised by the *enemy*.
King Richard III, act v. sc. 3.

Enemy—O that men should put an *enemy* in their mouths to steal away their brains.
Othello, act ii. sc. 3.

Enginer—For 'tis the sport to have the *enginer*
Hoist with his own petard. *Hamlet*, act iii. sc. 4.

England—This *England* never did, nor never shall,
Lie at the proud foot of a conqueror,
But when it first did help to wound itself,—
Come the three corners of the world in arms,
And we shall shock them ; nought shall make us rue,
If *England* to itself do rest but true.
King John, act v. sc. 7.

England—*England* is safe, if true within itself.
King Henry VI, part iii. act iv. sc. 1.

England—O *England!* model to thy inward greatness
Like little body with a mighty heart,
What might'st thou do, that honor would thee do,
Were all thy children kind and natural?
Chorus to King Henry V, act ii.

Enmity—'Tis death to me to be at *enmity;*
I hate it, and desire all good men's love.
King Richard III, act ii. sc. 1.

Enskyed—I hold you as a thing *enskyed* and sainted.
Measure for Measure, act i. sc. 5.

Enterprise— This sickness doth infect
The very life-blood of our *enterprise*.
King Henry IV, part i. act iv. sc. 1.

Ercles' vein—This is *Ercles' vein*.
Midsummer-Night's Dream, act i. sc. 2.

Eruption—This bodes some strange *eruption* to our state. *Hamlet*, act i. sc. 1.

Eruptions—Diseased nature oftentimes breaks forth
In strange *eruptions*.
King Henry IV, part i. act iii. sc. 1.

Eve—A child of our grandmother *Eve*, a female; or, for thy more sweet understanding, a woman.
Love's Labor's Lost, act i. sc. 1.

Evening—How still the *evening* is,
As hush'd on purpose to grace harmony!
Much Ado about Nothing, act ii. sc. 3.

Everlasting—Here comes the lady: O, so light a foot
Will ne'er wear out the *everlasting* flint.
Romeo and Juliet, act ii. sc. 6.

Evil—The *evil* that men do lives after them;
The good is oft interred with their bones.
Julius Cæsar, act iii. sc. 2.

Excellent—It is *excellent* to have a giant's strength;
But it is tyrannous to use it like a giant.
Measure for Measure, act ii. sc. 2.

Excellent— Her voice was ever soft,
Gentle, and low—an *excellent* thing in woman.
King Lear, act v. sc. 3.

Excess—To gild refined gold, to paint the lily,
To throw a perfume on the violet,
To smooth the ice, or add another hue
Unto the rainbow, or with taper-light
To seek the beauteous eye of heaven to garnish,
Is wasteful and ridiculous *excess*.
King John, act iv. sc. 2.

Expectation—He hath indeed better bettered *expectation*. *Much Ado about Nothing*, act i. sc. 1.

Expectation—Oft *expectation* fails, and most oft there
Where most it promises.
All's Well that Ends Well, act ii. sc. 1.

Experience—I had rather have a fool to make me merry than *experience* to make me sad.
As You Like It, act iv. sc. 1.

Exposition—I have an *exposition* of sleep come upon me. *Midsummer-Night's Dream*, act iv. sc. 1.

Extenuate—Speak of me as I am; nothing *extenuate*,
Nor set down aught in malice. Then must you speak
Of one that loved not wisely, but too well.
Othello, act v. sc. 2.

Eye—Into the *eye* and prospect of his soul.
Much Ado about Nothing, act iv. sc. 1.

Eye—In my mind's *eye*, Horatio. *Hamlet*, act i. sc. 2.

Eye— He drew a dial from his poke,
And looking on it with lack-lustre *eye*,
Says, very wisely, "It is ten o'clock.
Thus we may see," quoth he, "how the world wags."
As You Like It, act ii. sc. 7.

Eye—Alack! there lies more peril in thine *eye*
Than twenty of their swords.
Romeo and Juliet, act ii. sc. 2.

Eye—Friendship is constant in all other things,
Save in the office and affairs of love.
Therefore all hearts in love use their own tongues;
Let every *eye* negotiate for itself,
And trust no agent.
Much Ado about Nothing, act ii. sc. 1.

Eye—It adds a precious seeing to the *eye*.
Love's Labor's Lost, act iv. sc. 3.

Eye—Stabbed with a white wench's black *eye*.
Romeo and Juliet, act ii. sc. 4.

Eye—An *eye* like Mars, to threaten or command.
Hamlet, act iii. sc. 4.

Eyes—Thou hast no speculation in those *eyes*
Which thou dost glare with. *Macbeth*, act iii. sc. 4.

F

Face— There's no art
To find the mind's construction in the *face*.
Macbeth, act i. sc. 4.

Face—It is not night when I do see your *face*.
Midsummer-Night's Dream, act ii. sc. 2.

Face—A *face* without a heart. *Hamlet*, act iv. sc. 7.

Fair—*Fair* is foul, and foul is *fair*.
Macbeth, act i. sc. 1.

Fair—Is she not passing *fair*?
Two Gentlemen of Verona, act iv. sc. 4.

Fair-spoken—He was a scholar, and a ripe and good one:
Exceeding wise, *fair-spoken* and persuading;
Lofty and sour to them that loved him not,
But to those men that sought him, sweet as summer.
King Henry VIII, act iv. sc. 2.

Faith—There are no tricks in plain and simple *faith*.
Julius Cæsar, act iv. sc. 2.

Falcon—A *falcon*, towering in her pride of place,
Was by a mousing owl hawked at and killed.
Macbeth, act ii. sc. 4.

Fall— Great Cæsar fell.
O, what a *fall* was there, my countrymen!
Julius Cæsar, act iii. sc. 2.

Falling-off—O Hamlet, what a *falling-off* was there!
Hamlet, act i. sc. 5.

Falls—Vain pomp and glory of this world, I hate ye:
I feel my heart new open'd. O, how wretched
Is that poor man that hangs on princes' favors!
There is, betwixt that smile we would aspire to,
That sweet aspect of princes, and their ruin,
More pangs and fears than wars or women have:
And when he *falls*, he *falls* like Lucifer,
Never to hope again.
King Henry VIII, act iii. sc. 2.

False—*False* as dicers' oaths. *Hamlet*, act iii. sc. 4.

False— As for you,
Say what you can, my *false* o'erweighs your true.
Measure for Measure, act ii. sc. 4.

Falsehood—O, what a goodly outside *falsehood* hath!
Merchant of Venice, act i. sc. 3.

Fame—He lives in *fame* that died in virtue's cause.
Titus Andronicus, act i. sc. 2.

Fan—If I were now by this rascal, I could brain him with his lady's *fan*.
King Henry IV, part i. act ii. sc. 3.

Fancies— Not so sick, my lord,
As she is troubled with thick-coming *fancies*,
That keep her from her rest. *Macbeth*, act v. sc. 3.

Fancy—Tell me where is *fancy* bred,
Or in the heart, or in the head?
How begot, how nourished?
Merchant of Venice, act iii. sc. 2.

Fancy's course— All impediments in *fancy's course*
Are motives of more fancy.
All's Well that Ends Well, act v. sc. 3.

Fardels—Who would *fardels* bear,
To grunt and sweat under a weary life;
But that the dread of something after death,
The undiscovered country, from whose bourn
No traveller returns, puzzles the will;

And makes us rather bear those ills we have,
Than fly to others that we know not of?

Hamlet, act iii. sc. 1.

Farewell—If we do meet again, why we shall smile;
If not, why then this parting was well made.

Julius Cæsar, act v. sc. 5.

Farewell—*Farewell* the tranquil mind! *farewell* content!
Farewell the plumed troops, and the big wars
That make ambition virtue.
Farewell the neighing steed, and the shrill trump,
The spirit-stirring drum, the ear-piercing fife,
The royal banner; and all quality,
Pride, pomp, and circumstance of glorious war!
Farewell! Othello's occupation's gone!

Othello, act iii. sc. 3.

Farewell—*Farewell*, a long *farewell*, to all my greatness!
This is the state of man: to-day he puts forth
The tender leaves of hope, to-morrow blossoms,
And bears his blushing honors thick upon him:
The third day comes a frost, a killing frost;
And when he thinks, good easy man, full surely
His greatness is a-ripening—nips his root,
And then he falls, as I do.

King Henry VIII, act iii. sc. 2.

Fashion—The glass of *fashion*, and the mould of form,
The observed of all observers!

Hamlet, act iii. sc. 1.

Fast—*Fast* bind, *fast* find,
A proverb never stale in thrifty mind.

Merchant of Venice, act ii. sc. 5.

Fasting— Down on your knees,
And thank Heaven, *fasting*, for a good man's love.

As You Like It, act iii. sc. 5.

Fat—And duller shouldst thou be than the *fat* weed
That rots itself in ease on Lethe wharf.

Hamlet, act i. sc. 5.

Fatal—It was the owl that shrieked, the *fatal* bellman,
Which gives the stern'st good-night.
Macbeth, act ii. sc. 2.

Father—Oh, who would be a *father!*
Othello, act i. sc. 1.

Father—Art thou his *father?*
Ay, sir; so his mother says, if I may believe her.
Taming of the Shrew, act v. sc. 1.

Father—Old *father* antic the law.
King Henry IV, part i. act i. sc. 2.

Father—It is a wise *father* that knows his own child.
Merchant of Venice, act ii. sc. 2.

Father—My *father's* brother; but no more like my *father*
Than I to Hercules. *Hamlet*, act i. sc. 2.

Fault—And, oftentimes, excusing of a *fault*
Doth make the *fault* the worse by the excuse.
King John, act iv. sc. 2.

Fault—Every one *fault* seeming monstrous, till his fellow-fault came to match it.
As You Like It, act iii. sc. 2.

Faults—Oh, what a world of vile ill-favored *faults*
Looks handsome in three hundred pounds a-year!
Merry Wives of Windsor, act iii. sc. 4.

Faults—Every man has a bag hanging before him, in which he puts his neighbor's *faults*, and another behind him in which he stows his own.
Coriolanus, act ii. sc. 1.

Faults—O that you could turn your eyes towards the napes of your necks, and make but an interior survey of your good selves. *Coriolanus*, act ii. sc. 1.

Faults—Breathe his *faults* so quaintly,

That they may seem the taints of liberty:
The flash and outbreak of a fiery mind.
Hamlet, act ii. sc. 1.

Fear—Hang those that talk of *fear*.
Macbeth, act v. sc. 3.

Fears— When our actions do not,
Our *fears* do make us traitors.
Macbeth, act iv. sc. 2.

Feast—They have been at a great *feast* of languages, and stolen the scraps.
Love's Labor's Lost, act v. sc. 1.

Feast—The latter end of a fray, and the beginning of a *feast*,
Fits a dull fighter and a keen guest.
King Henry IV, part i. act iv. sc. 2.

Feasting—A *feasting* presence full of light.
Romeo and Juliet, act v. sc. 3.

Feeble—Let that suffice, most forcible *Feeble*.
King Henry IV, part ii. act iii. sc. 2.

Fellow—Alas, poor Yorick! I knew him, Horatio; a *fellow* of infinite jest, of most excellent fancy.
Hamlet, act v. sc. 1.

Fellow—A *fellow* that hath had losses; and one that hath two gowns, and everything handsome about him. *Much Ado about Nothing*, act iv. sc. 2.

Fellow—If he be not *fellow* with the best king, thou shalt find the best king of good fellows.
King Henry V, act v. sc. 2.

Fellow—A *fellow* almost damn'd in a fair wife.
Othello, act i. sc. 1.

Fie— *Fie*, foh, and fum,
I smell the blood of a British man.
King Lear, act iii. sc. 4.

Fife—Vile squeaking of the wry-necked *fife*.
Merchant of Venice, act ii. sc. 5.

Figure— But, alas! to make me
The fixed *figure* for the time, for scorn
To point his slow and moving finger at.
Othello, act iv. sc. 2.

Finger—In faith I'll break thy little *finger*, Harry,
An if thou wilt not tell me all things true.
King Henry IV, part i. act ii. sc. 3.

Finger—No man's pie is freed
From his ambitious *finger*.
King Henry VIII, act i. sc. 1.

Fire—The glowworm shows the matin to be near,
And 'gins to pale his uneffectual *fire*.
Hamlet, act i. sc. 5.

Fires—And where two raging *fires* meet together,
They do consume the thing that feeds their fury.
Taming of the Shrew, act ii. sc. 1.

Firmament—This brave o'erhanging *firmament*, this majestical roof fretted with golden fire, why, it appears no other thing to me than a foul and pestilent congregation of vapors. *Hamlet*, act ii. sc. 4.

Fit—Then comes my *fit* again. *Macbeth*, act iii. sc. 4.

Flashes—Where be your gibes now? your gambols? your songs? your *flashes* of merriment, that were wont to set the table on a roar.
Hamlet, act v. sc. 1.

Flatterers—But, when I tell him he hates *flatterers*,
He says he does; being then most flattered.
Julius Cæsar, act ii. sc. 1.

Flattering—Lay not that *flattering* unction to your soul. *Hamlet*, act iii. sc. 4.

Flattery—O, that men's ears should be
To counsel deaf, but not to *flattery*!
Timon of Athens, act i. sc. 2.

Flesh—O *flesh*, *flesh*, how art thou fishified!
Romeo and Juliet, act ii. sc. 4.

Flint— Weariness
Can snore upon the *flint*, when resty sloth
Finds the down pillow hard.
Cymbeline, act iii. sc. 6.

Flower—Maidens call it love in idleness—
Fetch me that *flower*.
Midsummer-Night's Dream, act ii. sc. 2.

Foggy—Like *foggy* south, puffing with wind and rain.
As You Like It, act iii. sc. 5.

Food—*Food* for powder, *food* for powder; they'll fill a pit as well as better.
King Henry IV, part i. act iv. sc. 2.

Fool—The *fool* doth think he is wise, but the wise man knows himself to be a *fool*.
As You Like It, act v. sc. 1.

Fool—A *fool*, a *fool!* I met a *fool* i' the forest,
A motley *fool;* a miserable world;
As I do live by food, I met a *fool;*
Who laid him down and bask'd him in the sun,
And rail'd on Lady Fortune in good terms,
In good set terms,—and yet a motley *fool*.
As You Like It, act ii. sc. 7.

Foolery—The little *foolery* that wise men have makes a great show. *As You Like It*, act i. sc. 2.

Foot—The inaudible and noiseless *foot* of Time.
All's Well that Ends Well, act v. sc. 3.

Foot—Come on, my lords, the better *foot* before.
Titus Andronicus, act ii. sc. 4.

Foot— So light a *foot*
Will ne'er wear out the everlasting flint.
Romeo and Juliet, act ii. sc. 6.

Foot—Nay, but make haste: the better *foot* before.
King John, act iv. sc. 2.

Footing—Dance on the sands, and yet no *footing* seen.
Venus and Adonis, stanza 25.

Forbear—*Forbear* to judge; for we are sinners all.
King Henry VI, part ii. act iii. sc. 3.

Fordoes— This is the night
That either makes me or *fordoes* me quite.
Othello, act v. sc. 1.

Forehead—With *forehead* villainous low.
Tempest, act iv. sc. 1.

Foremost—The *foremost* man of all this world.
Julius Cæsar, act iv. sc. 3.

Forget—Men are men; the best sometimes *forget.*
Othello, act ii. sc. 3.

Forgetfulness— O sleep, O gentle sleep,
Nature's soft nurse, how have I frighted thee,
That thou no more wilt weigh my eyelids down,
And steep my senses in *forgetfulness?*
King Henry IV, part ii. act iii. sc. 1.

Forgot—Have you *forgot* all sense of place and duty?
Othello, act ii. sc. 3.

Forked—Like a man made after supper of a cheese-paring; when he was naked, he was, for all the world, like a *forked* radish, with a head fantastically carved upon it with a knife.
King Henry IV, part ii. act iii. sc. 2.

Fortune—To be a well-favored man is the gift of *fortune;* but to write and read comes by nature.
Much Ado about Nothing, act iii. sc. 3.

Fortune— *Fortune* is merry,
And in this mood will give us any thing.
Julius Cæsar, act iii. sc. 2.

Fortune—All other doubts by time let them be clear'd
Fortune brings in some boats that are not steer'd.
Cymbeline, act iv. sc. 3.

Fortune—There is a tide in the affairs of men
Which, taken at the flood, leads on to *fortune;*
Omitted, all the voyage of their life
Is bound in shallows and in miseries.
Julius Cæsar, act iv. sc. 3.

Fortune— When *fortune* means to men most good,
She looks upon them with a threatening eye.
King John, act iii. sc. 4.

Fortune—And railed on lady *Fortune* in good terms,
In good set terms. *As You Like It*, act ii. sc. 7.

Fortune's buffets—A man, that *fortune's buffets* and rewards
Hast ta'en with equal thanks. *Hamlet*, act iii. sc. 2.

Fortunes—My pride fell with my *fortunes.*
As You Like It, act i. sc. 2.

Fountain—A woman moved is like a *fountain* troubled;
Muddy, ill-seeming, thick, bereft of beauty.
Taming of the Shrew, act v. sc. 2.

Frailty—*Frailty*, thy name is woman.
Hamlet, act i. sc. 2.

Framed—*Framed* to make women false.
Othello, act i. sc. 3.

Friend—I am not of that feather, to shake off
My *friend* when he most needs me.
Timon of Athens, act i. sc. 1.

Friend's infirmities—A friend should bear his *friend's infirmities;*
But Brutus makes mine greater than they are.
Julius Cæsar, act iv. sc. 3.

Friendship—*Friendship* is constant in all other things
Save in the office and affairs of love.
Much Ado about Nothing, act ii. sc. 1.

Fruit—The ripest *fruit* first falls.
King Richard II, act ii. sc. 1.

Fruits—*Fruits* that blossom first will first be ripe.
Othello, act ii. sc. 3.

Funeral—Thrift, thrift, Horatio! the *funeral* baked meats
Did coldly furnish forth the marriage tables.
Hamlet, act i. sc. 2.

Fury—Full of sound and *fury*,
Signifying nothing. *Macbeth*, act v. sc. 5.

G

Gall—Let there be *gall* enough in thy ink; though thou write with a goose-pen, no matter.
Twelfth Night, act iii. sc. 2.

Galled—Let the *galled* jade wince, our withers are unwrung. *Hamlet*, act iii. sc. 2.

Garish— When he shall die,
Take him and cut him out in little stars,
And he will make the face of heaven so fine
That all the world will be in love with night
And pay no worship to the *garish* sun.
Romeo and Juliet, act iii. sc. 2.

Garter—Mine host of the *Garter*.
Merry Wives of Windsor, act i. sc. 1.

Gentleman—The Prince of Darkness is a *gentleman*.
King Lear, act iii. sc. 4.

George—And if his name be *George*, I'll call him Peter;
For new-made honor doth forget men's names.
King John, act i. sc. 1.

Ghost—There needs no *ghost*, my lord, come from the grave
To tell us this. *Hamlet*, act i. sc. 5.

Ghost—Vex not his *ghost:* O, let him pass! he hates him
That would upon the rack of this rough world
Stretch him out longer. *King Lear*, act v. sc. 3.

Giant's strength— O, it is excellent
To have a *giant's strength*; but it is tyrannous
To use it like a giant.
Measure for Measure, act ii. sc. 2.

Gifts—*Shallow.* I know the young gentlewoman; she has good *gifts.*
Evans. Seven hundred pounds, and possibilities, is goot *gifts.* *Merry Wives of Windsor*, act i. sc. 1.

Girdle—I'll put a *girdle* round about the earth
In forty minutes.
Midsummer-Night's Dream, act ii. sc. 2.

Give—*Give* it an understanding, but no tongue.
Hamlet, act i. sc. 2.

Give—*Give* sorrow words; the grief that does not speak
Whispers the o'erfraught heart, and bids it break.
Macbeth, act iv. sc. 3.

Give—*Give* thy thoughts no tongue.
Hamlet, act i. sc. 3.

Give—*Give* me to drink mandragora.
That I might sleep out this great gap of time
My Antony is away.
Antony and Cleopatra, act i. sc. 5.

Give— *Give* me that man
That is not passion's slave, and I will wear him
In my heart's core, ay, in my heart of hearts,
As I do thee. *Hamlet*, act iii. sc. 2.

Glass— He was, indeed, the *glass*
Wherein the noble youth did dress themselves.
King Henry IV, part ii. act ii. sc. 3.

Gloves—*Gloves* as sweet as damask roses.
Winter's Tale, act iv. sc. 3.

Go—He must needs *go* that the devil drives.
All's Well that Ends Well, act i. sc. 3.

Go— 1. At once, good-night:—
Stand not upon the order of your going,
But *go* at once.
2. Good-night, and better health.
Macbeth, act iii. sc. 4.

Go—Master, *go* on; and I will follow thee,
To the last gasp, with truth and loyalty.
As You Like It, act ii. sc. 3.

God—The *god* of my idolatry.
Romeo and Juliet, act ii. sc. 2.

God—*God* save the mark!
King Henry IV, part i. act i. sc. 3.

God—Even so, or with much more contempt, men's eyes
Did scowl on Richard; no man cried *God* save him!
King Richard II, act v. sc. 2.

Gold—'Tis *gold* which buys admittance;—and 'tis *gold*
Which makes the true man kill'd, and saves the thief;
Nay, sometimes hangs both thief and true man;
What can it not do, and undo?
Cymbeline, act ii. sc. 3.

Gold—How quickly nature falls into revolt
When *gold* becomes her object!
King Henry IV, part ii. act iv. sc. 4.

Gold—All that glisters is not *gold*.
Merchant of Venice, act ii. sc. 7.

Golden— I have bought
Golden opinions from all sorts of people.
Macbeth, act i. sc. 7.

Good—Are you *good* men and true?
Much Ado about Nothing, act iii. sc. 3.

Good—*Good* name in man and woman, dear my lord,
Is the immediate jewel of their souls.
Who steals my purse, steals trash ; 'tis something, nothing ;
'Twas mine, 'tis his, and has been slave to thousands ;
But he that filches from me my good name
Robs me of that which not enriches him,
And makes me poor indeed. *Othello*, act iii. sc. 3.

Good—Nought so vile that on the earth doth live
But to the earth some special *good* doth give.
Romeo and Juliet, act ii. sc. 3.

Goodness—There is some soul of *goodness* in things evil,.
Would men observingly distil it out.
King Henry V, act iv. sc. 1.

Goodness—Virtue is bold, and *goodness* never fearful.
Measure for Measure, act iii. sc. 1.

Gory—Thou can'st not say I did it ; never shake
Thy *gory* locks at me. *Macbeth*, act iii. sc. 4.

Gossip—A long-tongued. babbling *gossip !*
Titus Andronicus, act iv. sc. 2.

Grandam—*Clown.* What is the opinion of Pythagoras concerning wild-fowl ?
Malvolio. That the soul of our *grandam* might haply inhabit a bird.
Clo. What thinkest thou of his opinion ?
Mal. I think nobly of the soul, and no way approve his opinion. *Twelfth Night*, act iv. sc. 2.

Grandsire—For I am proverbed with a *grandsire* phrase. *Romeo and Juliet*, act i. sc. 4.

Grave—Ask for me to-morrow, and you shall find me a *grave* man. *Romeo and Juliet*, act iii. sc. 1.

Graves—In the most high and palmy state of Rome,
A little ere the mightiest Julius fell,
The *graves* stood tenantless, and the sheeted dead
Did squeak and gibber in the Roman streets.
Hamlet, act i. sc. 1.

Great—In the perfum'd chamber of the *great*.
King Henry IV, part ii. act iii. sc. 1.

Great—Some are born *great*, some achieve greatness, and some have greatness thrust upon 'em.
Twelfth Night, act ii. sc. 5.

Greatness—Nay, then, farewell!
I have touch'd the highest point of all my *greatness;*
And from that full meridian of my glory,
I haste now to my setting. I shall fall
Like a bright exhalation in the evening,
And no man see me more.
King Henry VIII, act iii. sc. 2.

Greek—But, for mine own part, it was *Greek* to me.
Julius Cæsar, act i. sc. 2.

Greyhounds—I see you stand like *greyhounds* in the slips,
Straining upon the start.
King Henry V, act iii. sc. 1.

Grief—'Tis better to be lowly born,
And range with humble livers in content,
Than to be perk'd up in a glistering *grief*,
And wear a golden sorrow.
King Henry VIII, act ii. sc. 3.

Grief—Every one can master a *grief* but he that has it.
Much Ado about Nothing, act iii. sc. 2.

Grief—What's gone, and what's past help,
Should be past *grief*. *Winter's Tale*, act iii. sc. 2.

Griefs—Some *griefs* are med'cinable.
Cymbeline, act iii. sc. 2.

Griefs—When remedies are past, the *griefs* are ended.
Othello, act i. sc. 3.

Grim-visaged—*Grim-visaged* war hath smoothed his wrinkled front. *King Richard III*, act i. sc. 1.

Guests—Unbidden *guests*
Are often welcomest when they are gone.
King Henry VI, part i. act ii. sc. 2.

H

Habit—How use doth breed a *habit* in a man!
Two Gentlemen of Verona, act v. sc. 4.

Hand—Here is her *hand*, the agent of her heart.
Two Gentlemen of Verona, act i. sc. 3.

Hanged—If he be not born to be *hanged*, our case is miserable. *Tempest*, act i. sc. 1.

Hanged—I'll see thee *hanged* on Sunday first.
Taming of the Shrew, act ii. sc. 1.

Happiness—How bitter a thing it is to look into *happiness* through another man's eyes!
As You Like It, act v. sc. 2.

Harry—I saw young *Harry*, with his beaver on,
His cuisses on his thighs, gallantly arm'd,
Rise from the ground like feather'd Mercury,
And vaulted with such ease into his seat
As if an angel dropp'd down from the clouds,
To turn and wind a fiery Pegasus.
King Henry IV, part i. act iv. sc. 1.

Harvest—His chin, new reaped,
Shew'd like a stubble-land at *harvest* home.
King Henry IV, part i. act i. sc. 3.

Havock—Cry "*Havock*," and let slip the dogs of war.
Julius Cæsar, act iii. sc. 1.

Hawk—I know a *hawk* from a handsaw.
Hamlet, act ii. sc. 2.

Head—The *head* is not more native to the heart.
Hamlet, act i. sc. 2.

Head—The very *head* and front of my offending
Hath this extent; no more. *Othello*, act i. sc. 3.

Heart—Oh, tiger's *heart*, wrapp'd in a woman's hide!
King Henry VI, part iii. act i. sc. 4.

Heart—He hath a *heart* as sound as a bell, and his tongue is the clapper; for what his *heart* thinks his tongue speaks.
Much Ado about Nothing, act iii. sc. 2.

Heart—*Ferdinand*. Here's my hand.
Miranda. And mine, with my *heart* in 't.
Tempest, act iii. sc. 1.

Heart—A merry *heart* goes all the day,
Your sad tires in a mile-a.
Winter's Tale, act iv. sc. 2.

Heart—O, Hamlet! thou hast cleft my *heart* in twain.
O throw away the worser part of it,
And live the purer with the other half.
Hamlet, act iii. sc. 4.

Heaven— As sweet and musical
As bright Apollo's lute, strung with his hair;
And, when Love speaks, the voice of all the gods
Makes *heaven* drowsy with the harmony.
Love's Labor's Lost, act iv. sc. 3.

Heaven—But *heaven* hath a hand in these events;
To whose high will we bound our calm contents.
King Richard II, act v. sc. 2.

Heaven—So excellent a king! that was, to this,
Hyperion to a satyr! so loving to my mother,
That he might not beteem the winds of *heaven*
Visit her face too roughly. *Hamlet*, act i. sc. 2.

Heaven—A *heaven* on earth I have won, by wooing thee.
All's Well that Ends Well, act iv. sc. 2.

Heaven—*Heaven* is above all yet; there sits a judge
That no king can corrupt.
King Henry VIII, act iii. sc. 1.

Heavens—Hung be the *heavens* with black!
King Henry VI, part i. act i. sc. 1.

Hecuba—What's *Hecuba* to him, or he to *Hecuba*, that he should weep for her? *Hamlet*, act ii. sc. 2.

Help—'Tis not enough to *help* the feeble up,
But to support him after.
Timon of Athens, act i. sc. 1.

Hey-day— At your age
The *hey-day* in the blood is tame: it's humble.
Hamlet, act iii. sc. 4.

Highly— What thou wouldst *highly*,
That wouldst thou holily; wouldst not play false,
And yet wouldst wrongly win. *Macbeth*, act i. sc. 5.

Hind—The *hind* that would be mated by the lion
Must die for love.
All's Well that Ends Well, act i. sc. 1.

Hint—Upon this *hint* I spake. *Othello*, act i. sc. 3.

Hip—I have you on the *hip*.
Merchant of Venice, act iv. sc. 1.

History—There is a *history* in all men's lives,
Figuring the nature of the time deceas'd;
The which observ'd, a man may prophesy,
With a near aim, of the main chance of things
As yet not come to life; which in their seeds,
And weak beginnings, lie intreasured.
King Henry IV, part ii. act iii. sc. 1.

History—And what's her *History?*
A blank, my lord. *Twelfth Night*, act ii. sc. 4.

Hit—A *hit*, a very palpable *hit*. *Hamlet*, act v. sc. 2.

Home-keeping—*Home-keeping* youth have ever homely wits. *Two Gentlemen of Verona*, act i. sc. 1.

Honest—An *honest* tale speeds best, being plainly told.
King Richard III, act iv. sc. 4.

Honesty—There is no terror, Cassius, in your threats;
For I am armed so strong in *honesty*
That they pass by me as the idle wind,
Which I respect not. *Julius Cæsar*, act iv. sc. 3.

Honor—You stand upon your *honor!* Why, thou unconfinable baseness, it is as much as I can do to keep the terms of my *honor* precise. I myself sometimes, leaving the fear of heaven on the left hand, and hiding mine *honor* in my necessity, am fain to shuffle, to hedge, and to lurch; and yet you——!
Merry Wives of Windsor, act ii. sc. 2.

Honor—*Honor* pricks me on. Yea, but how if *honor* prick me off when I come on? how then? Can *honor* set to a leg? No. Or an arm? No. Or take away the grief of a wound? No. *Honor* hath no skill in surgery then? No. What is *honor?* A word. What is in that word, *honor?* What is that *honor?* Air. A trim reckoning! Who hath it? He that died o' Wednesday. Doth he feel it? No. Doth he hear it? No. 'Tis insensible then? Yea, to the dead. But will it not live with the living? No. Why? Detraction will not suffer it. Therefore I'll none of it. *Honor* is a mere scutcheon; and so ends my catechism.
King Henry IV, part i. act v. sc. 1.

Honors—This is the state of man: To-day he puts forth
The tender leaves of hope, to-morrow blossoms,
And bears his blushing *honors* thick upon him.
King Henry VIII, act iii. sc. 2.

Hope—True *hope* is swift, and flies with swallow's wings:
Kings it makes gods, and meaner creatures kings.
King Richard III, act v. sc. 2.

Hope—The miserable have no other medicine
But only *hope*. *Measure for Measure*, act iii. sc. 1.

Horatio—*Horatio*, thou art e'en as just a man
As e'er my conversation coped withal.
Hamlet, act iii. sc. 2.

Horrors—I have supp'd full with *horrors*.
Macbeth, act v. sc. 5.

Horror's head—On *horror's head* horrors accumulate.
Othello, act iii. sc. 3.

Horse—A *horse!* a *horse!* my kingdom for a *horse!*
King Richard III, act v. sc. 3.

Horsemanship—And witch the world with noble *horsemanship*. *King Henry IV*, part i. act iv. sc. 1.

Host—I follow, mine *host*, I follow.
Merry Wives of Windsor, act ii. sc. 1.

Host—1. Mine *host* of the Garter.
2. What says my bully-rook? Speak scholarly and wisely.
Merry Wives of Windsor, act i. sc. 3.

House—You take my *house* when you do take the prop
That doth sustain my *house*; you take my life
When you do take the means whereby I live.
Merchant of Venice, act iv. sc. 1.

Household— Then shall our names,
Familiar in their mouths as *household* words,
Harry the King, Bedford and Exeter,
Warwick and Talbot, Salisbury and Gloster,
Be in their flowing cups freshly remembered.
King Henry V, act iv. sc. 3.

Humor—The *humor* of it.
Merry Wives of Windsor, act ii. sc. 1.

I

Idea—The *idea* of her life shall sweetly creep
Into his study of imagination.
Much Ado about Nothing, act iv. sc. 1.

Ides—Beware the *Ides* of March.
Julius Cæsar, act i. sc. 2.

If—Your "*if*" is the only peacemaker; much virtue in "*if*." *As You Like It*, act v. sc. 4.

Ignorance—Let me not burst in *ignorance*.
Hamlet, act i. sc. 4.

Ill—*Ill* blows the wind that profits nobody.
King Henry VI, part iii. act ii. sc. 5.

Ill-favored—An *ill-favored* thing, sir, but mine own.
As You Like It, act v. sc. 4.

Ills—And makes us rather bear those *ills* we have
Than fly to others that we know not of.
Hamlet, act iii. sc. 1.

Imagination—The lunatic, the lover, and the poet
Are of *imagination* all compact.
Midsummer-Night's Dream, act v. sc. 1.

Immortality—So long as men can breathe, or eyes can see,
So long lives this, and this gives life to thee.
Sonnet, To his Love.

Imperfections—Unhousel'd, disappointed, unanel'd,
No reckoning made, but sent to my account
With all my *imperfections* on my head.
Hamlet, act i. sc. 5.

Infirm—*Infirm* of purpose. *Macbeth*, act ii. sc. 2.

Ingratitude—I hate *ingratitude* more in a man
Than lying, vainness, babbling, drunkenness,
Or any taint of vice. *Twelfth Night*, act iii. sc. 4.

Ingredient—*Cassio.* Every inordinate cup is unblessed, and the *ingredient* is a devil.

Iago. Come, come; good wine is a good familiar creature, if it be well used. *Othello*, act ii. sc. 3.

Inn—Shall I not take mine ease at mine *inn?*
King Henry IV, part i. act iii. sc. 3.

Instruments—The gods are just, and of our pleasant vices
Make *instruments* to plague us.
King Lear, act v. sc. 3.

Intolerable—*Intolerable*, not to be endured.
Taming of the Shrew, act. v. sc. 2.

Invisible—O thou *invisible* spirit of wine, if thou hast no name to be known by, let us call thee devil!
Othello, act ii. sc. 3.

Itching— You yourself
Are much condemned to have an *itching* palm.
Julius Cæsar, act iv. sc. 3.

J

Jack in Office—I do despise them,
For they do prank them in authority,
Against all noble sufferance.
Coriolanus, act iii. sc. 1.

Jealousy—O beware, my lord, of *jealousy*;
It is the green-eyed monster, which doth mock
The meat it feeds on. *Othello*, act iii. sc. 3.
Merchant of Venice, act iii. sc. 2.

Jest—A *jest's* prosperity lies in the ear
Of him that hears it, never in the tongue
Of him that makes it.
Love's Labor's Lost, act v. sc. 2.

Jew—I am a *Jew* else, an *Ebrew Jew*.
King Henry IV, part i. act ii. sc. 4.

Jew—I thank thee, *Jew*, for teaching me that word.
Merchant of Venice, act iv. sc. 1.

Jew—I am a *Jew*: hath not a *Jew* eyes? hath not a *Jew* hands, organs, dimensions, senses, affections, passions?
Merchant of Venice, act iii. sc. 1.

Job—As poor as *Job*.
Merry Wives of Windsor, act v. sc. 5.

Joint—The time is out of *joint*.
Hamlet, act i. sc. 5.

Journeys—*Journeys* end in lovers meeting,
Every wise man's son doth know.
Twelfth Night, act ii. sc. 3.

Judge—O noble *judge!* O excellent young man!
Merchant of Venice, act iv. sc. 1.

Judges—Thieves for their robbery have authority,
When *judges* steal themselves.
Measure for Measure, act ii. sc. 2.

Judicious—Though it make the unskilful laugh, cannot but make the *judicious* grieve.
Hamlet, act iii. sc. 2.

Jury—The *jury*, passing on the prisoner's life,
May in the sworn twelve have a thief or two,
Guiltier than him they try.
Measure for Measure, act ii. sc. 1.

Jurymen—They have been grand *jurymen* since before Noah was a sailor.
Twelfth Night, act iii. sc. 2.

Just—Be *just*, and fear not:
Let all the ends thou aim'st at be thy country's,
Thy God's, and truth's.
King Henry VIII, act iii. sc. 2.

Justice— And then, the *justice*;
In fair round belly, with good capon lined,
With eyes severe, and beard of formal cut,
Full of wise saws and modern instances,
And so he plays his part.
As You Like It, act ii. sc. 7.

K

Kin—A little more than *kin*, and less than kind.
Hamlet, act i. sc. 2.

King—Not all the water in the rough rude sea
Can wash the balm off from an anointed *king*.
King Richard II, act iii. sc. 2.

King—The *king's* name is a tower of strength.
King Richard III, act v. sc. 3.

King—Whiles he thought to steal the single ten,
The *King* was slyly finger'd from the deck.
King Henry VI, part iii. act v. sc. 1.

King— Do not fear our person:
There's such divinity doth hedge a *king*,
That treason can but peep to what it would,
Acts little of his will. *Hamlet*, act iv. sc. 5.

King—Ay, every inch a *king*.
King Lear, act iv. sc. 6.

King—Now lie I like a *king*.
King Henry V, act iv. sc. 1.

Kings—Such is the breath of *kings*.
King Richard II, act i. sc. 3.

Kings—It is the curse of *kings* to be attended
By slaves that take their humors for a warrant.
King John, act iv. sc. 2.

Knaves—Whip me such honest *knaves*.
Othello, act i. sc. 1.

Knell—Hear it not, Duncan; for it is a *knell*
That summons thee to heaven or to hell.
Macbeth, act ii. sc. 1.

Know—Lord, we *know* what we are, but *know* not what we may be. *Hamlet*, act iv. sc. 5.

L

Labor—I have had my *labor* for my travail.
Troilus and Cressida, act i. sc. 1.

Ladies— The *ladies* call him sweet:
The stairs, as he treads on them, kiss his feet.
Love's Labor's Lost, act v. sc. 2.

Lady—The *lady* doth protest too much, methinks.
Hamlet, act iii. sc. 2.

Laid—Well said; that was *laid* on with a trowel.
As You Like It, act i. sc. 2.

Lame—O most *lame* and impotent conclusion!
Othello, act ii. sc. 1.

Lards— Falstaff sweats to death,
And *lards* the lean earth as he walks along.
King Henry IV, part i. act ii. sc. 2.

Last—Though *last*, not least, in love.
Julius Cæsar, act iii. sc. 1.

Late—Too early seen unknown, and known too *late*.
Romeo and Juliet, act i. sc. 5.

Latin—Away with him, away with him! he speaks *Latin*.
King Henry VI, part ii. act iv. sc. 7.

Laugh—They *laugh* that win. *Othello*, act iv. sc. 2.

Law—Still you keep o' the windy side of the *law*.
Twelfth Night, act iii. sc. 4.

Law—1. But is this *law*?
2. Ay, marry is't; crowner's quest *law*.
Hamlet, act v. sc. 1.

Lawyers—The first thing we do, let's kill all the *lawyers*. *King Henry VI*, part ii. act iv. sc. 2.

Leap—Methinks, it were an easy *leap*
To pluck bright honor from the pale-faced moon.
King Henry IV, part i. act i. sc. 3.

Learning—O this *learning!* what a thing it is!
Taming of the Shrew, act i. sc. 2.

Leave— *Leave* her to Heaven,
And to those thorns that in her bosom lodge,
To prick and sting her. *Hamlet*, act i. sc. 5.

Liberty— I must have *liberty*
Withal, as large a charter as the wind,
To blow on whom I please.
As You Like It, act ii. sc. 7.

Lie—The *lie* circumstantial, and the *lie* direct.
As You Like It, act v. sc. 4.

Lie—If I do *lie*, and do no harm by it, though the gods hear, I hope they'll pardon it.
Cymbeline, act iv. sc. 2.

Lies—*Lies* like truth. *Macbeth*, act v. sc. 5.

Life— Reason thus with *life:*
If I lose thee, I do lose a thing
That none but fools would keep: a breath thou art,

(Servile to all the skyey influences,)
That dost this habitation, where thou keepest,
Hourly afflict. *Measure for Measure*, act iii. sc. 1.

Life—The wine of *life* is drawn, and the mere lees
Is left this vault to brag of. *Macbeth*, act ii. sc. 3.

Life—The web of our *life* is of a mingled yarn, good and ill together.
All's Well that Ends Well, act iv. sc. 3.

Light—But, soft! what *light* through yonder window
breaks?
It is the east, and Juliet is my sun!
Romeo and Juliet, act ii. sc. 2.

Light—*Light*, seeking *light*, doth *light* of *light* beguile.
Love's Labor's Lost, act i. sc. 1.

Lion—Dost thou hear the Nemean *lion* roar?
Love's Labor's Lost, act iv. sc. 1.

Lion—Hear the *lion* roar. *King John*, act ii. sc. 1.

Lips—Their *lips* were four red roses on a stalk.
King Richard III, act iv. sc. 3.

Loaf— And easy it is
Of a cut *loaf* to steal a shive, we know.
Titus Andronicus, act ii. sc. 1.

Looked—No sooner met, but they *looked*; no sooner *looked*, but they loved; no sooner loved, but they sighed; no sooner sighed, but they asked one another the reason. *As You Like It*, act v. sc. 2.

Looker-on— My business in this state
Made me a *looker-on* here in Vienna.
Measure for Measure, act v. sc. 1.

Lord—*Lord* of thy presence, and no land beside.
King John, act i. sc. 1.

Love—Fie, fie! how wayward is this foolish *love*,
That, like a testy babe, will scratch the nurse,
And presently all humbled, kiss the rod!
Two Gentlemen of Verona, act i. sc. 2.

Love—But *love* is blind, and lovers cannot see
The pretty follies that themselves commit.
Merchant of Venice, act ii. sc. 6.

Love—Stony limits cannot hold *love* out;
And what *love* can do, that dares *love* attempt.
Romeo and Juliet, act ii. sc. 2.

Love—How to know a man in *love*—your hose should be ungartered, your bonnet unbanded, your sleeve unbuttoned, your shoe untied, and every thing about you demonstrating a careless desolation.
As You Like It, act iii. sc. 2.

Love—*Love* sought is good, but given unsought is better. *Twelfth Night*, act iii. sc. 1.

Love—*Love* thyself last.
King Henry VIII, act iii. sc. 2.

Lov'd—Who ever *lov'd* that *lov'd* not at first sight?
As You Like it, act iii. sc. 5.

Lowliness—*Lowliness* is young ambition's ladder,
Whereto the climber upward turns his face;
But when he once attains the utmost round,
He then unto the ladder turns his back,
Looks in the clouds, scorning the base degrees
By which he did ascend. *Julius Cæsar*, act ii. sc. 1.

Lunes—In his old *lunes* again.
Merry Wives of Windsor, act iv. sc. 2.

Lure—O, for a falconer's voice
To *lure* this tassel-gentle back again.
Romeo and Juliet, act ii. sc. 2.

Lying—Lord, lord, how the world is given to *lying!*
I grant you I was down, and out of breath; and so

was he: but we rose both at an instant, and fought a long hour by Shrewsbury clock.
King Henry IV, part i. act v. sc. 4.

M

Macduff— Lay on, *Macduff;*
And damned be him that first cries, Hold, enough!
Macbeth, act v. sc. 8.

Mad— By mine honesty,
If she be *mad*, as I believe no other,
Her madness hath the oddest frame of sense
(Such a dependency of thing on thing)
As e'er I heard in madness.
Measure for Measure, act v. sc. 1.

Mad—That he is *mad*, 'tis true; 'tis true, 'tis pity;
And pity 'tis 'tis true. *Hamlet*, act ii. sc. 2.

Madness—Why this is very midsummer *madness*.
Twelfth Night, act iii. sc. 4.

Madness—Though this be *madness*, yet there's method in it. *Hamlet*, act ii. sc. 2.

Madness— It shall be so;
Madness in great ones must not unwatch'd go.
Hamlet, act iii. sc. 1.

Madness— Bring me to the test,
And I the matter will re-word: which *madness*
Would gambol from. *Hamlet*, act iii. sc. 4.

Maid—The chariest *maid* is prodigal enough,
If she unmask her beauty to the moon;
Virtue itself 'scapes not calumnious strokes.
Hamlet, act i. sc. 3.

Maiden—In *maiden* meditation, fancy free.
Midsummer-Night's Dream, act ii. sc. 1.

Man—What a piece of work is *man!* how noble in reason! how infinite in faculty! in form and moving, how express and admirable! in action how like an angel, in apprehension how like a God!
Hamlet, act ii. sc. 2.

Man—A proper *man*, as one shall see in a summer's day. *Midsummer-Night's Dream*, act i. sc. 2.

Man—A poor, infirm, weak, and despised old *man*.
King Lear, act iii. sc. 2.

Man—Life is as tedious as a twice-told tale,
Vexing the dull ear of a drowsy *man*.
King John, act iii. sc. 4.

Man—*Man* delights not me,—no, nor woman neither.
Hamlet, act ii. sc. 2.

Man—A good old *man*, sir; he will be talking.
Much Ado about Nothing, act iii. sc. 5.

Man—God made him, and therefore let him pass for a *man*. *Merchant of Venice*, act i. sc. 2.

Man—And now am I, if a *man* should speak truly, little better than one of the wicked.
King Henry IV, part i. act i. sc. 2.

Man—A needy, hollow-eyed, sharp-looking wretch,
A living dead *man*. *Comedy of Errors*, act v. sc. 1.

Man—A *man* of my kidney.
Merry Wives of Windsor, act iii. sc. 5.

Man—He was a *man*, take him for all in all,
I shall not look upon his like again.
Hamlet, act i. sc. 2.

Man—That *man* that hath a tongue, I say, is no *man!*
If with his tongue he cannot win a woman.
Two Gentlemen of Verona, act iii. sc. 1.

Many— *Many* a time and oft,
In the Rialto, you have rated me.
Merchant of Venice, act i. sc. 3.

March—Remember *March*, the ides of *March* remember! *Julius Cæsar*, act iv. sc. 3.

Marigold—The *marigold*, that goes to bed with the sun,
And with him rises weeping.
Winter's Tale, act iv. sc. 3.

Married—As a walled town is more worthier than a village, so is the forehead of a *married* man more honorable than the bare brow of a bachelor.
As You Like It, act iii. sc. 3.

Marry—I will *marry* her, sir, at your request; but if there be no great love in the beginning, yet Heaven may decrease it upon better acquaintance:—I hope, upon familiarity will grow more contempt;——I will *marry* her, that I am freely dissolved, and dissolutely. *Merry Wives of Windsor*, act i. sc. 1.

Marshal'st—Thou *marshal'st* me the way that I was going. *Macbeth*, act ii. sc. 1.

Master—Think of that, *Master* Brook.
Merry Wives of Windsor, act iii. sc. 5.

Matter—I'll read you *matter* deep and dangerous.
King Henry IV, part i. act i. sc. 3.

Medicine—The miserable have no other *medicine*,
But only hope. *Measure for Measure*, act iii. sc. 1.

Medicines—If the rascal have not given me *medicines* to make me love him, I'll be hanged.
King Henry IV, part i. act ii. sc. 2.

Melting—Albeit unused to the *melting* mood.
Othello, act v. sc. 2.

Memory— Remember thee?
Ay, thou poor ghost, while *memory* holds a seat
In this distracted globe. Remember thee?

Yea, from the table of my *memory*
I'll wipe away all trivial, fond records.
Hamlet, act i. sc. 5.

Men—Play the *men*. *Tempest*, act i. sc. 1.

Men— *Men* must endure
Their going hence, even as their coming hither.
King Lear, act v. sc. 2.

Men—*Men* are April when they woo, December when they wed. *As You Like It*, act iv. sc. 1.

Men—*Men* have died, from time to time, and worms have eaten them; but not for love.
As You Like It, act iv. sc. 1.

Men—O, what *men* dare do! what *men* may do! what *men* daily do! not knowing what they do.
Much Ado about Nothing, act iv. sc. 1.

Mercy—Sweet *Mercy* is nobility's true badge.
Titus Andronicus, act i. sc. 2.

Mercy—There is no more *mercy* in him than there is milk in a male tiger. *Coriolanus*, act v. sc. 4.

Merry—I am not *merry;* but I do beguile
The thing I am, by seeming otherwise.
Othello, act ii. sc. 1.

Merry—I am never *merry* when I hear sweet music.
Merchant of Venice, act v. sc. 1.

Merry—How oft, when men are at the point of death,
Have they been *merry?*
Romeo and Juliet, act v. sc. 3.

Merry—And if you can be *merry* then, I'll say
A man may weep upon his wedding day.
King Henry VIII, Prologue.

Metal—Here's *metal* more attractive.
Hamlet, act iii. sc. 2.

Micher—Shall the blessed sun of heaven prove a *micher* and eat blackberries?
King Henry IV, part i. act ii. sc. 4.

Miching—This is *miching* mallecho; it means mischief.
Hamlet, act iii. sc. 2.

Mildly—Well, *mildly* be it then, *mildly*.
Coriolanus, act iii. sc. 2.

Mile— They have measured many a *mile*
To tread a measure with you on this grass.
Love's Labor's Lost, act v. sc. 2.

Milk— Yet do I fear thy nature;
It is too full of the *milk* of human kindness.
Macbeth, act i. sc. 5.

Mind—O, what a noble *mind* is here o'erthrown!
The courtier's, soldier's, scholar's eye, tongue, sword.
Hamlet, act iii. sc. 1.

Mind—'Tis the *mind* that makes the body rich.
Taming of the Shrew, act iv. sc. 3.

Minister—Canst thou not *minister* to a mind diseas'd?
Pluck from the memory a rooted sorrow;
Raze out the written troubles of the brain;
And, with some sweet oblivious antidote,
Cleanse the stuff'd bosom of that perilous stuff,
Which weighs upon the heart?
Macbeth, act v. sc. 3.

Minnows—Hear you this Triton of the *minnows?*
Coriolanus, act iii. sc. 1.

Mirror—To hold, as 'twere, the *mirror* up to nature.
Hamlet, act iii. sc. 2.

Mirth— A merrier man
Within the limit of becoming *mirth*
I never spent an hour's talk withal.
Love's Labor's Lost, act ii. sc. 1.

Mirth—From the crown of his head to the sole of his foot he is all *mirth*.
Much Ado about Nothing, act iii. sc. 2.

Mirth—I have of late (but, wherefore, I know not) lost all my *mirth*, foregone all custom of exercises.
Hamlet, act ii. sc. 2.

Mirth—Prepare for *mirth*, for *mirth* becomes a feast.
Pericles, act ii. sc. 3.

Mischief—To mourn a *mischief* that is past and gone,
Is the next way to draw new *mischief* on.
Othello, act i. sc. 3.

Misery— *Misery* doth part
The flux of company; anon, a careless herd,
Full of the pasture, jumps along by him,
And never stays to greet him: "Ay," quoth Jaques,
"Sweep on, you fat and greasy citizens;
'Tis just the fashion: wherefore do you look
Upon that poor and broken bankrupt there?"
As You Like It, act ii. sc. 1.

Moan— Let us pay betimes
A moiety of that mass of *moan* to come.
Troilus and Cressida, act ii. sc. 2.

Mockery—Unreal *mockery*, hence!
Macbeth, act iii. sc. 4.

Money—He that wants *money*, means, and content, is without three good friends.
As You Like It, act iii. sc. 2.

Monster— O beware, my lord, of jealousy;
It is the green-ey'd *monster*, which doth mock
The meat it feeds on. *Othello*, act iii. sc. 3.

Month—A little *month*, ere yet those shoes were old.
Hamlet, act i. sc. 2.

Monument—When old Time shall lead him to his end,
Goodness and he fill up one *monument*.
King Henry VIII, act ii. sc. 1.

Moonlight—How sweet the *moonlight* sleeps upon this bank! *Merchant of Venice*, act v. sc. 1.

Morn—The *morn*, in russet mantle clad,
Walks o'er the dew of yon high eastward hill.
Hamlet, act i. sc. 1.

Mother—That would hang us every *mother's* son.
Midsummer-Night's Dream, act i. sc. 2.

Motley—*Motley's* the only wear.
As You Like It, act ii. sc. 7.

Mouths— Your name is great
In *mouths* of wisest censure. *Othello*, act ii. sc. 3.

Murder will out— Foul deeds will rise,
Tho' all the earth o'erwhelm them, to men's eyes.
Hamlet, act i. sc. 2.

Murder—For *murder*, though it have no tongue, will speak
With most miraculous organ. *Hamlet*, act ii. sc. 2.

Murther—*Murther* most foul, as in the best it is.
Hamlet, act i. sc. 5.

Music—If *music* be the food of love, play on,
Give me excess of it; that surfeiting,
The appetite may sicken, and so die.
That strain again;—it had a dying fall:
O, it came o'er my ear like the sweet sound
That breathes upon a bank of violets,
Stealing and giving odor.
Twelfth Night, act i. sc. 1.

Music—When griping grief the heart doth wound,
And doleful dumps the mind oppress,
Then *music*, with his silver sound
With speedy help doth lend redress.
Romeo and Juliet, act iv. sc. 5.

Mystery—Pluck out the heart of my *mystery*.
Hamlet, act iii. sc. 2.

N

Naked—And thus I clothe my *naked* villainy
With old odd ends, stol'n out of holy writ,
And seem a saint when most I play the devil.
King Richard III, act i. sc. 3.

Name—*Auf.* What is thy *name?*
Cor. A name unmusical to Volscian's ears,
And harsh in sound to thine.
Coriolanus, act iv. sc. 5.

Nature— Now, by two-headed Janus,
Nature hath framed strange fellows in her time.
Merchant of Venice, act i. sc. 1.

Nature—One touch of *Nature* makes the whole world kin. *Troilus and Cressida*, act iii. sc. 3.

Necessity—Are you content to be our general?
To make a virtue of *necessity*,
And live, as we do, in this wilderness?
Two Gentlemen of Verona, act iv. sc. 1.

Necessity—I'd rather dwell in my *necessity*.
Merchant of Venice, act i. sc. 3.

Necessity's pinch— And choose
To wage against the enmity o' the air;
To be a comrade with the wolf and owl,—
Necessity's sharp *pinch!* *King Lear*, act ii. sc. 4.

Neither—'Tis *neither* here nor there.
Othello, act iv. sc. 3.

Nestor—Though *Nestor* swear the jest be laughable.
Merchant of Venice, act i. sc. 1.

News—The first bringer of unwelcome *news*
Hath but a losing office.
King Henry IV, part ii. act i. sc. 1.

Night—Making *night* hideous. *Hamlet*, act i. sc. 4.

Night— This sweaty haste
Doth make the *night* joint-laborer with the day.
Hamlet, act i. sc. 1.

Night—The *night* is long that never finds the day.
Macbeth, act iv. sc. 3.

Ninth—But, in the way of bargain, mark ye me,
I'll cavil on the *ninth* part of a hair.
King Henry IV, part i. act iii. sc. 1.

Niobe—Like *Niobe*, all tears. *Hamlet*, act i. sc. 2.

No—*No* more of that, Hal, and thou lovest me.
King Henry IV, part i. act ii. sc. 4.

Not—Thou troublest me; I am *not* in the vein.
King Richard III, act iv. sc. 2.

Note—I'll *note* you in my book of memory.
King Henry VI, part i. act ii. sc. 4.

Note— *Note* this before my notes.
There's not a *note* of mine that's worth the noting.
Much Ado about Nothing, act ii. sc. 3.

Note-book—I will make a prief of it in my *note-book*.
Merry Wives of Windsor, act i. sc. 1.

Nothing—When I told you
My state was *nothing*, I should then have told you
That I was worse than *nothing*.
Merchant of Venice, act iii. sc. 2.

Nothing—Gratiano speaks an infinite deal of *nothing*.
Merchant of Venice, act i. sc. 1.

Nothing— *Nothing* in his life
Became him like the leaving it.
Macbeth, act i. sc. 4.

Nunnery—Get thee to a *nunnery*.
Hamlet, act iii. sc. 1.

Nymph— *Nymph*, in thy orisons
Be all my sins remembered. *Hamlet*, act iii. sc. 1.

O

Oath—A good mouth-filling *oath*.
King Henry IV, part i. act iii. sc. 1.

Obey—I shall in all my best *obey* you, madam.
Hamlet, act i. sc. 2.

Obscure—And my large kingdom for a little grave,
A little, little grave, an *obscure* grave.
King Richard II, act iii. sc. 3.

Off—*Off* with his head! so much for Buckingham.
King Richard III, act iv. sc. 3.

Offence—All's not *offence* that indiscretion finds.
King Lear, act ii. sc. 4.

Offence—Every *offence* is not a hate at first.
Merchant of Venice, act iv. sc. 1.

Offence—Oh, my *offence* is rank, it smells to heaven!
Hamlet, act iii. sc. 3.

Old—*Old* John of Gaunt, time-honor'd Lancaster.
King Richard II, act i. sc. 1.

Old—An *old* man is twice a child.
Hamlet, act ii. sc. 2.

Opinion—A plague of *opinion!* a man may wear it on both sides, like a leathern jerkin.
Troilus and Cressida, act iii. sc. 3.

Oracle—I am *Sir Oracle*,
And when I ope my lips let no dog bark!
Merchant of Venice, act i. sc. 1.

Orators—Very good *orators*: when they are out, they will spit. *As You Like It*, act iv. sc. 1.

Othello's occupation—*Othello's occupation's* gone.
Othello, act iii. sc. 3.

Out-Herods—It *out-Herods* Herod.
Hamlet, act iii. sc. 2.

Out—*Out*; damned spot! *out* I say.
Macbeth, act v. sc. 1.

Out—*Out*, *out*, brief candle! *Macbeth*, act v. sc. 5.

Out—*Out* of my door, you witch!
Merry Wives of Windsor, act iv. sc. 2.

Oyster—Why, then the world's mine *oyster*,
Which I with sword will open.
Merry Wives of Windsor, act ii. sc. 2.

Oyster—I will not be sworn but love may transform me to an *oyster*: but I'll take my oath on it, till he have made an *oyster* of me he shall never make me such a fool. *Much Ado about Nothing*, act ii. sc. 3.

P

Paddle—Did'st thou see her *paddle* with the palm
Of his hand? did'st not mark that?
Othello, act ii. sc. 1.

Paddling—But to be *paddling* palms, and pinching fingers,
As now they are; and making practis'd smiles,
As in a looking-glass; and then to sigh——
O, that is entertainment
My bosom likes not, nor my brows!
Winter's Tale, act i. sc. 2.

Paid—He is well *paid* that is well satisfied.
Merchant of Venice, act iv. sc. 1.

Pain—The labor we delight in physics *pain*.
Macbeth, act ii. sc. 3.

Palpable—A hit, a very *palpable* hit!
Hamlet, act v. sc. 2.

Palsied—*Palsied* eld.
Measure for Measure, act iii. sc. 1.

Pansies—There's rosemary: that's for remembrance;
. . . . and there is *pansies:* that's for thoughts.
Hamlet, act iv. sc. 5.

Paper-mill—Thou hast most traitorously corrupted the youth of the realm, in erecting a grammar-school: and whereas, before, our forefathers had no other books but the score and the tally, thou hast caused printing to be used; and, contrary to the King, his crown and dignity, thou hast built a *paper-mill.*
King Henry VI, part ii. act iv. sc. 7.

Paragon'd—*Paragon'd* o' the world.
King Henry VIII, act ii. sc. 4.

Parchment—Is not this a lamentable thing, that of the skin of an innocent lamb should be made *parchment?* that *parchment*, being scribbled o'er, should undo a man? *King Henry VI*, part ii. act iv. sc. 2.

Parish—The why is plain as way to *parish* church.
As You Like It, act ii. sc. 7.

Parting—Good-night, good-night! *parting* is such sweet sorrow,
That I shall say good-night till it be morrow.
Romeo and Juliet, act ii. sc. 2.

Parting—This *parting* heart strikes poor lovers dumb.
Two Gentlemen of Verona, act ii. sc. 2.

Passeth—But I have that within which *passeth* show;
These but the trappings and the suits of woe.
Hamlet, act i. sc. 2.

Passing— My story being done,
She gave me for my pains a world of sighs:
She swore, in faith, 'twas strange, 'twas *passing* strange;

'Twas pitiful, 'twas wondrous pitiful;
She wished she had not heard it: yet she wished
That heaven had made her such a man.
Othello, act i. sc. 3.

Past—*Past* corporal toil. *King Henry V*, act i. sc. 1.

Past—*Iago*. What! are you hurt, lieutenant?
Cassio. Ay, *past* all surgery.
Othello, act ii. sc. 3.

Patches—A king of shreds and *patches*.
Hamlet, act iii. sc. 4.

Patience— *Patience* and sorrow strove
Who should express her goodliest.
King Lear, act iv. sc. 3.

Patience— 'Tis all men's office to speak *patience*
To those that wring under the load of sorrow;
But no man's virtue, nor sufficiency,
To be so moral, when he shall endure
The like himself.
Much Ado about Nothing, act v. sc. 1.

Patient— Therein the *patient*
Must minister to himself. *Macbeth*, act v. sc. 3.

Paunches—Fat *paunches* have lean pates; and dainty bits
Make rich the ribs, but bankerout the wits.
Love's Labor's Lost, act i. sc. 1.

Pause—I *pause* for a reply.
Julius Cæsar, act iii. sc. 2.

Pays—Base is the slave that *pays*.
King Henry V, act ii. sc. 1.

Peace—He gave his honors to the world again,
His blessed part to Heaven, and slept in *peace*.
King Henry VIII, act iv. sc. 2.

Peace— *Peace*, sit you down,
And let me wring your heart: for so I shall,
If it be made of penetrable stuff.
Hamlet, act iii. sc. 4.

Peace—Why, I, in this weak piping time of *peace*,
Have no delight to pass away the time.
King Richard III, act i. sc. 1.

Pearl— Of one whose hand,
Like the base Indian, threw a *pearl* away
Richer than all his tribe. *Othello*, act v. sc. 2.

Peers—Brave *peers* of England, pillars of the state.
King Henry VI, part ii. act i. sc. 1.

Pelting—Poor naked wretches, wheresoe'er you are,
That bide the *pelting* of this pitiless storm,
How shall your houseless heads, and unfed sides,
Your looped and windowed raggedness, defend you
From seasons such as these?
King Lear, act iii. sc. 4.

Perilous—That's a *perilous* shot out of an elder gun.
King Henry V, act iv. sc. 1.

Perjuries— At lover's *perjuries*,
They say, Jove laughs.
Romeo and Juliet, act ii. sc. 2.

Perjury—Shall I lay *perjury* upon my soul?
No, not for Venice.
Merchant of Venice, act iv. sc. 1.

Perusal—He falls to such *perusal* of my face
As he would draw it. *Hamlet*, act ii. sc. 1.

Philippi—I will see thee at *Philippi* then.
Julius Cæsar, act iv. sc. 3.

Philosopher—For there was never yet *philosopher*
That could endure the toothache patiently.
Much Ado about Nothing, act v. sc. 1.

Philosophy—Hast any *philosophy* in thee, shepherd?
As You Like It, act iii. sc. 2.

Phœbus—Hark! hark! the lark at heaven's gate sings,
And *Phœbus'* gins arise. *Cymbeline*, act ii. sc. 3.

Physic— Take *physic*, pomp;
Expose thyself to feel what wretches feel.
King Lear, act iii. sc. 4.

Pia mater—These are begot in the ventricle of memory, nourished in the womb of *pia mater*, and delivered upon the mellowing of occasion.
Love's Labor's Lost, act iv. sc. 2.

Pictures—The sleeping and the dead
Are but as *pictures*. *Macbeth*, act ii. sc. 2.

Pinch— Along with them
They brought one *Pinch*, a hungry, lean-faced villain,
A mere anatomy, a mountebank.
Comedy of Errors, act v. sc. 1.

Pin's fee—I do not set my life at a *pin's fee*.
Hamlet, act i. sc. 4.

Pipe—They are not a *pipe* for Fortune's finger
To sound what stop she please. Give me that man
That is not passion's slave, and I will wear him
In my heart's core, ay, in my heart of heart,
As I do thee. *Hamlet*, act iii. sc. 2.

Pity—Are not within the leaf of *pity* writ.
Timon of Athens, act iv. sc. 3.

Pity—But yet the *pity* of it, Iago! O Iago, the *pity* of it, Iago! *Othello*, act iv. sc. 1.

Plain—Mark, now, how a *plain* tale shall put you down.
King Henry IV, part i. act ii. sc. 1.

Play— The *play's* the thing,
Wherein I'll catch the conscience of the king.
Hamlet, act ii. sc. 2.

Players—O, there be *players* that I have seen play, and heard others praise, and that highly, not to speak it profanely, that, neither having the accent of Christians, nor the gait of Christian, pagan, nor man, have so strutted and bellowed, that I have thought some of Nature's journeymen had made men, and not made them well, they imitated humanity so abominably. *Hamlet*, act iii. sc. 2.

Plentiful—They have a *plentiful* lack of wit.
Hamlet, act ii. sc. 2.

Plummet—Deeper than did ever *plummet* sound,
I'll drown my book. *Tempest*, act v. sc. 1.

Poetical—Truly, I would the gods had made thee *poetical!* *As You Like It*, act iii. sc. 3.

Poison—Sweet, sweet, sweet *poison* for the age's tooth.
King John, act i. sc. 1.

Pool—The green mantle of the standing *pool*.
King Lear, act iii. sc. 4.

Poor—*Poor* and content, is rich, and rich enough;
But riches, fineless, is as poor as winter,
To him that ever fears he shall be *poor*.
Othello, act iii. sc. 3.

Poppy— Not *poppy* nor mandragora,
Nor all the drowsy syrups of the world,
Shall ever medicine thee to that sweet sleep
Which thou ow'dst yesterday. *Othello*, act iii. sc. 3.

Ports—All places that the eye of Heaven visits
Are to a wise man *ports* and happy havens.
King Richard II, act i. sc. 3.

Potations—*Potations* pottle deep. *Othello*, act ii. sc. 3.

Potent—Most *potent*, grave, and reverend signiors.
Othello, act i. sc. 3.

Poverty—My *poverty*, but not my will, consents.
Romeo and Juliet, act v. sc. 1.

Poverty—Steeped me in *poverty* to the very lips.
Othello, act iv. sc. 2.

Praising— *Praising* what is lost
Makes the remembrance dear.
All's Well that Ends Well, act v. sc. 3.

Prayer-book—See, where his grace stands 'tween two clergymen!
And, see, a *book of prayer* in his hand!
True ornaments to know a holy man.
King Richard III, act iii. sc. 7.

Present— *Present* fears
Are less than horrible imaginings.
Macbeth, act i. sc. 3.

Press—*Press* not a falling man too far.
King Henry VIII, act iii. sc. 2.

Presumption—It is *presumption* in us, when
The help of heaven we count the act of men.
All's Well that Ends Well, act ii. sc. 1.

Prey— If I do prove her haggard,
Though that her jesses were my dear heart-strings,
I'd whistle her off, and let her down the wind
To *prey* at fortune. *Othello*, act iii. sc. 3.

Priam's curtain—Even such a man, so faint, so spiritless,
So dull, so dead in looks, so woe-begone,
Drew *Priam's curtain* in the dead of night,
And would have told him half his Troy was burned.
King Henry IV, part ii. act i. sc. 1.

Pricking—By the *pricking* of my thumbs,
Something wicked this way comes.
Macbeth, act iv. sc. 1.

Pride—*Pride*, pomp, and circumstance of glorious war.
Othello, act iii. sc. 3.

Pride—My *pride* fell with my fortunes.
As You Like It, act i. sc. 2.

Prize— It so falls out,
That what we have we *prize* not to the worth
Whiles we enjoy it; but being lack'd and lost,
Why then we rack the value; then we find
The virtue that possession would not show us
Whiles it was ours.
Much Ado about Nothing, act ii. sc. 1.

Prodigal—Shall I keep your hogs, and eat husks with them? What *prodigal* portion have I spent, that I should come to such penury?
As You Like It, act i. sc. 1.

Profit—No *profit* grows where is no pleasure ta'en;
In brief, sir, study what you most affect.
Taming of the Shrew, act i. sc. 1.

Prologues— Two truths are told,
As happy *prologues* to the swelling act
Of the imperial theme. *Macbeth*, act i. sc. 3.

Promotion—O good old man, how well in thee appears
The constant service of the antique world,
When service sweat for duty, not for meed!
Thou art not for the fashion of these times,
Where none will sweat but for *promotion*,
As You Like It, act ii. sc. 3.

Proof—Give me the ocular *proof*.
Othello, act iii. sc. 3.

Prophetic—O my *prophetic* soul! my uncle!
Hamlet, act i. sc. 5.

Proportion—I, that am curtailed of this fair *proportion*,
Cheated of feature by dissembling nature,
Deformed, unfinished, sent before my time
Into this breathing world, scarce half made up.
King Richard III, act i. sc. 1.

Prosperity—A jest's *prosperity* lies in the ear
Of him that hears it, never in the tongue
Of him that makes it.
Love's Labor's Lost, act v. sc. 2.

Proud—*Proud* setter-up and puller-down of kings.
King Henry VI, part iii. act iii. sc. 3.

Prouder—*Prouder* than rustling in unpaid-for silk.
Cymbeline, act iii. sc. 3.

Prove—I will *prove* it legitimate, sir, upon the oaths of judgment and reason.
Twelfth Night, act iii. sc. 2.

Purge—*Purge*, and leave sack, and live cleanly.
King Henry IV, part i. act v. sc. 4.

Puritan—But one *Puritan* amongst them, and he sings psalms to hornpipes.
Winter's Tale, act iv. sc. 2.

Purpose—Infirm of *purpose*. *Macbeth*, act ii. sc. 2.

Purse—Put money in thy *purse*. *Othello*, act i. sc. 3.

Purses—Lies in their *purses*; and whoso empties them,
By so much fills their hearts with deadly hate.
King Richard II, act ii. sc. 2.

Q

Quality—Come, give us a taste of your *quality*.
Hamlet, act ii. sc. 2.

Quarrel—Put we our *quarrel* to the will of Heaven,
Who, when he sees the hours ripe on earth,
Will rain hot vengeance on offenders' heads.
King Richard II, act i. sc. 2.

Quarrel—Greatly to find *quarrel* in a straw,
When honor's at the stake. *Hamlet*, act iv. sc. 4.

Quarrels—Thy head is as full of *quarrels* as an egg is full of meat. *Romeo and Juliet*, act iii. sc. 1.

Quarry—Your castle is surprised; your wife and babes
Savagely slaughtered: to relate the manner
Were, on the *quarry* of these murdered deer,
To add the death of you. *Macbeth*, act iv. sc. 3.

Question'd—Her father loved me; oft invited me;
Still *question'd* me the story of my life
From year to year; the battles, sieges, fortunes,
That I have pass'd. *Othello*, act i. sc. 3.

R

Rain—The quality of mercy is not strained;
It droppeth, as the gentle *rain* from heaven
Upon the place beneath: it is twice blessed;
It blesseth him that gives, and him that takes.
'Tis mightiest in the mightiest; it becomes
The throned monarch better than his crown:
His sceptre shows the force of temporal power,
The attribute to awe and majesty,
Wherein doth sit the dread and fear of kings:
But mercy is above this sceptred sway;
It is enthroned in the hearts of kings,
It is an attribute to God Himself;
And earthly power doth then show likest God's
When mercy seasons justice. Therefore, Jew,
Though justice be thy plea, consider this,—
That in the course of justice none of us
Should see salvation; we do pray for mercy;
And that same prayer doth teach us all to render
The deeds of mercy.
Merchant of Venice, act iv. sc. 1.

Rascals—And put in every honest hand a whip,
To lash the *rascals* naked through the world.
Othello, act iv. sc. 2.

Razure— 'Gainst the tooth of time
And *razure* of oblivion.
Measure for Measure, act v. sc. 1.

Reason—I have no other but a woman's *reason*:
I think him so, because I think him so.
Two Gentlemen of Verona, act i. sc. 2.

Reason—Neither rhyme nor *reason* can express how much. *As You Like It*, act iii. sc. 2.

Reason— The insane root
That takes the *reason* prisoner.
Macbeth, act i. sc. 3.

Reasons—His *reasons* are two grains of wheat hid in two bushels of chaff; you shall seek all day ere you find them; and when you have found them they are not worth the search
Merchant of Venice, act i. sc. 1.

Reckoning—I am ill at *reckoning*; it fits the spirit of a tapster. *Love's Labor's Lost*, act i. sc. 2.

Reckoning—Ruminates like an hostess that hath no arithmetic but her brain to set down her *reckoning*.
Troilus and Cressida, act iii. sc. 3.

Reform—O, *reform* it altogether.
Hamlet, act iii. sc. 2.

Relief—For this *relief*, much thanks.
Hamlet, act i. sc. 1.

Remedies—Our *remedies* oft in ourselves do lie
Which we ascribe to Heaven.
All's Well that Ends Well, act i. sc. 1.

Remedy— Things without all *remedy*
Should be without regard: what's done is done.
Macbeth, act iii. sc. 2.

Remuneration—Biron. What is a *remuneration?*
Costard. Marry, sir, halfpenny farthing.
Love's Labor's Lost, act iii. sc. 1.

Report—Report me and my cause aright.
Hamlet, act v. sc. 2.

Reproof—I have a touch of your condition,
That cannot brook the accent of *reproof.*
King Richard III, act iv. sc. 4.

Reputation—Thou liest in *reputation* sick.
King Richard II, act ii. sc. 1.

Respect—You have too much *respect* upon the world:
They lose it that do buy it with much care.
Merchant of Venice, act i. sc. 1.

Rest—Rest thy unrest on England's lawful earth.
King Richard III, act iv. sc. 4.

Rest—So may he *rest;* his faults lie gently on him!
King Henry VIII, act iv. sc. 2.

Rest—One that was a woman, sir, but, *rest* her soul, she's dead. *Hamlet*, act v. sc. 1.

Rest—Sleep dwell upon thine eyes, peace in thy breast!—
Would I were sleep and peace, so sweet to *rest.*
Romeo and Juliet, act ii. sc. 2.

Retort—The *retort* courteous.
As You Like It, act v. sc. 4.

Revenge—Haste me to know it; that I, with wings as swift
As meditation, or the thoughts of love,
May sweep to my *revenge.* *Hamlet*, act i. sc. 5.

Rhyme and Reason—D. In *Reason* nothing.
B. Something then in *Rhyme.*
Love's Labor's Lost, act i. sc. 1.

Rich—Rich gifts wax poor when givers prove unkind.
Hamlet, act iii. sc. 1.

Ripe—From hour to hour, we *ripe* and *ripe*,
And then, from hour to hour, we rot and rot,
And thereby hangs a tale.
As You Like It, act ii. sc. 7.

Rob—*Rob* me the Exchequer the first thing thou doest.
King Henry IV, part i. act iii. sc. 3.

Robbed—He that is *robbed*, not wanting what is stolen,
Let him not know it, and he is not *robbed* at all.
Othello, act iii. sc. 3.

Robbed—The *robbed* that smiles steals something from the thief. *Othello*, act i. sc. 3.

Robes—Through tattered clothes small vices do appear;
Robes and furred gowns hide all.
King Lear, act iv. sc. 6.

Rod—Take thy correction mildly. Kiss the *rod*.
King Richard II, act v. sc. 1.

Roll—I am not in the *roll* of common men.
King Henry IV, part i. act iii. sc. 1.

Roman—This was the noblest *Roman* of them all.
Julius Cæsar, act v. sc. 5.

Romans—The last of all the *Romans*, fare thee well.
Julius Cæsar, act v. sc. 3.

Rome—*Rome* indeed, and room enough,
When there is in it but one only man.
Julius Cæsar, act i. sc. 2.

Romeo—O *Romeo, Romeo!* wherefore art thou *Romeo?*
Romeo and Juliet, act ii. sc. 2.

Rose—What's in a name? that which we call a *rose*
By any other name would smell as sweet.
Romeo and Juliet, act ii. sc. 2.

Roses—*Roses* have thorns, and silver fountains mud.
Sonnets.

Round—I will a *round*, unvarnished tale deliver
Of my whole course of love. *Othello*, act i. sc. 3.

Rude— *Rude* am I in my speech
And little bless'd with the soft phrase of peace.
Othello, act i. sc. 3.

Rumination—It is a melancholy of mine own, compounded of many simples, ... which, by often *rumination*, wraps me in a most humorous sadness.
As You Like It, act iv. sc. 1.

Run—But yet I *run* before my horse to market.
King Richard III, act i. sc. 2.

Russia—This will last out a night in *Russia*,
When nights are longest there.
Measure for Measure, act ii. sc. 1.

S

Sack—Oh, monstrous! but one halfpenny-worth of bread to this intolerable deal of *sack*.
King Henry IV, part i. act ii. sc. 4.

Sad—And nothing can we call our own but death,
And that small module of the barren earth
Which serves as paste and cover to our bones.
For Heaven's sake, let us sit upon the ground,
And tell *sad* stories of the death of kings.
King Richard II, act iii. sc. 2.

Salvation— About some act
That has no relish of *salvation* in't.
Hamlet, act iii. sc. 3.

Samphire— Half-way down
Hangs one that gathers *samphire*; dreadful trade!
Methinks he seems no bigger than his head:

The fishermen that walk upon the beach
Appear like mice. *King Lear*, act iv. sc. 6.

Sands—Now our *sands* are almost run.
Pericles, Prince of Tyre, act v. sc. 2.

Scandal— You know
That I do fawn on men, and hug them hard,
And after *scandal* them. *Julius Cæsar*, act i. sc. 2.

Scar— I'll not shed her blood;
Nor *scar* that whiter skin of hers than snow,
And smooth as alabaster. *Othello*, act v. sc. 2.

Scars—He jests at *scars* that never felt a wound.
Romeo and Juliet, act ii. sc. 2.

Scotched—We have *scotched* the snake, not killed it.
Macbeth, act iii. sc. 2.

Sea-maid's music—And certain stars shot madly from their spheres,
To hear the *sea-maid's music*.
Midsummer-Night's Dream, act ii. sc. 2.

Seals—Take, O take those lips away
That so sweetly were forsworn;
And those eyes, the break of day,
Lights that do mislead the morn;
But my kisses bring again, bring again,
Seals of love, but sealed in vain, sealed in vain.
Measure for Measure, act iv. sc. 1.

Seas— My hand will rather
The multitudinous *seas* incarnadine,
Making the green one red. *Macbeth*, act ii. sc. 2.

Season—*Season* your admiration for a while
With an attent ear. *Hamlet*, act i. sc. 2.

Season—How many things by *season* seasoned are
To their right praise and true perfection!
Merchant of Venice, act v. sc. 1.

Seated—And make my *seated* heart knock at my ribs.
Macbeth, act i. sc. 3.

Secrets— But that I am forbid
To tell the *secrets* of my prison-house,
I could a tale unfold whose lightest word
Would harrow up thy soul, freeze thy young blood,
Make thy two eyes, like stars, start from their spheres,
Thy knotted and combined locks to part.
Hamlet, act i. sc. 5.

Seeds—If you can look into the *seeds* of time,
And say which grain will grow, and which will not.
Macbeth, act i. sc. 3.

Seem—Men should be what they *seem*.
Othello, act iii. sc. 3.

Seems—*Seems*, madam! nay, it is; I know not "*seems*."
Hamlet, act i. sc. 2.

Sense—You cram these words into mine ears, against the stomach of my *sense*. *Tempest*, act ii. sc. 1.

Serpent—What! wouldst thou have a *serpent* sting thee twice? *Merchant of Venice*, act iv. sc. 1.

Serpent—He is a very *serpent* in my way.
King John, act iii. sc. 3.

Serpent—A *serpent* that will sting thee to the heart.
King Richard II, act v. sc. 3.

Service—I have done the state some *service*, and they know it. *Othello*, act v. sc. 2.

Servile—*Servile* to all the skyey influences.
Measure for Measure, act iii. sc. 1.

Shadow—Shine out, fair sun, till I have bought a glass,
That I may see my *shadow* as I pass.
King Richard III, act i. sc. 2.

Shadow—Love like a *shadow* flies, when substance love pursues;
Pursuing that that flies, and flying what pursues.
Merry Wives of Windsor, act ii. sc. 2.

Shadows— *Shadows* to night
Have struck more terror to the soul of Richard
Than can the substance of ten thousand soldiers,
Arm'd in proof, and led by shallow Richmond.
King Richard III, act v. sc. 3.

Shaft—In my school-days, when I had lost one *shaft*,
I shot his fellow of the self-same flight,
The self-same way, with more advised watch,
To find the other forth; and by adventuring both
I oft found both. *Merchant of Venice*, act i. sc. 1.

Shall— *Shall* remain!
Hear you this Triton of the minnows? mark you
His absolute *shall?* *Coriolanus*, act iii. sc. 1.

Shame—O *shame!* where is thy blush?
Hamlet, act iii. sc. 4.

Shape—Be thy intents wicked or charitable,
Thou comest in such a questionable *shape*,
That I will speak to thee. *Hamlet*, act i. sc. 4.

Shape—Take any *shape* but that, and my firm nerves
Shall never tremble. *Macbeth*, act iii. sc. 4.

Show—I have that within that passeth *show*.
Hamlet, act i. sc. 2.

Sigh—*Sigh* no more, ladies, *sigh* no more:
Men were deceivers ever;
One foot in sea, and one on shore,
To one thing constant never.
Much Ado about Nothing, act ii. sc. 3.

Silence—*Silence* is the perfectest herald of joy; I were but little happy if I could say how much.
Much Ado about Nothing, act ii. sc. 1.

Sin—Some rise by *sin*, and some by virtue fall.
Measure for Measure, act ii. sc. 1.

Sin—*Sin* from my lips? O trespass sweetly urged!
Give me my *sin* again.
Romeo and Juliet, act i. sc. 5.

Sing—O she will *sing* the savageness out of a bear!
Othello, act iv. sc. 1.

Singularity—Put thyself into the trick of *singularity*.
Twelfth Night, act ii. sc. 5.

Sinned— I am a man
More *sinned* against than sinning.
King Lear, act iii. sc. 2.

Skirmish—A *skirmish* of wit between them.
Much Ado about Nothing, act i. sc. 1.

Skull—That *skull* had a tongue in it, and could sing once.
Hamlet, act v. sc. 1.

Slander— *Slander*——
Whose edge is sharper than the sword.
Cymbeline, act iii. sc. 4.

Slander—For *slander* lives upon succession;
For ever housed where it gets possession.
Comedy of Errors, act iii. sc. 1.

Slander—I will be hang'd if some eternal villain,
Some busy and insinuating rogue,
Some cogging cozening slave, to get some office,
Have not devised this *slander*.
Othello, act iv. sc. 2.

Sleep—And *sleep* in dull, cold marble.
King Henry VIII, act iii. sc. 2.

Sleep—*Sleep*, that sometimes shuts up sorrow's eye.
Midsummer-Night's Dream, act iii. sc. 2.

Sleep—Shake off this downy *sleep*, death's counterfeit,
And look on death itself. *Macbeth*, act ii. sc. 3.

Slipp'd—If he had been as you,
And you as he, you would have *slipp'd* like him.
Measure for Measure, act ii. sc. 2.

Slippery—And he that stands upon a *slippery* place
Makes nice of no vile hold to stay him up.
King John, act iii. sc. 4.

Slow—Wisely and *slow*: they stumble that run fast.
Romeo and Juliet, act ii. sc. 3.

Smallest—The *smallest* worm will turn, being trodden on. *King Henry VI*, part iii. act ii. sc. 2.

Smell—The rankest compound of villanous *smell* that ever offended nostril.
Merry Wives of Windsor, act iii. sc. 5.

Smelt—And *smelt* so? pah! *Hamlet*, act v. sc. 1.

Smile—My tables, my tables,—meet it is I set it down,
That one may *smile*, and *smile*, and be a villain.
Hamlet, act i. sc. 5.

Smile—Seldom he smiles; and smiles in such a sort,
As if he mock'd himself, and scorn'd his spirit,
That could be moved to *smile* at any thing.
Julius Cæsar, act i. sc. 2.

Smile—I can *smile*, and murther while I *smile*.
King Henry VI, part iii. act iii. sc. 2.

Smiling—A villain with a *smiling* cheek.
Merchant of Venice, act i. sc. 3.

Smith—I saw a *smith* stand with his hammer, thus,
The whilst his iron did on the anvil cool,
With open mouth swallowing a tailor's news.
King John, act iv. sc. 2.

Snow—When *snow* the pasture sheets.
Antony and Cleopatra, act i. sc. 4.

Society—I am ill, but your being by me cannot amend me; *society* is no comfort to one not sociable:
Cymbeline, act iv. sc. 3.

Soldier—He is a *soldier* fit to stand by Cæsar,
And give direction. *Othello*, act ii. sc. 3.

Soldiers— 'Tis the *soldiers'* life
To have their balmy slumbers waked with strife.
Othello, act ii. sc. 3.

Solicitor—Bold of your worthiness, we single you
As our best-moving, fair *solicitor.*
Love's Labor's Lost, act ii. sc. 1.

Something—*Something* too much of this.
Hamlet, act iii. sc. 2.

Son—He talks to me that never had a *son.*
King John, act iii. sc. 4.

Sorrow—Some unborn *sorrow*, ripe in fortune's womb,
Is coming towards me.
King Richard II, act ii. sc. 2.

Sorrow—*Sorrow* conceal'd, like an oven stopp'd,
Doth burn the heart to cinders.
Titus Andronicus, act ii. sc. 5.

Sorrow—*Sorrow* ends not when it seemeth done.
King Richard II, act i. sc. 2.

Sorrow— Down, thou climbing *sorrow*,
Thy element's below. *King Lear*, act ii. sc. 4.

Sorrow—Affliction may one day smile again, and till then sit thee down, *sorrow!*
Love's Labor's Lost, act i. sc. 1.

Sorrows— Here I and *sorrows* sit;
Here is my throne: bid kings come bow to it.
King John, act iii. sc. 1.

Soul—Every subject's duty is the king's; but every subject's *soul* is his own.
King Henry V, act iv. sc. 1.

Soul— Within this wall of flesh
There is a *soul* counts thee her creditor,
And with advantage means to pay thy love.
King John, act iii. sc. 3.

Soul—That unlettered, small-knowing *soul.*
Love's Labor's Lost, act i. sc. 1.

Souls—Why, all the *souls* that were, were forfeit once,
And He that might the vantage best have took
Found out the remedy.
Measure for Measure, act ii. sc. 2.

Sound—He goes but to see a noise that he heard, and is to come again.
Midsummer-Night's Dream, act iii. sc. 1.

Sound—To hear by the nose, it is dulcet in contagion.
Twelfth Night, act ii. sc. 3.

Sparrow—There is a special providence in the fall of a *sparrow*. *Hamlet*, act v. sc. 2.

Speak—*Speak* then to me, who neither beg nor fear
Your favors, nor your hate. *Macbeth*, act i. sc. 3.

Speak—*Speak*, I'll go no further.
Hamlet, act i. sc. 5.

Speak—Mistake me not, I *speak* but as I find.
Taming of the Shrew, act ii. sc. 1.

Speak—A heavier task could not have been imposed,
Than I to *speak* my griefs unspeakable.
Comedy of Errors, act i. sc. 1.

Speak—Not to *speak* it profanely.
Hamlet, act iii. sc. 2.

Speak—I come not, friends, to steal away your hearts;
I am no orator, as Brutus is,
. . . . I only *speak* right on.
Julius Cæsar, act iii. sc. 2.

Speak—*Lys*. He hath rid his prologue like a rough colt; he knows not the stop. It is not enough to *speak*, but to *speak* true.

Hip. Indeed he hath played on his prologue like a child on a recorder; a sound, but not in government.

The. His speech was like a tangled chain; nothing impaired but all disordered.
Midsummer-Night's Dream, act v. sc. 1.

Speak—All tongues *speak* of him.
Coriolanus, act ii. sc. 1.

Speaking—*Speaking* thick, which nature made his blemish. *King Henry IV*, part ii. act ii. sc. 3.

Spectacles—What a pair of *spectacles* is here!
Troilus and Cressida, act iv. sc. 4.

Sphere—Two stars keep not their motion in one *sphere.*
King Henry IV, part i. act v. sc. 4.

Spirit—I do lack some part of that quick *spirit* that is in Antony. *Julius Cæsar*, act i. sc. 2.

Spirit—There's nothing ill can dwell in such a temple:
If the ill *spirit* have so fair a house,
Good things will strive to dwell with 't.
Tempest, act i. sc. 2.

Spirit—This morning, like the *spirit* of a youth
That means to be of note, begins betimes.
Antony and Cleopatra, act iv. sc. 4.

Splenetive—For, though I am not *splenetive* and rash,
Yet have I something in me dangerous.
Hamlet, act v. sc. 1.

Spoon—This is a devil, and no monster; I will leave him;
I have no long *spoon.* *Tempest*, act ii. sc. 2.

Spoon—He must have a long *spoon* that must eat with the devil. *Comedy of Errors*, act iv. sc. 3.

Sport—It is the first time that ever I heard breaking of ribs was *sport* for ladies.
As You Like It. act i. sc. 2.

Spread—Masters, *spread* yourselves.
Midsummer-Night's Dream, act i. sc. 2.

Spring— The *spring*, the summer,
The childing autumn, angry winter, change
Their wonted liveries.
Midsummer-Night's Dream, act ii. sc. 1.

Springes—*Springes* to catch woodcocks.
Hamlet, act i. sc. 3.

Spur—What need we any *spur* but our own cause
To prick us to redress? *Julius Cæsar*, act ii. sc. 1.

Stage—I hold the world but as the world, Gratiano;
A *stage*, where every man must play a part,
And mine a sad one.
Merchant of Venice, act i. sc. 1.

Stage— All the world's a *stage*,
And all the men and women merely players;
They have their exits, and their entrances,
And one man in his time plays many parts,
His acts being seven ages.
As You Like It, act ii. sc. 1.

Stand—*Stand* not upon the order of your going,
But go at once. *Macbeth*, act iii. sc. 4.

Stands—*Stands* Scotland where it did?
Macbeth, act iv. sc. 3.

Star—Look, the unfolding *star* calls up the shepherd.
Measure for Measure, act iv. sc. 2.

Stars—Men at some time are masters of their fates;
The fault, dear Brutus, is not in our *stars*,
But in ourselves, that we are underlings.
Julius Cæsar, act i. sc. 2.

Stars—Those gold candles fix'd in heaven's air.
Sonnet 21.

Stars—Let all the number of the *stars* give light
To thy fair way!
Antony and Cleopatra, act iii. sc. 2.

Stars—Witness, you ever-burning lights above!
Othello, act iii. sc. 3.

Started—And then it *started* like a guilty thing
Upon a fearful summons. *Hamlet*, act i. sc. 1.

Stay'd— 1. *Stay'd* it long?
2. While one with moderate haste might tell a hundred.
3. Longer, Longer!
2. Not when I saw it. *Hamlet*, act i. sc. 2.

Steel—My man's as true as *steel*.
Romeo and Juliet, act ii. sc. 4.

Steel—*Steel* to the very back.
Titus Andronicus, act iv. sc. 3.

Steel—Like a man of *steel*.
Antony and Cleopatra, act iv. sc. 4.

Stephen—As *Stephen Sly*, and old John Naps of Greece,
And Peter Turf and Henry Pimpernell;
And twenty more such names and men as these,
Which never were, nor no man ever saw.
Taming of the Shrew, *Induction*, sc. 2.

Stir—We may as well push against Powle's as *stir* 'em.
King Henry VIII, act v. sc. 4.

Stomach— He was a man
Of an unbounded *stomach*.
King Henry VIII, act iv. sc. 2.

Stone— At this sight
My heart is turned to *stone*.
King Henry VI, part ii. act v. sc. 2.

Straining—*Straining* harsh discords and unpleasing sharps, *Romeo and Juliet*, act iii. sc. 5.

Strange—But 'tis *strange*:
And oftentimes to win us to our harm,

The instruments of darkness tell us truths;
Win us with honest trifles, to betray us
In deepest consequence. *Macbeth*, act i. sc. 3.

Strawberry—The *strawberry* grows underneath the nettle;
And wholesome berries thrive and ripen best
Neighbor'd by fruit of baser quality.
King Henry V, act i. sc. 1.

Strength—The king's name is a tower of *strength*.
King Richard III, act v. sc. 3.

Strike—*Strike* now, or else the iron cools.
King Henry VI, part iii. act v. sc. 1.

Striving—*Striving* to better, oft we mar what's well.
King Lear, act i. sc. 4.

Stuffing—*Stuffing* the ears of men with false reports.
King Henry IV, part ii. *Induction*.

Success—And on a love-book pray for my *success*.
Two Gentlemen of Verona, act i. sc. 1.

Success— Didst thou never hear,
That things ill got had ever bad *success?*
King Henry VI, part iii. act ii. sc. 2.

Suggestion—For all the rest,
They'll take a *suggestion* as a cat laps milk.
Tempest, act ii. sc. 1.

Sum—"Poor deer," quoth he, "thou mak'st a testament,
As worldlings do, giving thy *sum* of more
To that which had too much."
As You Like It, act ii. sc. 1.

Summer— For men, like butterflies,
Show not their mealy wings but to the *summer*.
Troilus and Cressida, act iii. sc. 3.

Sun—The self-same *sun* that shines upon his court,
Hides not his visage from our cottage, but
Looks on alike. *Winter's Tale*, act iv. sc. 3.

Sun—Men shut their doors against the setting *sun*.
Timon of Athens, act i. sc. 2.

Sun—I 'gin to be a-weary of the *sun*.
Macbeth, act v. sc. 5.

Sun— And teach me how
To name the bigger light, and how the less,
That burn by day and night. *Tempest*, act i. sc. 2.

Sunday—Does not divide the *Sunday* from the week.
Hamlet, act i. sc. 1.

Suns—*Edw.* Dazzle mine eyes, or do I see three *suns?*
Rich. Three glorious *suns*, each one a perfect sun;
See, see! they join, embrace, and seem to kiss;
Now are they but one.
King Henry VI, part iii. act ii. sc. 1.

Supped—I have *supped* full with horrors.
Macbeth, act v. sc. 5.

Supposed—Or in the night, imagining some fear,
How easy is a bush *supposed* a bear!
Midsummer-Night's Dream, act v. sc. 1.

Surrey—Saddle white *Surrey* for the field to-morrow.
King Richard III, act v. sc. 3.

Swashing—We'll have a *swashing* and a martial outside. *As You Like It*, act i. sc. 3.

Swear—*Romeo.* Lady, by yonder blessed moon I *swear*,
That tips with silver all these fruit-tree tops—
Juliet. O, *swear* not by the moon, the inconstant moon,
That monthly changes in her circled orb,
Lest that thy love prove likewise variable.
Romeo and Juliet, act ii. sc. 2.

Swearing—Nay, let me alone for *swearing*.
Twelfth Night, act iii. sc. 4.

Sweets—*Sweets* to the sweet. *Hamlet*, act v. sc. 1.

Sylvia—Except I be by *Sylvia* in the night,
There is no music in the nightingale.
Two Gentlemen of Verona, act iii. sc. 1.

T

Take—*Take* thy auld cloak about thee.
Othello, act ii. sc. 3.

Talbot—Is this the scourge of France?
Is this the *Talbot* so much fear'd abroad,
That with his name the mothers still their babes?
King Henry VI, part i. act ii. sc. 3.

Tale—And thereby hangs a *tale*.
Taming of the Shrew, act iv. sc. 1.

Tale—This act is an ancient *tale* new told;
And, in the last repeating, troublesome,
Being urged at a time unreasonable.
King John, act iv. sc. 2.

Talk—If I chance to *talk* a little wild, forgive me;
I had it from my father.
King Henry VIII, act i. sc. 4.

Talkers—*Talkers* are no good doers.
King Richard III, act i. sc. 3.

Taste—*Taste* your legs, sir; put them to motion.
Twelfth Night, act iii. sc. 1.

Taste—I have heard of some kind of men that put quarrels purposely on others, to *taste* their valor.
Twelfth Night, act iii. sc. 4.

Team—The heavenly-harness'd *team*
Begins his golden progress in the east.
King Henry IV, part i. act iii. sc. 1.

Tears—And often did beguile her of her *tears*.
Othello, act i. sc. 3.

Tears— The big round *tears*
Cours'd one another down his innocent nose
In piteous chase. *As You Like It*, act ii. sc. 1.

Tears—If you have *tears*, prepare to shed them now.
Julius Cæsar, act iii. sc. 2.

Tears—The tide is now: nay, not thy tide of *tears*,
That tide will stay me longer than I should.
Two Gentlemen of Verona, act ii. sc. 2.

Tears—And all my mother came into mine eyes,
And gave me up to *tears*.
King Henry V, act iv. sc. 6.

Tears—Venus smiles not in a house of *tears*.
Romeo and Juliet, act iv. sc. 1.

Tears—He has strangled his language in his *tears*.
King Henry VIII, act v. sc. 1.

Tedious—O, he's as *tedious*
As is a tired horse!
King Henry IV, part i. act iii. sc. 1.

Tedious—1. Neighbors you are *tedious*.
2. It pleases your worship to say so; but truly, for mine own part, if I were as *tedious* as a king, I could find in my heart to bestow it all of your worship. *Much Ado about Nothing*, act iii. sc. 5.

Tempest—O, then began the *tempest* of my soul!
King Richard III, act i. sc. 4.

Tented—In the *tented* field. *Othello*, act i. sc. 3.

Thanks—Your love deserves my *thanks*.
King Richard III, act iii. sc. 7.

Thanks—I can no other answer make but *thanks*,
And *thanks*; and ever oft good turns
Are shuffled off with such uncurrent pay.
Twelfth Night, act iii. sc. 3.

That—*That* it should come to this.
Hamlet, act i. sc. 2.

Theban—I'll talk a word with this same learned *Theban*:
What is your study? *King Lear*, act iii. sc. 4.

Thievery—Master be one of them;
It is an honorable kind of *thievery*.
Two Gentlemen of Verona, act iv. sc. 1.

Thing—A *thing* devised by the enemy.
King Richard III, act v. sc. 3.

Thing—I had a *thing* to say;
But I will fit it with some better tune.
King John, act iii. sc. 3.

Thing—Thou *thing* of no bowels, thou!
Troilus and Cressida, act ii. sc. 1.

Things—*Things* bad begun make strong themselves by ill. *Macbeth*, act iii. sc. 2.

Thought—Thy wish was father, Harry, to that *thought*.
King Henry IV, part ii. act iv. sc. 4.

Thoughts— From this time forth
My *thoughts* be bloody, or be nothing worth!
Hamlet, act iv. sc. 4.

Threaten—Be stirring as the time, be fire with fire;
Threaten the threat'ner, and outface the brow
Of bragging horror. *King John*, act v. sc. 1.

Thrice—*Thrice* the brinded cat hath mew'd.
Macbeth, act iv. sc. 1.

Thunder—*Witch*. When shall we three meet again—
In *thunder*, lightning, or in rain?
Macbeth, act i. sc. 1.

Tidings—Prithee take the cork out of thy mouth, that I may drink thy *tidings*.
As You Like It, act iii. sc. 2.

Time—There's a *time* for all things.
Comedy of Errors, act ii. sc. 2.

Time—*Time* comes stealing on by night and day.
Comedy of Errors, act iv. sc. 2.

Time— Nor *time*, nor place,
Did then adhere. *Macbeth*, act i. sc. 7.

Time—*Time* must friend or end.
Troilus and Cressida, act i. sc. 2.

Time—1. Now, Hal, what *time* of day is it, lad?
2. I see no reason why thou should'st be so superfluous to demand the *time* of the day.
King Henry IV, part i. act i. sc. 2.

Time—I wasted *time*, and now doth *time* waste me.
King Richard II, act v. sc. 5.

Time—The clock upbraids me with the waste of *time*.
Twelfth Night, act iii. sc. 1.

Time—*Time* hath set a blot upon my pride.
King Richard II, act iii. sc. 2.

Time—*Time* doth transfix the flourish set on youth,
And delves the parallels in beauty's brow.
Sonnet 60.

Time—*Time* is the nurse and breeder of all good.
Two Gentlemen of Verona, act iii. sc. 1.

Tongue—Think you a little din can daunt mine ears?
Have I not in my time heard lions roar?
Have I not heard the sea, puff'd up with wind,
Rage like an angry boar, chafed with sweat?
Have I not heard great ordnance in the field,
And heaven's artillery thunder in the skies?
Have I not in a pitched battle heard
Loud 'larums, neighing steeds, and trumpets clang?
And do you tell me of a woman's *tongue?*
Taming of the Shrew, act i. sc. 2.

Tongue—A maiden hath no *tongue* but thought.
Merchant of Venice, act iii. sc. 2.

Tongues—They say the *tongues* of dying men
Enforce attention, like deep harmony;
When words are scarce, they're seldom spent in vain:
For they breathe truth that breathe their words in pain. *King Richard II*, act ii. sc. 1.

Tongues—*Tongues* I'll hang on every tree,
That shall civil sayings show.
As You Like It, act iii. sc. 2.

Towering—Into a *towering* passion.
Hamlet, act v. sc. 2.

Towers—Yon *towers*, whose wanton tops do buss the clouds. *Troilus and Cressida*, act iv. sc. 5.

Travellers—When I was at home, I was in a better place;
But *travellers* must be content.
As You Like It, act ii. sc. 4.

Trencherman—A very valiant *trencherman*.
Much Ado about Nothing, act i. sc. 1.

Trick—I know a *trick* worth two of that.
King Henry IV, part i. act ii. sc. 1.

Trifles—A snapper-up of unconsidered *trifles*.
Winter's Tale, act iv. sc. 2.

Trifles—Come, gentlemen, we sit too long on *trifles*,
And waste the time, which looks for other revels.
Pericles, act ii. sc. 3.

True—More strange than *true*.
Midsummer-Night's Dream, act v. sc. 1.

Trumpet—Be thou the *trumpet* of our wrath,
And sullen presage of your own decay.
King John, act i. sc. 1.

Truth— ***Truth* is *truth***
To the end of reckoning.
Measure for Measure, act v. sc. 1.

Truths—I hope there be *truths.*
Measure for Measure, act ii. sc. 1.

Turn—Ay; you did wish that I would make her *turn;*
Sir, she can *turn* and *turn*, and yet go on,
And *turn* again. *Othello*, act iv. sc. 1.

U

Uncle— Tut, tut!
Grace me no grace, nor *uncle* me no *uncle.*
King Richard II, act ii. sc. 3.

Unexpressive—The fair, the chaste, and *unexpressive* she. *As You Like It*, act iii. sc. 2.

Unkennel—*Unkennel* the fox.
Merry Wives of Windsor, act iii. sc. 3.

Unkindness—Sharp-tooth'd *unkindness.*
King Lear, act ii. sc. 4.

Unkindness— *Unkindness* may do much,
And his *unkindness* may defeat my life,
But never taint my love. *Othello*, act iv. sc. 2.

Unkindness—Drink down all *unkindness.*
Merry Wives of Windsor, act i. sc. 1.

Unkindness— Give me a bowl of wine—
In this I bury all *unkindness*, Cassius.
Julius Cæsar, act iv. sc. 3.

Use—*Use* can almost change the stamp of nature.
Hamlet, act iii. sc. 4.

V

Vale— Declined
Into the *vale* of years. *Othello*, act iii. sc. 3.

Vanish—Go; *vanish* into air: away!
Othello, act iii. sc. 1.

Vanish—*Vanish* like hailstones, go!
Merry Wives of Windsor, act i. sc. 3.

Vanity—Hal, I prithee trouble me no more with *vanity*.
King Henry IV, part i. act i. sc. 2.

Ventured— I have *ventured*,
Like little wanton boys that swim on bladders,
This many summers in a sea of glory,
But far beyond my depth: my high-blown pride
At length broke under me, and now has left me,
Weary and old with service, to the mercy
Of a rude stream, that must for ever hide me.
King Henry VIII, act iii. sc. 2.

Vex'd—As mad as the *vex'd* sea.
King Lear, act iv. sc. 4.

Vice—Virtue itself turns *vice*, being misapplied;
And *vice* sometimes by action dignified.
Romeo and Juliet, act ii. sc. 3.

Victory—Thus far our fortune keeps an upward course
And we are graced with wreaths of *victory*.
King Henry VI, part iii. act v. sc. 3.

Victory—And either *victory*, or else a grave.
King Henry VI, part iii. act ii. sc. 2.

Villain—*Villain* and he be many miles asunder.
Romeo and Juliet, act iii. sc. 5.

Villany—A very excellent piece of *villany*.
Titus Andronicus, act ii. sc. 3.

Virtue— Calumny will sear
Virtue itself: these shrugs, these hums, and ha's.
Winter's Tale, act ii. sc. 1.

Virtue—A *virtue* that was never seen in you.
King Henry IV, part i. act iii. sc. 1.

Visage—I saw Othello's *visage* in his mind.
Othello, act i. sc. 3.

Vocation—Why, Hal, 'tis my *vocation*.
Hal. 'Tis no sin for a man to labor in his *vocation*.
King Henry IV, part i. act i. sc. 2.

W

Wall—The weakest goes to the *wall*.
Romeo and Juliet, act i. sc. 1.

War—List his discourse of *war*, and you shall hear
A fearful battle render'd you in music.
King Henry V, act i. sc. 1.

War—The harsh and boist'rous tongue of *war*.
King Henry IV, part ii. act iv. sc. 1.

War—Horribly stuff'd with epithets of *war*.
Othello, act i. sc. 1.

War—Like, or find fault; do as your pleasures are;
Now good or bad, 'tis but the chance of *war*.
Troilus and Cressida, Prologue.

Water—Smooth runs the *water* where the brook is deep. *King Henry VI*, part ii. act iii. sc. 1.

Wave— When you do dance, I wish you
A *wave* o' the sea, that you might ever do
Nothing but that. *Winter's Tale*, act iv. sc. 3.

Weakest—He that of greatest works is finisher,
Oft does them by the *weakest* minister;
So holy writ in babes hath judgment shewn,
When judges have been babes.
All's Well that Ends Well, act ii. sc. 1.

Wealth—Who would not wish to be from *wealth* exempt,
Since riches point to misery and contempt?
Timon of Athens, act iv. sc. 2.

Wear—*Wear* this for me.
As You Like It, act i. sc. 2.

Weeds—Sweet flowers are slow, and *weeds* make haste.
Small herbs have grace, great *weeds* do grow apace.
King Richard III, act ii. sc. 4.

Welcome—A tableful of *welcome* makes scarce one dainty dish. *Comedy of Errors*, act iii. sc. 1.

Welcome—To say you are *welcome*, would be superfluous. *Pericles*, act iii. sc. 3.

Wenches—This gallant pins the *wenches* on his sleeve;
Had he been Adam, he had tempted Eve:
He can carve too, and lisp.
Love's Labor's Lost, act v. sc. 2.

What—We know *what* we are, but know not *what* we may be. *Hamlet*, act iv. sc. 5.

What's—*What's* done cannot be undone.
Macbeth, act v. sc. 1.

What's—*What's* done cannot be now amended.
King Richard III, act iv. sc. 4.

Whip—*Whip* me such honest knaves.
Othello, act i. sc. 1.

Whistle—Hear the shrill *whistle*, which doth order give
To sounds confused.
King Henry V, Chorus to act iii.

Wind—What *wind* blew you hither, Pistol?
Not the ill *wind* which blows no man to good.
King Henry IV, part ii. act v. sc. 3.

Wind—Now sits the *wind* fair, and we will aboard.
King Henry V, act ii. sc. 2.

Window— Mistress, look on me,
Behold the *window* of mine heart, mine eye,
What humble suit attends thy answer there?
Love's Labor's Lost, act v. sc. 2.

Windows—Ere I let fall the *windows* of mine eyes.
King Richard III, act v. sc. 3.

Windows—Thy eyes' *windows* fall,
Like death, when he shuts up the day of life.
Romeo and Juliet, act iv. sc. 1.

Windows—Her two blue *windows* faintly she upheaveth.
Venus and Adonis, Verse 81.

Winter—When great leaves fall, then *winter* is at hand.
King Richard III, act ii. sc. 3.

Wisdom— Full oft we see
Cold *wisdom* waiting on superfluous folly.
All's Well that Ends Well, act i. sc. 1.

Wise—So *wise*, so young, they say, do ne'er live long.
King Richard III, act iii. sc. 1.

Wit—*Pro.* Beshrew me, but you have a quick *wit.*
Speed. And yet cannot overtake your slow purse.
Two Gentlemen of Verona, act i. sc. 1.

Wit—I shall ne'er be 'ware of mine own *wit* till I break my shins against it.
As You Like It, act ii. sc. 4.

Wither—Such short-lived wits do *wither* as they grow.
Love's Labor's Lost, act ii. sc. 1.

Wits—It is meat and drink to me to see a clown: By my troth, we that have good *wits* have much to answer for. *As You Like It*, act v. sc. 1.

Woe—One *woe* doth tread upon another's heel,
So fast they follow. *Hamlet*, act iv. sc. 7.

Woman—A *woman*, that is like a German clock,
Still a repairing; ever out of frame;
And never going aright; being a watch,
But being watch'd that it may still go right!
Love's Labor's Lost, act iii. sc. 1.

Woman—Was ever *woman* in this humor wooed?
Was ever *woman* in this humor won?
King Richard III, act i. sc. 2.

Woman— Be that you are,
That is, a *woman*; if you be more, you're none.
Measure for Measure, act ii. sc. 4.

Woman—Relenting fool, and shallow, changing *woman!*
King Richard III, act iv. sc. 4.

Woman's—To be slow in words is a *woman's* only virtue. *Two Gentlemen of Verona*, act iii. sc. 1.

Women—Two *women* placed together make cold weather. *King Henry VIII*, act i. sc. 4.

Women's weapons—And let not *women's weapons*, water-drops,
Stain my man's cheeks. *King Lear*, act ii. sc. 4.

Wonder—I *wonder* men dare trust themselves with men. *Timon of Athens*, act i. sc. 2.

Wonderful—O *wonderful wonderful*, and most *wonderful wonderful*, and yet again *wonderful*, and after that out of all whooping.
As You Like It, act iii. sc. 2.

Word—And but one *word* with one of us? Couple it with something.
Make it a word and a blow.
Romeo and Juliet, act iii. sc. 1.

Word—I'll take the ghost's *word* for a thousand pounds. *Hamlet*, act iii. sc. 2.

Word—I'll take thy *word* for faith, not ask thine oath;
Who shuns not to break one, will sure crack both.
Pericles, act i. sc. 2.

Words—My *words* fly up, my thoughts remain below;
Words, without thoughts, never to heaven go.
Hamlet, act iii. sc. 3.

Words—When I would pray and think, I think and pray
To several subjects: heaven hath my empty *words*.
Measure for Measure, act ii. sc. 4.

Words—*Polonius*. What do you read, my lord?
Hamlet. *Words*, *words*, *words*.
Hamlet, act ii. sc. 2.

Words—1. Sir, if you spend word for word with me, I shall make your wit bankrupt.
2. I know it well, sir; you have an exchequer of *words*.
Two Gentlemen of Verona, act ii. sc. 4.

Words—*Words* are grown so false I am loath to prove reason with them. *Twelfth Night*, act iii. sc. 1.

Words of Mercury—The *words of Mercury* are harsh after the songs of Apollo,
Love's Labor's Lost, act v. sc. 2.

World—O, what a *world* is this, when what is comely
Envenoms him that bears it!
As You Like It, act ii. sc. 3.

World—No: the *world* must be peopled.
Much Ado about Nothing, act ii. sc. 3.

World— I am one, my liege,
Whom the vile blows and buffets of the *world*
Have so incens'd, that I am reckless what
I do, to spite the world. *Macbeth*, act iii. sc. 1.

Worm—Your *worm* is your only emperor for diet; we fat all creatures else to fat us, and we fat ourselves for maggots. *Hamlet*, act iv. sc. 3.

Worm—A man may fish with the *worm* that hath eat of a king. *Hamlet*, act iv. sc. 3.

Worst—Things at the *worst* will cease, or else climb upward
To what they were before. *Macbeth*, act iv. sc. 2.

Worth—I know my price; I am *worth* no worse a place. *Othello*, act i. sc. 1.

Wound—The private *wound* is deepest. *Two Gentlemen of Verona*, act v. sc. 4.

Wrong—It may be right; but you are in the *wrong*
To speak before your time. *Measure for Measure*, act v. sc. 1.

Wrong'd—He hath *wrong'd* me, master Page. *Merry Wives of Windsor*, act i. sc. 1.

Y

Years— Jumping o'er times,
Turning the accomplishment of many *years*
Into an hour-glass. *King Henry V*, Chorus.

Youth—Crabbed age and *youth*
Cannot live together. *Passionate Pilgrim*, viii.

Youth—In the very May-morn of his *youth*,
Ripe for exploits and mighty enterprises. *King Henry V*, act i. sc. 2.

Youth—He wears the rose
Of *youth* upon him; from which the world should note
Something particular. *Antony and Cleopatra*, act iii. sc. 4.

Worm—A man may fish with the worm that hath eat of a king. *Hamlet*, act iv. sc. 3.

Worst—Things at the worst will cease, or else climb upward
To what they were before. *Macbeth*, act iv. sc. 2.

Worth—I know my price; I am worth no worse a place. [illegible]

[illegible]

[illegible]

[illegible]

Y

Years— [illegible] Jumping o'er times,
Turning the accomplishment of many years
Into an hour-glass. *King Henry V*, Chorus.

Youth—Crabbed age and youth
Cannot live together. *Passionate Pilgrim*, viii.

Youth—In the very May-morn of his youth,
Ripe for exploits and mighty enterprises.
King Henry V, act i. sc. 2.

Youth—He wears the rose
Of youth upon him; from which the world should note
Something particular.
Antony and Cleopatra, act iii. sc. 4.

INDEX.

D

H

M

N

O

P

Q

R

S

T

U

V

W

Y

INDEX TO THE CHARACTERS

IN

SHAKESPEARE'S DRAMATIC WORKS.

Aaron,	A Moor, beloved by Tamora,	Titus Andronicus.
Abbot of Westminster,		Richard II.
Abergavenny, Lord,		King Henry VIII.
Abhorson,	An Executioner,	Measure for Measure.
Abram,	Servant of Montague,	Romeo and Juliet.
Achilles,	A Grecian Commander,	Troilus and Cressida.
Adam,	Servant to Oliver,	As You Like it.
Adrian,	A Lord of Naples,	Tempest.
Adriana,	Wife of Antipholus of Ephesus,	Comedy of Errors.
Ægeon,	A Merchant of Syracuse,	Comedy of Errors.
Æmilia,	An Abbess at Ephesus,	Comedy of Errors.
Æmilius,	A Noble Roman,	Titus Andronicus.
Æmilius Lepidus.	A Roman Triumvir,	Julius Cæsar.
Æneas,	A Trojan Commander,	Troilus and Cressida.
Agamemnon,	A Grecian General,	Troilus and Cressida.
Agrippa,	A Friend of Cæsar,	Antony and Cleopatra.
Agrippa Menenius,	Friend of Coriolanus,	Coriolanus.
Ague-cheek, Sir Andrew		Twelfth Night.
Ajax,	A Grecian Commander,	Troilus and Cressida.
Alarbus,	Son of Tamora,	Titus Andronicus.
Albany, Duke of		King Lear.
Alcibiades.	An Athenian General,	Timon of Athens.
Alencon, Duke of,		King Henry VI., Part I.
Alexander,	Servant to Cressida,	Troilus and Cressida.
Alexander Iden,	A Kentish Gentleman,	King Henry VI., Part II.
Alexas,	Attendant on Cleopatra,	Antony and Cleopatra.
Alice,	Attendant on Prin. Katharine,	King Henry V.
Alonso,	King of Naples,	Tempest.
Amiens,	Attendant on Exiled Duke,	As You Like it.
Andromache,	Wife of Hector,	Troilus and Cressida.
Andronicus, Marcus,	Tribune, Brother of Titus,	Titus Andronicus.
Andronicus, Titus,	General against the Goths,	Titus Andronicus.
Angelo,	A Goldsmith,	Comedy of Errors.
Angelo,	Deputy of Duke of Vienna,	Measure for Measure.
Angus,	A Scottish Nobleman,	Macbeth.
Anne, Lady,	Widow of Edward Prin. of Wales,	King Richard III.
Anne Bullen,	Afterwards Queen,	King Henry VIII.
Antenor.	A Trojan Commander,	Troilus and Cressida.
Antigonus,	A Sicilian Lord,	Winter's Tale.
Antiochus,	King of Antioch,	Pericles.
Antiochus,	Daughter of	Pericles.

Antipholus of Ephesus, Antipholus of Syracuse,	Twin Brothers; unknown to each other,	Comedy of Errors.
Antonio,	The Merchant of Venice,	Merchant of Venice.
Antonio,	Usurping Duke of Milan,	Tempest.
Antonio,	A Sea Captain,	Twelfth Night.
Antonio,	Brother of Leonato,	Much Ado About Nothing.
Antonio,	Father of Proteus,	Two Gentlemen of Verona.
Antony, Marc,	A Triumvir,	Antony and Cleopatra.
Apemantus,	A Churlish Philosopher,	Timon of Athens.
Apothecary, An,		Romeo and Juliet.
Archb. of Canterbury,	Cranmer,	King Henry VIII.
Archb. of Canterbury,	Cardinal Bouchier,	King Richard III.
Archb. of Canterbury,		King Henry II.
Archbishop of York,	Scroop,	Henry IV., Parts I., II.
Archbishop of York,	Thomas Rotheram,	King Richard III.
Archduke of Austria,		King John.
Archibald,	Earl of Douglas,	Henry IV., Parts I., II.
Archidamus,	A Bohemian Lord,	Winter's Tale.
Ariel,	An Airy Spirit,	Tempest.
Armado, Don Adriano	A Fantastical Spaniard,	Love's Labour Lost.
Arragon, Prince of,	Suitor to Portia,	Merchant of Venice.
Arthur,	Elder Brother of King John,	King John.
Artimidorus,	A Sophist of Cnidos,	Julius Cæsar.
Arviragus,	Son of Cymbeline,	Cymbeline.
Audrey,	A Country Wench,	As You Like it.
Aufidius Tullus,	Volscian General,	Coriolanus.
Aumerle, Duke of	Son of Duke of York,	King Richard II.
Autolycus,	A Rogue,	Winter's Tale.
Auvergne, Countess of,		King Henry VI., Part I.
Bagot,	"Creature" of Richard II.,	King Richard II.
Balthazar,	A Merchant,	Comedy of Errors.
Balthazar,	Servant to Portia,	Merchant of Venice.
Balthazar,	Servant to Don Pedro,	Much Ado About Nothing.
Balthazar,	Servant to Romeo,	Romeo and Juliet.
Banquo,	A General,	Macbeth.
Banished Duke,		As You Like it.
Baptista,	A Rich Gentleman of Padua,	Taming of the Shrew.
Bardolph,	Soldier in King's Army,	King Henry II.
Bardolph,	A Follower of Falstaff,	Merry Wives of Windsor.
Bardolph,	Follower of Sir John Falstaff,	Henry IV., Parts I., II.
Bardolph, Lord,	Enemy to the King,	King Henry IV., Part II.
Barnardine,	A Dissolute Prisoner,	Measure for Measure.
Basset,	Of the Red Rose Faction,	King Henry VI., Part I.
Bassanio,	Friend of Antonio,	Merchant of Venice.
Bassanius,	Brother of Saturninus,	Titus Andronicus.
Bastard of Orleans,		King Henry VI., Part I.
Bates,	Soldier in King's Army,	King Henry V.
Beatrice,	Niece of Leonato,	Much Ado About Nothing.
Beau, Le,	A Courtier,	As You Like it.
Beaufort, Cardinal,	Bishop of Winchester,	King Henry VI., Part II.
Beaufort, Henry,	Bishop of Winchester,	King Henry VI., Part I.
Beaufort, John,	Earl of Somerset,	King Henry VI., Part I.
Beaufort, Thomas,	Duke of Exeter,	King Henry VI., Part I.
Bedford, Duke of,	Brother of Henry V.,	King Henry V.
Bedford, Duke of,	Regent of France,	King Henry VI., Part I.
Belarius,	A Banished Lord,	Cymbeline.
Belch, Sir Toby,	Uncle of Olivia,	Twelfth Night.
Benedick,	A Young Lord of Padua,	Much Ado About Nothing.

Benvolio, . .	. Friend of Romeo, . .	. Romeo and Juliet.
Berkley, Earl, .	. . . .	. King Richard II.
Bernardo, . .	. An Officer, . . .	. Hamlet.
Bertram, . .	. Count of Rousillon, .	. All's Well that Ends Well.
Bianca, . .	. Mistress of Cassio, . .	. Othello.
Bianca, . .	. Sister of Katherine, .	. Taming of the Shrew.
Bigot, Robert, .	. Earl of Norfolk, . .	. King John.
Biondello, . .	. Servant of Lucentio, .	. Taming of the Shrew.
Biron, . .	. Attendant on King of Navarre,	Love's Labour Lost.
Bishop of Carlisle,	. . . .	. King Richard II.
Bishop of Ely, .	. . . .	. King Henry V.
Bishop of Ely, .	. John Morton, . . .	. King Richard III.
Bishop of Lincoln,	. . . .	. King Henry VIII.
Bishop of Winchester,	Gardiner, ...	. King Henry VIII.
Blanch, . .	. Niece of King John, .	. King John.
Blount, Sir James,	. . . .	. King Richard III.
Blunt, Sir Walter,	. Friend of Henry IV., .	. Henry IV., Parts I., II.
Bolingbroke, .	. A Conjurer, . . .	. King Henry VI., Part II.
Bolingbroke, .	. Afterwards Henry IV. .	. King Richard II.
Bona, . . .	. Sister of the French Queen,	. Henry VI., Part III.
Borachio, . .	. Follower of Don John, .	. Much Ado About Nothing
Bottom, . .	. The Weaver, . . .	. Midsummer Night's Dream
Boult, . .	. A Servant, . . .	. Pericles.
Bourbon, Duke of,	. . . .	. King Henry V.
Bouchier, Cardinal,	. Archbishop of Canterbury,	. King Richard III.
Boyet, . .	. Attendant on Princess of France,	Love's Labour Lost.
Brabantio, . .	. A Senator, . . .	. Othello.
Brakenbury, Sir Robt.,	Lieutenant of the Tower,	. King Richard III.
Brandon, . .	. . . .	. King Henry VIII.
Brutus, Junius, .	. Tribune of the People, .	. Coriolanus.
Brutus, Marcus,	. A Roman Conspirator, .	. Julius Cæsar.
Buckingham, Duke of,	. . . .	. King Richard III.
Buckingham, Duke of,	Of the King's Party, .	. King Henry VI., Part II.
Buckingham, Duke of,	. . . .	. King Henry VIII.
Bullcalf, . .	. A Recruit, . . .	. King Henry IV., Part II.
Bullen, Anne, .	. Afterwards Queen, . .	. King Henry VIII.
Burgundy, Duke of,	. . . .	. King Henry V.
Burgundy, Duke of,	. . . .	. King Henry VI., Part I.
Burgundy, Duke of,	. . . .	. King Lear.
Bushy, . .	. "Creature" of Richard II.,	. King Richard II.
Butts, Dr., . .	. Physician to Henry VIII.,	. King Henry VIII.
Cade, Jack, .	. A Rebel, ...	. King Henry VI., Part II.
Cadwal, . .	. Arviragus in Disguise, .	. Cymbeline.
Cæsar, Octavius,	. A Triumvir, . . .	. Antony and Cleopatra.
Caithness, . .	. A Scottish Nobleman, .	. Macbeth.
Caius, Dr., . .	. A French Physician, .	. Merry Wives of Windsor
Caius, Lucius, .	. General of Roman Forces,	. Cymbeline.
Caius M. Coriolanus,	. A Noble Roman, . .	. Coriolanus.
Calchas, . .	. A Trojan Priest, . .	. Troilus and Cressida.
Caliban, . .	. A Savage and Deformed Slave,	The Tempest.
Calphurnia, .	. Wife of Cæsar, . .	. Julius Cæsar.
Cambridge, Earl of,	. A Conspirator, . .	. King Henry V.
Camillo, . .	. A Sicilian Lord, . .	. Winter's Tale.
Campeius, Cardinal,	. . . .	. King Henry VIII.
Canidius, . .	. Lieutenant-General of Antony,	Antony and Cleopatra.
Canterbury, Archb. of,	Cardinal Bouchier, . .	. King Richard III.
Canterbury, Archb. of,	. . . .	. King Henry V.
Canterbury Archb. of,	Cranmer, ...	. King Henry VIII.

Count of Rousillon,		All's Well that Ends Well.
Countess of Auvergne,		King Henry VI., Part I.
Countess of Rousillon,	Mother of Bertram,	All's Well that Ends Well.
Court,	Soldier in King's Army,	King Henry V.
Cranmer,	Archbishop of Canterbury,	King Henry VIII.
Cressida,	Daughter to Chalcas,	Troilus and Cressida.
Cromwell,	Servant to Wolsey,	King Henry VIII.
Curan,	A Courtier,	King Lear.
Curio,	Attendant on Duke of Illyria,	Twelfth Night.
Curtis,	Servant to Petruchio,	Taming of the Shrew.
Cymbeline,	King of Britain,	Cymbeline.
Dame Quickly,	Hostess of a Tavern,	King Henry IV., Pts. I & II.
Dardanius,	Servant to Brutus,	Julius Cæsar.
Dauphin, The,	Louis,	King John.
Davy,	Servant to Shallow,	King Henry IV., Part II.
Decius Brutus,	A Roman Conspirator,	Julius Cæsar.
Deiphobus,	Son to Priam,	Troilus and Cressida.
Demetrius,	Friend to Antony,	Antony and Cleopatra.
Demetrius,	In Love with Hermione,	Midsummer Nights Dream
Demetrius,	Son to Tamora,	Titus Andronicus.
Dennis,	Servant to Oliver,	As You Like it.
Denny, Sir Anthony,		King Henry VIII.
Dercetas,	Friend to Antony,	Antony and Cleopatra.
Desdemona,	Wife to Othello,	Othello.
Diana,	Daughter to Widow,	All's Well that Ends Well.
Diana,		Pericles.
Dick,	A Follower of Jack Cade,	King Henry VI., Part II.
Diomedes,	A Grecian Commander,	Troilus and Cressida.
Diomedes,	Attendant on Cleopatra,	Antony and Cleopatra.
Dion,	A Sicilian Lord,	Winter's Tale.
Dionyza,	Wife to Cleon,	Pericles.
Doctor Butts,	Physician to Henry VIII.,	King Henry VIII.
Doctor Caius,	A French Physician,	Merry Wives of Windsor.
Dogberry,	A Foolish Officer,	Much Ado About Nothing.
Doll Tearsheet,	A Bawd,	King Henry IV., Part II.
Dolabella,	Friend to Cæsar,	Antony and Cleopatra.
Domitius Enobarbus,	Friend to Antony,	Antony and Cleopatra.
Don Adriano de Armado,	A Fantastical Spaniard,	Love's Labour Lost.
Don John,	Bastard Brother to Don Pedro,	Much Ado About Nothing.
Don Pedro,	Prince of Aragon,	Much Ado About Nothing.
Donaldbain,	Son to King Duncan,	Macbeth.
Dorcas,	A Shepherdess,	Winter's Tale.
Dorset, Marquis of,		King Richard III.
Douglas, Earl of,	Archibald,	King Henry IV., Part I.
Dromio of Ephesus, Dromio of Syracuse,	Twin Brothers: Attendants on the two Antipholuses,	Comedy of Errors.
Duchess of Gloster,		King Richard II.
Duchess of York,		King Richard II.
Duchess of York,	Mother to King Edward IV.,	King Richard III.
Duke, The,	Living in Exile,	As You Like it.
Duke of Albany,		King Lear.
Duke of Alencon,		King Henry VI., Part I.
Duke of Aumerle,	Son to Duke of York,	King Richard II.
Duke of Bedford,	Brother to King Henry V.,	King Henry V.
Duke of Bedford,	Regent of France,	King Henry VI., Part I.
Duke of Bourbon,		King Henry V.
Duke of Buckingham,		King Richard III.
Duke of Buckingham,	Of the King's Party,	King Henry VI., Part I.

Duke of Buckingham,		King Henry VIII.
Duke of Burgundy,		King Lear.
Duke of Burgundy,		King Henry V.
Duke of Burgundy,		King Henry VI., Part I.
Duke of Clarence,	Brother to King Edward IV.,	King Richard III.
Duke of Clarence,	Son to King Henry IV.,	King Henry IV., Part II.
Duke of Cornwall,		King Lear.
Duke of Exeter,	Uncle to King Henry V.,	King Henry V.
Duke of Exeter,	Of the King's Party,	King Henry VI., Pt. III.
Duke of Florence,		All's Well that Ends Well.
Duke of Gloster,	Afterwards King Richard III.,	King Richard III.
Duke of Gloster,	Brother to King Henry V.,	King Henry V.
Duke of Gloster,	Uncle to King Henry VI.,	Henry VI., Part III.
Duke of Lancaster,	Uncle to King Richard II.,	King Richard II.
Duke of Milan,	Father to Silvia,	Two Gentlemen of Verona.
Duke of Norfolk,	Thomas Mowbray,	King Richard II.
Duke of Norfolk,		King Richard III.
Duke of Norfolk,	Of the Duke's Party,	Henry VI., Part III.
Duke of Norfolk,		King Henry VIII.
Duke of Orleans,		King Henry V.
Duke of Oxford,	Of the King's Party,	Henry VI., Part III.
Duke of Somerset,	Of the King's Party,	Henry VI., Parts II., III.
Duke of Suffolk,	Of the King's Party,	King Henry VI., Part II.
Duke of Suffolk,		King Henry VIII.
Duke of Surrey,		King Richard II.
Duke of Venice,		Merchant of Venice.
Duke of Venice,		Othello.
Duke of York,	Cousin to the King,	King Henry V.
Duke of York,	Uncle to King Richard II.,	King Richard II.
Duke of York,	Son to King Edward IV.,	King Richard III.
Dull,	A Constable,	Love's Labour Lost.
Dumain,	Attendant on King of Navarre,	Love's Labour Lost.
Duncan,	King of Scotland,	Macbeth.
Earl Berkley,		King Richard II.
Earl of Cambridge,	A Conspirator,	King Henry V.
Earl of Douglas,	Archibald,	King Henry IV., Part I.
Earl of Essex,	Geoffrey Fitz-Peter,	King John.
Earl of Gloster,		King Lear.
Earl of Kent,		King Lear.
Earl of March,	Edward Mortimer,	King Henry IV., Part I.
Earl of March,	Afterwards King Edward IV.,	Henry VI., Part III.
Earl of Northumberland		King Richard II.
Earl of Northumberland	Henry Percy,	Henry IV., Parts I., II.
Earl of Northumberland	Enemy to the King,	King Henry IV., Part II.
Earl of Northumberland	Of the King's Party,	Henry VI., Part III.
Earl of Oxford,		King Richard III.
Earl of Pembroke,	William Mareshall,	King John.
Earl of Pembroke,	Of the Duke's Party,	Henry VI., Part III.
Earl of Richmond,		King Richard III.
Earl of Salisbury,	William Longsword,	King John.
Earl of Salisbury,		King Richard II.
Earl of Salisbury,		King Henry V.
Earl of Salisbury,	Of the York Faction,	Henry VI., Parts I., II.
Earl of Suffolk,		King Henry VI., Part I.
Earl of Surrey,	Son to Duke of Norfolk,	King Richard III.
Earl of Surrey,		King Henry VIII.
Earl of Warwick,	Of the King's Party,	King Henry IV., Part II.
Earl of Warwick,		King Henry V.

Earl of Warwick,	Of the York Faction,	Henry VI., Pts. I., II., III.
Earl of Westmoreland,	Friend to King Henry IV.,	Henry IV., Parts I., II.
Earl of Westmoreland,		King Henry V.
Earl of Westmoreland,	Of the King's Party,	Henry VI., Part III.
Earl of Worcester,	Thomas Percy,	Henry IV., Parts I. II.
Earl Rivers,		King Richard III.
Edgar,	Son to Gloster,	King Lear.
Edmund,	Earl of Rutland,	Henry VI., Part III.
Edmund,	Bastard Son to Gloster,	King Lear.
Edmund Mortimer,	Earl of March,	King Henry IV., Part I.
Edmund Mortimer,	Earl of March,	King Henry VI., Part I.
Edmund of Langley,	Duke of York,	King Richard II.
Edward,	Prince of Wales,	King Richard III.
Edward,	Son to Plantagenet,	King Henry VI., Part II.
Edward Prince of Wales,	Son to King Henry VI.,	Henry VI., Part III.
Edward IV., King,		King Richard III.
Edward Earl of March,	Afterwards King Edward IV.,	Henry VI., Part III.
Egeus,	Father to Hermia,	Midsummer Nights Dream
Eglamour,	Agent for Silvia,	Two Gentlemen of Verona.
Elbow,	A Simple Constable,	Measure for Measure.
Eleanor,	Duchess of Gloster,	King Henry VI., Part II.
Elinor,	Mother to King John,	King John.
Elizabeth,	Queen to King Edward IV.,	King Richard III.
Ely, Bishop of,	John Morton,	King Richard III.
Ely, Bishop of,		King Henry V.
Emilia,	Wife to Iago,	Othello.
Emilia,	A Lady,	Winter's Tale.
Enobarbus, Domitius,	Friend to Antony,	Antony and Cleopatra.
Eros,	Friend to Antony,	Antony and Cleopatra.
Erpingham, Sir Thomas,	Officer in the King's Army,	King Henry V.
Escalus,	A Lord of Vienna,	Measure for Measure.
Escalus,	Prince of Verona,	Romeo and Juliet.
Escanes,	A Lord of Tyre,	Pericles.
Essex, Earl of,	Geoffrey Fitz-Peter,	King John.
Euphronius,	An Ambassador,	Antony and Cleopatra.
Evans, Sir Hugh,	A Welsh Parson,	Merry Wives of Windsor.
Exeter, Duke of,	Uncle to Henry V.,	King Henry V.
Exeter, Duke of,	Of the King's Party,	Henry VI., Part III.
Exiled Duke,		As You Like it.
Fabian,	Servant to Olivia,	Twelfth Night.
Falstaff, Sir John,		Henry IV., Parts I., II.
Falstaff, Sir John,		Merry Wives of Windsor.
Fang,	A Sheriff's Officer,	King Henry IV., Part II.
Fastolfe, Sir John,		King Henry VI., Part I.
Falconbridge, Lady,	Mother to Robert and Philip,	King John.
Falconbridge, Philip,	Bastard Son to King Richard I.,	King John.
Falconbridge, Robert,	Son to Sir Robert Falconbridge,	King John.
Feeble,	A Recruit,	King Henry IV., Part II.
Fenton,	A Young Gentleman,	Merry Wives of Windsor.
Ferdinand,	King of Navarre,	Love's Labour Lost.
Ferdinand,	Son to the King of Naples,	The Tempest.
Fitz-Peter, Geoffrey,	Earl of Essex,	King John.
Fitzwater, Lord,		King Richard II.
Flaminius,	Servant to Timon,	Timon of Athens.
Flavius,	A Roman Tribune,	Julius Cæsar.
Flavius,	Steward to Timon,	Timon of Athens.
Fleance,	Son to Banquo,	Macbeth.
Florence, Duke of,		All's Well that Ends Well.

Hamlet, . . .	Prince of Denmark, . .	Hamlet.
Harcourt, . . .	Of the King's Party, . .	King Henry IV., Part II.
Hastings, Lord,	Enemy to the King, . .	King Henry IV., Part II.
Hastings, Lord,	Of the Duke's Party, . .	Henry VI., Part III.
Hastings, Lord,	. . . .	King Richard III.
Hecate, . . .	A Witch, ...	Macbeth.
Hector, . . .	Son to Priam, ...	Troilus and Cressida.
Helen, . . .	Woman to Imogen, . .	Cymbeline.
Helen, . . .	Wife to Menelaus, . . .	Troilus and Cressida.
Helena, . . .	A Gentlewoman, . . .	All's Well that Ends Well.
Helena, . . .	In Love with Demetrius, .	MidsummerNightsDream
Helenus, . . .	Son to Priam, ...	Troilus and Cressida.
Helicanus, . . .	A Lord of Tyre, . . .	Pericles.
Henry, . . .	Earl of Richmond, . . .	King Richard III.
Henry Bolingbroke, .	Afterwards King Henry IV., .	King Richard II.
Henry, Earl Richmond,	A Youth, ...	Henry VI., Part III.
Henry Percy, . .	Son to Earl of Northumberland,	King Richard II.
Henry Percy (Hotspur),	Son to Earl of Northumberland,	Henry IV., Parts I., II.
Henry Percy, . .	Earl of Northumberland, .	Henry IV., Parts I., II.
Henry, Prince, . .	Son to King John, . . .	King John.
Henry, Prince of Wales,	Son to King Henry IV., . .	Henry IV., Parts I., II.
Henry IV., King,	. . . .	Henry IV., Parts I., II.
Henry V., King,	. . . .	King Henry V.
Henry VI., King,	. . . .	Henry VI., Parts I., II.
Henry VIII., King, .	. . . .	King Henry VIII.
Herbert, Sir Walter, .	. . . .	King Richard III.
Hermia, . . .	Daughter to Egeus, . .	MidsummerNightsDream
Hermione, . . .	Queen to Sicilia, . . .	Winter's Tale.
Hero, . . .	Daughter to Leonato, . .	Much AdoAboutNothing.
Hippolyta, . .	Queen of the Amazons, . .	MidsummerNightsDream
Holofernes, . .	A Schoolmaster, . . .	Love's Labour Lost.
Horatio, . . .	Friend to Hamlet, . . .	Hamlet.
Horner, Thomas, .	An Armourer, ...	King Henry VI., Part II.
Hortensio, . . .	Suitor to Bianca, . . .	Taming of the Shrew.
Hortensius, . .	A Servant, ...	Timon of Athens.
Hostess, . . .	Character in the Induction, .	Taming of the Shrew.
Hostess Quickly, .	Hostess of a Tavern, . .	Henry IV., Parts I., II.
Hotspur (Henry Percy),	Son to Earl of Northumberland,	Henry IV., Parts I., II.
Hubert de Burgh, .	Chamberlain to King John, .	King John.
Hume, ...	A Priest, ...	King Henry VI., Part II.
Humphrey, D. of Gloster	Uncle to King Henry VI., .	King Henry VI., Part II.
Humphrey, Pr. of Gloster	Son to King Henry IV., .	King Henry IV., Part II.
Huntsmen, . . .	Characters in the Induction, .	Taming of the Shrew.
Iachimo, . . .	Friend to Philario, . . .	Cymbeline.
Iago, ...	Ancient to Othello, . .	Othello.
Iden, Alexander, .	A Kentish Gentleman, . .	King Henry VI., Part II.
Imogen, . . .	Daughter to Cymbeline, . .	Cymbeline.
Iras, ...	Attendant on Cleopatra, .	Antony and Cleopatra.
Iris, ...	A Spirit, ...	The Tempest.
Isabel, . . .	Queen of France, . . .	King Henry V.
Isabella, . . .	Sister to Claudio, . . .	Measure for Measure.
Jack Cade, . . .	A Rebel, ...	King Henry IV., Part II.
James Gurney, . .	Servant to Lady Falconbridge,	King John.
Jamy, . . .	Officer in King's Army, . .	King Henry V.
Jaquenetta, . .	A Country Wench, . . .	Love's Labour Lost.
Jaques, . . .	Son to Sir Roland de Bois, .	As You Like it.
Jaques, . . .	An attendant on Exiled Duke,	As You Like it.

Character	Description	Play
Jessica,	Daughter to Shylock,	Merchant of Venice.
Joan la Pucelle,	Joan of Arc,	King Henry VI., Part I.
John,	A Follower of Cade,	King Henry IV., Part II.
John, Don,	Bastard Brother to Don Pedro,	Much Ado About Nothing.
John, Friar,	A Franciscan,	Romeo and Juliet.
John, King,		King John.
John of Gaunt,	Duke of Lancaster,	King Richard II.
John, Pr. of Lancaster,	Son to King Henry IV.,	Henry IV., Parts I., II.
John Talbot,	Son to Lord Talbot,	King Henry VI., Part I.
Jourdain, Margery,	A witch,	King Henry VI., Part II.
Julia,	A Lady of Verona,	Two Gentlemen of Verona.
Juliet,		Measure for Measure.
Juliet.	Daughter to Capulet,	Romeo and Juliet.
Julius Cæsar,		Julius Cæsar.
Junius Brutus,	Tribune of the People,	Coriolanus.
Juno,	A Spirit,	The Tempest.
Justice Shallow,	A Country Justice,	King Henry IV., Part II.
Katharina,	The Shrew,	Taming of the Shrew.
Katharine,	Attendant on Princess of France	Love's Labour Lost.
Katharine, Princess,	Daughter to Charles VI.,	King Henry V.
Katharine, Queen,	Wife to King Henry VIII.,	King Henry VIII.
Kent, Earl of,		King Lear.
King Edward IV.,		King Richard III.
King Henry IV.,		Henry IV., Parts I., II.
King Henry V.,		King Henry V.
King Henry VI.,		Henry VI., Pts. I., II., III.
King Henry VIII.,		King Henry VIII.
King John,		King John.
King of France,		All's Well that Ends Well.
King of France,		King Lear.
King Richard II.,		King Richard II.
King Richard III.,		King Richard III.
Lady Anne,	Widow to Edward Pr. of Wales,	King Richard III.
Lady Capulet,	Wife to Capulet,	Romeo and Juliet.
Lady Falconbridge,	Mother to Robert and Philip,	King John.
Lady Grey,	Queen to Edward IV.,	Henry VI., Part III.
Lady Macbeth,	Wife to Macbeth,	Macbeth.
Lady Macduff,	Wife to Macduff,	Macbeth.
Lady Montague,	Wife to Montague,	Romeo and Juliet.
Lady Mortimer,	Daughter to Glendower,	King Henry IV., Part I.
Lady Northumberland,		King Henry IV., Part II.
Lady Percy,	Wife to Hotspur,	King Henry IV., Part I.
Laertes,	Son to Polonius,	Hamlet.
Lafeu,	An Old Lord,	All's Well that Ends Well.
Lancaster, Duke of,	Uncle to King Richard II.,	King Richard II.
Lancaster, Pr. John of,	Son to King Henry IV.,	Henry IV., Parts I., II.
Launce,	Servant to Proteus,	Two Gentlemen of Verona.
Launcelot Gobbo,	Servant to Shylock,	Merchant of Venice.
Lawrence, Friar,	A Franciscan,	Romeo and Juliet.
Lavinia,	Daughter to Titus,	Titus Andronicus.
Lear,	King of Britain,	King Lear.
Le Beau,	A Courtier,	As You Like it.
Lennox,	A Scottish Nobleman,	Macbeth.
Leonardo,	Servant to Bassanio,	Merchant of Venice.
Leonato,	Governor of Messina,	Much Ado About Nothing.
Leonatus Posthumus,	Husband to Imogen,	Cymbeline.
Leonine,	Servant to Dionyza,	Pericles.

Leontes,	King of Sicilia,	Winter's Tale.
Lepidus, M. Æmilius,	A Triumvir,	Antony and Cleopatra.
Ligarius,	A Roman Conspirator,	Julius Cæsar.
Lincoln, Bishop of,		King Henry VIII.
Lion,	A Character in the Interlude,	MidsummerNightsDream
Lodovico,	Kinsman to Brabantio,	Othello.
Longaville,	Attendant on King of Navarre,	Love's Labour Lost.
Longsword, William,	Earl of Salisbury,	King John.
Lord, A,	Character in the Induction,	Taming of the Shrew.
Lord Abergavenny,		King Henry VIII.
Lord Bardolph,	Enemy to the King,	King Henry IV., Part II.
Lord Chief-Justice,	Of the King's Bench,	King Henry IV., Part II.
Lord Clifford,	Of the King's Party,	Henry VI., Parts II., III.
Lord Fitzwater,		King Richard II.
Lord Grey,	Son to Lady Grey,	King Richard III.
Lord Hastings,		King Richard III.
Lord Hastings,	Enemy to the King,	King Henry IV., Part II.
Lord Hastings,	Of the Duke's Party,	Henry VI., Part III.
Lord Lovel,		King Richard III.
Lord Mowbray,	Enemy to the King.	King Henry IV., Part II.
Lord Rivers,	Brother to Lady Grey,	Henry VI., Part III.
Lord Ross,		King Richard II.
Lord Sands,		King Henry VIII.
Lord Says,		King Henry VI., Part II.
Lord Scales,	Governor of the Tower,	King Henry VI., Part II.
Lord Scroop,	A Conspirator,	King Henry V.
Lord Stafford,	Of the Duke's Party,	Henry VI., Part III.
Lord Stanley,		King Richard III.
Lord Talbot,	Afterwards Earl of Shrewsbury,	King Henry VI., Part I.
Lord Willoughby,		King Richard II.
Lorenzo,	The Lover of Jessica,	Merchant of Venice.
Louis, the Dauphin,		King John.
Louis, the Dauphin,		King Henry V.
Louis XI.,	King of France,	Henry VI., Part III.
Lovel, Lord,		King Richard III.
Lovell, Sir Thomas,		King Henry VIII.
Luce,	Servant to Luciana,	Comedy of Errors.
Lucentio,	Son to Vincentio,	Taming of the Shrew.
Lucetta,	Waiting-woman to Julia,	TwoGentlemenofVerona.
Luciana,	Sister to Adriana,	Comedy of Errors.
Lucilius,	Friend to Brutus and Cassius,	Julius Cæsar.
Lucilius,	Servant to Timon,	Timon of Athens.
Lucio,	A Fantastic,	Measure for Measure.
Lucius,	A Lord: Flatterer of Timon,	Timon of Athens.
Lucius,	A Servant,	Timon of Athens.
Lucius,	Servant to Brutus,	Julius Cæsar.
Lucius,	Son to Titus,	Titus Andronicus.
Lucullus,	A Lord: Flatterer of Timon,	Timon of Athens.
Lucy, Sir William,		King Henry VI., Part I.
Lychorida,	Nurse to Marina.	Pericles.
Lysander,	In Love with Hermione,	MidsummerNightsDream
Lysimachus,	Governor of Mitylene,	Pericles.
Macbeth,	General of the King's Army,	Macbeth.
Macbeth, Lady,	Wife to Macbeth,	Macbeth.
Macduff,	A Scottish Nobleman,	Macbeth.
Macduff, Lady,	Wife to Macduff,	Macbeth.
Macmorris,	Officer in King's Army,	King Henry V.
Malcolm,	Son to King Duncan,	Macbeth.

Malvolio,	Steward to Olivia,	Twelfth Night.
Mamillius,	Son to Leontes,	Winter's Tale.
Marc Antony,	A Triumvir,	Antony and Cleopatra.
Marcellus,	An Officer,	Hamlet.
March, Earl of,	Edward Mortimer,	King Henry IV., Part I.
Marcius, Young,	Son to Coriolanus,	Coriolanus.
Marcus Andronicus,	Tribune: Brother to Titus,	Titus Andronicus.
Marcus Antonius,	A Roman Triumvir,	Julius Cæsar.
Marcus Brutus,	A Roman Conspirator,	Julius Cæsar.
Mardian,	Attendant on Cleopatra,	Antony and Cleopatra.
Mareshall, William,	Earl of Pembroke,	King John.
Margarelon,	Bastard Son to Priam,	Troilus and Cressida.
Margaret,	Daughter to Reignier,	King Henry VI., Part I.
Margaret,	Queen to King Henry VI.,	King Henry VI., Part II.
Margaret,	Widow to King Henry VI.,	King Richard III.
Margaret, Queen,		King Henry VI., Pt. III.
Margaret,	Attendant on Hero,	Much Ado About Nothing.
Margery Jourdain,	A Witch,	King Henry VI., Part II.
Maria,	Attendant on Princess of France,	Love's Labour Lost.
Maria,	Attendant on Olivia,	Twelfth Night.
Mariana,	Neighbour to Widow of Florence,	All's Well that Ends Well.
Mariana,	The Betrothed of Angelo,	Measure for Measure.
Marina,	Daughter to Pericles,	Pericles.
Marquis of Dorset,	Son to Lady Grey,	King Richard III.
Marquis of Montagne,	Of the Duke's Party,	Henry VI., Part III.
Martext, Sir Oliver,	A Vicar,	As You Like it.
Martius,	Son to Titus,	Titus Andronicus.
Marullus,	A Roman Tribune,	Julius Cæsar.
Mecænas,	Friend to Cæsar,	Antony and Cleopatra.
Melun,	A French Lord,	King John.
Menas,	Friend to Pompey,	Antony and Cleopatra.
Menecrates,	Friend to Pompey,	Antony and Cleopatra.
Menelaus,	Brother to Agamemnon,	Troilus and Cressida.
Menenius Agrippa,	Friend to Coriolanus,	Coriolanus.
Menteith,	A Scottish Nobleman,	Macbeth.
Mercade,	Attendant on Princess of France,	Love's Labour Lost.
Mercutio,	Friend to Romeo,	Romeo and Juliet.
Messala,	Friend to Brutus and Cassius,	Julius Cæsar.
Metellus Cimber,	A Roman Conspirator,	Julius Cæsar.
Michael,	A Follower of Cade,	King Henry VI., Part II.
Michael, Sir,	Friend to Archbishop of York,	Henry IV., Parts I., II.
Milan, Duke of,	Father to Silvia.	Two Gentlemen of Verona.
Miranda,	Daughter to Prospero,	The Tempest.
Mr. Ford,	Gentleman dwelling at Windsor,	Merry Wives of Windsor.
Mrs. Ford,		Merry Wives of Windsor.
Mrs. Overdone	A Bawd,	Measure for Measure.
Mr. Page,	Gentleman dwelling at Windsor,	Merry Wives of Windsor.
Mrs. Page,		Merry Wives of Windsor.
Mrs. Anne Page,	Daughter to Mrs. Page,	Merry Wives of Windsor.
Mrs. Quickly,	Hostess of a Tavern.	Henry IV., Parts I., II.
Mrs. Quickly,	A hostess: Wife to Pistol,	King Henry V.
Mrs. Quickly,	Servant to Dr. Caius,	Merry Wives of Windsor.
Montague,	At variance with Capulet,	Romeo and Juliet.
Montague, Marquis of,	Of the Duke's Party,	Henry VI., Part III.
Montague, Lady,	Wife to Montague,	Romeo and Juliet.
Montano,	Othello's Predecessor in Office,	Othello.
Montgomery, Sir John,		Henry VI., Part III.
Moonshine,	A Character in the Interlude,	Midsummer Nights Dream
Mopsa,	A Shepherdess,	Winter's Tale.

Morgan, . . .	. Belarius in disguise, . .	. Cymbeline.
Morocco, Prince of,	. Suitor to Portia, . . .	. Merchant of Venice.
Mortimer, Edmund,	. Earl of March, . . .	. King Henry IV., Part I.
Mortimer, Edmund,	. Earl of March, . . .	. King Henry VI., Part I.
Mortimer, Lady,	. Daughter to Glendower,	. King Henry IV., Part I.
Mortimer, Sir Hugh,	Uncle to Duke of York, .	. Henry VI., Part III.
Mortimer, Sir John,	. Uncle to Duke of York, .	. Henry VI., Part III.
Morton, John, .	. Bishop of Ely, ...	. King Richard III.
Morton, . . .	. Servant to Northumberland,	. King Henry IV., Part II.
Moth, . . .	. A Fairy, ...	. MidsummerNightsDream
Moth, . . .	. Page to Armado, . . .	. Love's Labour Lost.
Mouldy, . . .	. A Recruit, ...	. King Henry IV., Part II.
Mountjoy, . . .	. A French Herald, . . .	. King Henry V.
Mowbray, Thomas,	. Duke of Norfolk, . . .	. King Richard II.
Mowbray, Lord,	. Enemy to the King, . .	. King Henry VI., Part II.
Mustardseed, .	. A Fairy, ...	. MidsummerNightsDream
Mutius,. . .	. Son to Titus, ...	. Titus Andronicus.
Nathaniel, Sir, .	. A Curate, ...	. Love's Labour Lost.
Nerissa, . . .	. Waiting-maid to Portia, .	. Merchant of Venice.
Nestor, . . .	. A Grecian Commander, .	. Troilus and Cressida.
Norfolk, Duke of,	. . . .	. King Richard II. & III.
Norfolk, Duke of,	. Of the Duke's Party, .	. Henry VI., Part III.
Norfolk, Duke of,	. . . .	. King Henry VIII.
Northumberland, Lady,	. . . .	. King Henry IV., Part II.
Northumberland, Earl of,	. . . .	. King Richard II.
Northumberland, Earl of,	Enemy to the King, . .	. King Henry IV., Part II.
Northumberland, Earl of,	Henry Percy, . . .	. King Henry IV., Pts. I & II.
Northumberland, Earl of,	Of the King's Party, . .	. Henry VI., Part III.
Nurse of Juliet, .	. . . .	. Romeo and Juliet.
Nym, ...	. Soldier in King's Army, .	. King Henry V.
Nym, ...	. A Follower of Falstaff, .	. Merry Wives of Windsor.
Oberon, . . .	. King of the Fairies, . .	. MidsummerNightsDream
Octavia, . . .	. Wife to Antony, . . .	. Antony and Cleopatra.
Octavius Cæsar,	. A Roman Triumvir, . .	. Julius Cæsar.
Octavius Cæsar,	. A Roman Triumvir, . .	. Antony and Cleopatra.
Old Gobbo, .	. Father to Launcelot Gobbo,	. Merchant of Venice.
Oliver, . . .	. Son to Sir Rowland de Bois,	. As You Like it.
Olivia, . . .	. A Rich Countess, . . .	. Twelfth Night.
Ophelia, . . .	. Daughter to Polonius, . .	. Hamlet.
Orlando, . . .	. Son to Sir Rowland de Bois,	. As You Like it.
Orleans, Duke of,	. . . .	. King Henry V.
Orsino, . . .	. Duke of Illyria, . . .	. Twelfth Night.
Orsic, ...	. A Courtier, ...	. Hamlet.
Oswald, . . .	. Steward to Goneril, . .	. King Lear.
Othello, . . .	. The Moor, ...	. Othello.
Overdone, Mrs. .	. A Bawd, ...	. Measure for Measure.
Owen Glendower,	. . . .	. King Henry IV., Part I.
Oxford, Duke of,	. Of the King's Party, .	. Henry VI., Part III.
Oxford, Earl of,	. . . .	. King Richard III.
Page, Mr., . .	. Gentleman dwelling at Windsor,	Merry Wives of Windsor.
Page, Mrs., .	. . . .	. Merry Wives of Windsor
Page, Mrs. Anne,	. Daughter to Mrs. Page, .	. Merry Wives of Windsor.
Page, William, .	. Son to Mr. Page, . . .	. Merry Wives of Windsor.
Pandarus, . . .	. Uncle to Cressida, . . .	. Troilus and Cressida.
Pandulph, Cardinal,	. The Pope's Legate, . .	. King John.
Panthino, . . .	. Servant to Antonio, . .	. TwoGentleman ofVerona.

Princess Katharine,	Daughter to King Charles VI.,	King Henry V.
Princess of France,		Love's Labour Lost.
Proculeius,	Friend to Cæsar,	Antony and Cleopatra.
Prophetess,	Cassandra,	Troilus and Cressida.
Prospero,	Rightful Duke of Milan,	The Tempest.
Proteus,	A Gentleman of Verona,	Two Gentlemen of Verona.
Publius,	A Roman Senator,	Julius Cæsar.
Publius,	Son to Marcus,	Titus Andronicus.
Pucelle, Joan la,	Joan of Arc,	King Henry VI., Part I.
Puck,	A Fairy,	MidsummerNightsDream
Pyramus,	A Character in the Interlude,	MidsummerNightsDream
Queen,	Wife to Cymbeline,	Cymbeline.
Queen Elizabeth,	Queen to King Edward IV.,	King Richard III.
Queen Katharine,	Wife to King Henry VIII.,	King Henry VIII.
Queen Margaret,	Wife to King Henry VI.,	Henry VI., Part III.
Queen of Richard II.,		King Richard II.
Quickly, Mrs.,	Hostess of a Tavern,	Henry IV., Parts I., II.,
Quickly, Mrs.,	A Hostess: Wife to Pistol,	King Henry V.
Quickly, Mrs.	Servant to Dr. Caius,	Merry Wives of Windsor.
Quince,	The Carpenter,	MidsummerNightsDream
Quintus,	Son to Titus,	Titus Andronicus.
Rambures,	A French Lord,	King Henry V.
Ratcliff, Sir Richard,		King Richard III.
Regan,	Daughter to King Lear,	King Lear.
Reignier,	Duke of Anjou,	King Henry VI., Part I.
Reynaldo,	Servant to Polonius,	Hamlet.
Richard,	Son to Plantagenet,	King Henry VI., Part II.
Richard,	Afterwards Duke of Gloster,	Henry VI., Part III.
Richard, Duke of Gloster	Afterwards King Richard III.,	King Richard III.
Richard, Duke of York,	Son to King Edward IV.,	King Richard III.
Richard Plantagenet,	Duke of York,	Henry VI., Pts. I., II., III.
Richard II., King,		King Richard II.
Richard III., King,		King Richard III.
Richmond, Earl of,	Afterwards King Henry VII.,	King Richard III.
Rivers, Earl,	Brother to Lady Grey,	King Richard III.
Rivers, Lord,	Brother to Lady Grey,	Henry VI., Part III.
Robert Bigot,	Earl of Norfolk,	King John.
Robert Falconbridge,	Son to Sir Robert Falconbridge,	King John.
Robin,	A Page to Sir John Falstaff,	Merry Wives of Windsor.
Robin Goodfellow (Puck),	A Fairy,	MidsummerNightsDream
Roderigo,	A Venetian Gentleman,	Othello.
Rogero,	A Sicilian Gentleman,	Winter's Tale.
Romeo,	Son to Montague,	Romeo and Juliet.
Rosalind,	Daughter to the Banished Duke,	As You Like it.
Rosaline,	Attendant on Princess of France,	Love's Labour Lost.
Rosencrantz,	A Courtier,	Hamlet.
Ross, Lord,		King Richard II.
Ross,	A Scottish Nobleman,	Macbeth.
Rotheram, Thomas,	Archbishop of York,	King Richard III.
Rousillon, Count of,	Bertram,	All's Well that Ends Well.
Rousillon, Countess of,	Mother to Bertram,	All's Well that Ends Well.
Rugby,	Servant to Dr. Caius,	Merry Wives of Windsor.
Rumour,	As a Prologue,	King Henry IV., Part II.
Salanio,	Friend to Antonio and Bassanio,	Merchant of Venice.
Salarino,	Friend to Antonio and Bassanio,	Merchant of Venice.
Salerio,	A Messenger from Venice,	Merchant of Venice.

Salisbury, Earl of,	William Longsword,	King John.
Salisbury, Earl of,		King Henry V.
Salisbury, Earl of,	Of the York Faction,	Henry VI., Parts I., II.
Salisbury, Earl of,		King Richard II.
Sampson,	Servant to Capulet,	Romeo and Juliet.
Sands, Lord,		King Henry VIII.
Saturninus,	Emperor of Rome,	Titus Andronicus.
Say, Lord,		King Henry VI., Part II.
Scales, Lord,	Governor of the Tower,	King Henry VI., Part II.
Scarus,	Friend to Antony,	Antony and Cleopatra.
Scroop,	Archbishop of York,	Henry IV., Parts I., II.
Scroop, Lord,	A Conspirator,	King Henry V.
Scroop, Sir Stephen,		King Richard II.
Sebastian,	Brother to the King of Naples,	The Tempest.
Sebastian,	Brother to Viola,	Twelfth Night.
Seleucus,	Attendant on Cleopatra,	Antony and Cleopatra.
Sempronius,	A Lord: Flatterer of Timon,	Timon of Athens.
Servilius,	Servant to Timon,	Timon of Athens.
Sextus Pompeius,	Friend to Antony,	Antony and Cleopatra.
Seyton,	Officer attending on Macbeth,	Macbeth.
Shadow,	A Recruit,	King Henry IV., Part II.
Shallow,	A Country Justice,	King Henry IV., Part II.
Shallow,	A Country Justice,	Merry Wives of Windsor.
Shylock,	A Jew,	Merchant of Venice.
Sicinius Velutus,	Tribune of the People,	Coriolanus.
Silence,	A Country Justice,	King Henry IV., Part II.
Silius,	An Officer of Ventidius's Army,	Antony and Cleopatra.
Silvia,	Daughter to the Duke of Milan,	Two Gentlemen of Verona.
Simonides,	King of Pentapolis,	Pericles.
Simpcox,	An Impostor,	King Henry VI., Part II.
Simple,	Servant to Slender,	Merry Wives of Windsor.
Sir Andrew Aguecheek,		Twelfth Night.
Sir Anthony Denny,		King Henry VIII.
Sir Henry Guildford,		King Henry VIII.
Sir Hugh Evans,	A Welsh Parson,	Merry Wives of Windsor.
Sir Hugh Mortimer,	Uncle to Duke of York,	Henry VI., Part III.
Sir Humphrey Stafford,		King Henry VI., Part II.
Sir James Blount,		King Richard III.
Sir James Tyrrell,		King Richard III.
Sir John Coleville,	Enemy to the King,	King Henry IV., Part II.
Sir John Falstaff,		Henry IV., Parts I., II.
Sir John Falstaff,		Merry Wives of Windsor.
Sir John Fastolfe,		King Henry VI , Part I.
Sir John Montgomery,		Henry VI., Part III.
Sir John Mortimer,	Uncle to Duke of York,	Henry VI., Part III.
Sir John Somerville,		Henry VI., Part III.
Sir John Stanley,		King Henry VI., Part II.
Sir Michael,	Friend to Archbishop of York,	Henry VI., Parts I., II.
Sir Nathaniel,	A Curate,	Love's Labour Lost.
Sir Nicholas Vaux,		King Henry VIII.
Sir Oliver Martext,	A Vicar,	As You Like it.
Sir Pierce of Exton,		King Richard II.
Sir Richard Ratcliff,		King Richard III.
Sir Richard Vernon,		King Henry IV., Part I.
Sir Robert Brakenbury,	Lieutenant of the Tower,	King Richard III.
Sir Stephen Scroop,		King Richard II.
Sir Thomas Erpingham,	Officer in King's Army,	King Henry V.
Sir Thomas Gargrave,		King Henry VI., Part I.
Sir Thomas Grey,	A Conspirator,	King Henry V.

Sir Thomas Lovell,		King Henry VIII.
Sir Thomas Vaughan,		King Richard III.
Sir Toby Belch,	Uncle to Olivia,	Twelfth Night.
Sir Walter Blunt,	Friend to King Henry IV.,	Henry IV., Parts I., II.
Sir Walter Herbert,		King Richard III.
Sir William Catesby,		King Richard III.
Sir William Glandsale,		King Henry VI., Part I.
Sir William Lucy,		King Henry VI., Part I.
Sir William Stanley,		Henry VI., Part III.
Siward,	Earl of Northumberland,	Macbeth.
Siward, Young,	Son to Siward,	Macbeth.
Slender,	Cousin to Justice Shallow,	Merry Wives of Windsor.
Smith the Weaver,	A Follower of Cade,	King Henry VI., Part II.
Snare,	A Sheriff's Officer,	King Henry IV., Part II.
Snout,	The Tinker,	MidsummerNightsDream
Snug,	The Joiner,	MidsummerNightsDream
Solinus,	Duke of Ephesus,	Comedy of Errors.
Somerset, Duke of,	Of the King's Party,	Henry VI., Parts II., III.
Somerville, Sir John,		Henry VI., Part III.
Southwell,	A Priest,	King Henry VI., Part II.
Speed,	A Clownish Servant,	Two Gentlemen of Verona.
Stafford, Lord,	Of the Duke's Party,	Henry VI., Part III.
Stafford, Sir Humphrey,		King Henry VI., Part II.
Stanley, Lord,		King Richard III.
Stanley, Sir John,		King Henry VI., Part II.
Stanley, Sir William,		Henry VI., Part III.
Starveling,	The Tailor,	MidsummerNightsDream
Stephano,	A Drunken Butler,	The Tempest.
Stephano,	Servant to Portia,	Merchant of Venice.
Strato,	Servant to Brutus,	Julius Cæsar.
Suffolk, Duke of,	Of the King's Party,	King Henry VI., Part II.
Suffolk, Duke of,		King Henry VIII.
Suffolk, Earl of,		King Henry VI., Part I.
Surrey, Duke of,		King Richard II.
Surrey, Earl of,	Son to Duke of Norfolk,	King Richard III.
Surrey, Earl of,		King Henry VIII.
Sylvius,	A Shepherd,	As You Like it.
Talbot, John,	Son to Lord Talbot,	King Henry VI., Part I.
Talbot, Lord,	Afterwards Earl of Shrewsbury,	King Henry VI., Part I.
Tamora,	Queen of the Goths,	Titus Andronicus.
Taurus,	Lieutenant-General to Cæsar,	Antony and Cleopatra.
Tearsheet, Doll,	A Bawd,	King Henry IV., Part II.
Thaisa,	Daughter to Simonides,	Pericles.
Thaliard,	A Lord of Antioch,	Pericles.
Thersites,	A Deformed Grecian,	Troilus and Cressida.
Theseus,	Duke of Athens,	MidsummerNightsDream
Thisbe,	A Character in the Interlude,	MidsummerNightsDream
Thomas,	A Friar,	Measure for Measure.
Thomas, D. of Clarence,	Son to King Henry IV.,	King Henry IV., Part II.
Thomas Horner,	An Armourer,	King Henry VI., Part II.
Three Witches,		Macbeth.
Thurio,	Rival to Valentine,	Two Gentlemen of Verona.
Thyreus,	Friend to Cæsar,	Antony and Cleopatra.
Timandra,	Mistress to Alcibiades,	Timon of Athens.
Time,	As Chorus,	Winter's Tale.
Timon,	A Noble Athenian,	Timon of Athens.
Titania,	Queen of the Fairies,	MidsummerNightsDream
Titinius,	Friend to Brutus and Cassius,	Julius Cæsar.

Titus Andronicus,	General against the Goths,	Titus Andronicus.
Titus Lartius,	General against the Volscians,	Coriolanus.
Touchstone,	A Clown,	As You Like it.
Tranio,	Servant to Lucentio,	Taming of the Shrew.
Travers,	Servant to Northumberland,	King Henry IV., Part II.
Trebonius,	A Roman Conspirator,	Julius Cæsar.
Trinculo,	A Jester,	The Tempest.
Troilus,	Son to Priam,	Troilus and Cressida.
Tubal,	A Jew, Friend to Shylock,	Merchant of Venice.
Tullus Aufidius,	Volscian General,	Coriolanus.
Tybalt,	Nephew to Capulet,	Romeo and Juliet.
Tyrrel, Sir James,		King Richard III.
Ulysses,	A Grecian Commander,	Troilus and Cressida.
Ursula,	Attendant on Hero,	Much Ado About Nothing.
Urswick, Christopher,	A Priest,	King Richard III.
Valentine,	A Gentleman of Verona,	Two Gentlemen of Verona.
Valentine,	Attendant on Duke of Illyria,	Twelfth Night.
Valeria,	Friend to Virgilia,	Coriolanus.
Varrius,	Friend to Pompey,	Antony and Cleopatra.
Varrius,	Servant to Duke of Vienna,	Measure for Measure.
Varro,	Servant to Brutus,	Julius Cæsar.
Vaughan, Sir Thomas,		King Richard III.
Vaux,		King Henry VI., Part II.
Vaux, Sir Nicholas,		King Henry VIII.
Veletus, Sicinius,	Tribune of the People,	Coriolanus.
Venice, Duke of,		Merchant of Venice.
Ventidius,	A False Friend,	Timon of Athens.
Ventidius,	Friend to Antony,	Antony and Cleopatra.
Verges,	A Foolish Officer,	Much Ado About Nothing.
Vernon,	Of the White-Rose Faction,	King Henry VI., Part I.
Vernon, Sir Richard,		King Henry IV., Part I.
Vicentio,	Duke of Vienna,	Measure for Measure.
Vincentio,	An Old Gentleman of Pisa,	Taming of the Shrew.
Viola,	In love with the Duke of Illyria,	Twelfth Night.
Violenta,	Neighbour to Widow of Florence,	All's Well that Ends Well.
Virgilia,	Wife to Coriolanus,	Coriolanus.
Voltimand,	A Courtier,	Hamlet.
Volumnia,	Mother to Coriolanus,	Coriolanus.
Volumnius,	Friend to Brutus and Cassius,	Julius Cæsar.
Wales, Henry, Pr. of,	Son to King Henry IV.,	Henry IV., Parts I., II.
Wales, Prince of,	Son to King Edward IV.,	King Richard III.
Walter Whitmore,		King Henry VI., Part II.
Wart,	A Recruit,	King Henry IV., Part II.
Warwick, Earl of,	Of the King's Party,	King Henry IV., Part II.
Warwick, Earl of,		King Henry V.
Warwick, Earl of,	Of the York Faction,	Henry VI., Pts. I., II., III.
Westminster, Abbot of,		King Richard II.
Westmoreland, Earl of,		King Henry V.
Westmoreland, Earl of,	Friend to King Henry IV.,	Henry IV., Parts I., II.
Westmoreland, Earl of,	Of the King's Party,	Henry VI., Part III.
Whitmore, Walter,		King Henry VI., Part II.
William,	A Country Fellow,	As You Like it.
William Longsword,	Earl of Salisbury,	King John.
William Mareshall,	Earl of Pembroke,	King John.
William Page,	Son to Mrs. Page,	Merry Wives of Windsor.
Williams,	Soldier in King's Army,	King Henry V.

Willoughby, Lord,	. . . . . .	King Richard II.
Winchester, Bishop of,	Gardiner, ...	King Henry VIII.
Wolsey, Cardinal,	. . . . . .	King Henry VIII.
Woodville, . .	Lieutenant of the Tower,	King Henry VI., Part I.
Worcester, Earl of,	Thomas Percy, . .	Henry VI., Parts I., II.
York, Archbishop of,	Scroop, ...	Henry IV., Parts I., II.
York, Archbishop of,	Thomas Rotheram, . .	King Richard III.
York, Duchess of,	. . . . . .	King Richard II.
York, Duchess of,	Mother to King Edward IV.,	King Richard III.
York, Duke of, .	Cousin to the King, .	King Henry V.
York, Duke of, .	Uncle to King Richard II.,	King Richard II.
York, Duke of, .	Son to King Edward IV.,	King Richard III.
Young Cato, .	Friend to Brutus and Cassius,	Julius Cæsar.
Young Clifford, .	Son to Lord Clifford, .	King Henry VI., Part II.
Young Marcius,	Son to Coriolanus, . .	Coriolanus.
Young Siward, .	Son to Siward, . .	Macbeth.

Lightning Source UK Ltd.
Milton Keynes UK
UKHW051850070119
335139UK00006BA/202/P